# PIPE FITTINGS

P9-CEE-403

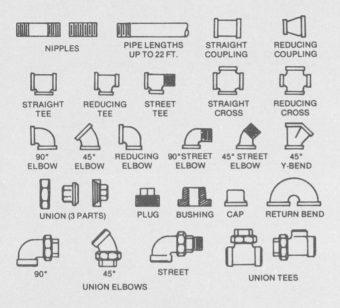

Here are the common steel pipe fittings. Nipples are simply short lengths of pipe threaded on both ends. Reducing fittings join two different sizes of pipe.

Compression fittings of the flared-tube type are the easiest for the novice to handle when working with copper tubing.

## STANDARD STEEL PIPE
### (All Dimensions in Inches)

| Nominal Size | Outside Diameter | Inside Diameter | Nominal Size | Outside Diameter | Inside Diameter |
|---|---|---|---|---|---|
| 1/8 | 0.405 | 0.269 | 1 | 1.315 | 1.049 |
| 1/4 | 0.540 | 0.364 | 1 1/4 | 1.660 | 1.380 |
| 3/8 | 0.675 | 0.493 | 1 1/2 | 1.900 | 1.610 |
| 1/2 | 0.840 | 0.622 | 2 | 2.375 | 2.067 |
| 3/4 | 1.050 | 0.824 | 2 1/2 | 2.875 | 2.469 |

## SQUARE MEASURE
144 sq in = 1 sq ft
9 sq ft = 1 sq yd
272.25 sq ft = 1 sq rod
160 sq rods = 1 acre

## VOLUME MEASURE
1728 cu in = 1 cu ft
27 cu ft = 1 cu yd

## MEASURES OF CAPACITY
1 cup = 8 fl oz
2 cups = 1 pint
2 pints = 1 quart
4 quarts = 1 gallon
2 gallons = 1 peck
4 pecks = 1 bushel

# WOOD SCREWS

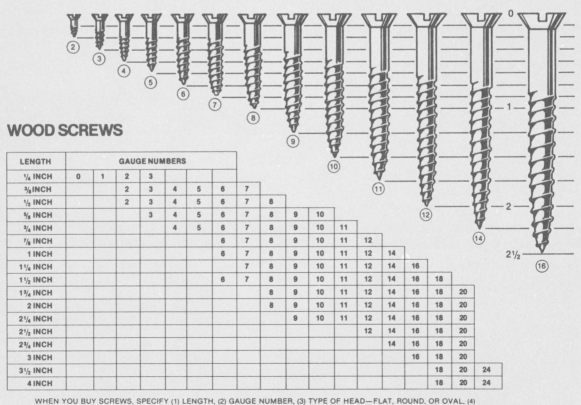

| LENGTH | GAUGE NUMBERS | | | | | | | | | | | | | |
|---|---|---|---|---|---|---|---|---|---|---|---|---|---|---|
| 1/4 INCH | 0 | 1 | 2 | 3 | | | | | | | | | | |
| 3/8 INCH | | | 2 | 3 | 4 | 5 | 6 | 7 | | | | | | |
| 1/2 INCH | | | 2 | 3 | 4 | 5 | 6 | 7 | 8 | | | | | |
| 5/8 INCH | | | | 3 | 4 | 5 | 6 | 7 | 8 | 9 | 10 | | | |
| 3/4 INCH | | | | | 4 | 5 | 6 | 7 | 8 | 9 | 10 | 11 | | |
| 7/8 INCH | | | | | | | 6 | 7 | 8 | 9 | 10 | 11 | 12 | |
| 1 INCH | | | | | | | 6 | 7 | 8 | 9 | 10 | 11 | 12 | 14 |
| 1 1/4 INCH | | | | | | | | 7 | 8 | 9 | 10 | 11 | 12 | 14 | 16 |
| 1 1/2 INCH | | | | | | | 6 | 7 | 8 | 9 | 10 | 11 | 12 | 14 | 16 | 18 |
| 1 3/4 INCH | | | | | | | | | 8 | 9 | 10 | 11 | 12 | 14 | 16 | 18 | 20 |
| 2 INCH | | | | | | | | | 8 | 9 | 10 | 11 | 12 | 14 | 16 | 18 | 20 |
| 2 1/4 INCH | | | | | | | | | | 9 | 10 | 11 | 12 | 14 | 16 | 18 | 20 |
| 2 1/2 INCH | | | | | | | | | | | | | 12 | 14 | 16 | 18 | 20 |
| 2 3/4 INCH | | | | | | | | | | | | | | 14 | 16 | 18 | 20 |
| 3 INCH | | | | | | | | | | | | | | | 16 | 18 | 20 |
| 3 1/2 INCH | | | | | | | | | | | | | | | | 18 | 20 | 24 |
| 4 INCH | | | | | | | | | | | | | | | | 18 | 20 | 24 |

WHEN YOU BUY SCREWS, SPECIFY (1) LENGTH, (2) GAUGE NUMBER, (3) TYPE OF HEAD—FLAT, ROUND, OR OVAL, (4) MATERIAL—STEEL, BRASS, BRONZE, ETC., (5) FINISH—BRIGHT, STEEL BLUED, CADMIUM, NICKEL, OR CHROMIUM PLATED.

# Popular Mechanics

## do-it-yourself yearbook

The best illustrated home reference guide from the world's most authoritative source for today's how-to-do-it information.

## 1994

HEARST DIRECT BOOKS

This book is published with the consent and cooperation of POPULAR MECHANICS Magazine.

POPULAR MECHANICS Staff:
   *Editor-in-Chief:* Joe Oldham
   *Managing Editor:* Deborah Frank
   *Graphics Director:* Bryan Canniff
   *Home Improvement Editor:* Steven Willson
   *Electronics/Photography Editor:* Frank Visard
   *Boating/Outdoors Editor:* Joe Skorupa
   *Editorial Production:* John Bostonian Jr.
   *Copy Editors:* Peter Burns, Nancy Coggins

**POPULAR MECHANICS ENCYCLOPEDIA
1994 YEARBOOK**
*Editor:*
   C. Edward Cavert
*Manufacturing:*
   Ron Schoenfeld
*Book Design and Production:*
   The Bookmaker
   Fairfax, Virginia
*Editorial Assistance:*
   Wilma Cavert
*Cover Photo:*
   Cy DeCosse, Inc.
*Cover Design:*
   Harold Perry

©1994 by The Hearst Corporation

All rights reserved. No part of this book may be reproduced in any manner whatsoever without permission of the publisher.

ISBN 0–87851–121–0
Library of Congress Catalog Card Number: 85–81760
GST Hearst Registration No. R105218291


10 9 8 7 6 5 4 3 2 1
Printed in the United States of America

Although every effort has been made to ensure the accuracy and completeness of the information in this book, Hearst Direct Books and Popular Mechanics Magazine make no guarantees, stated or implied, nor will they be liable in the event of misinterpretation or human error made by the reader or for any typographical errors that may appear. Plans for projects illustrated in this book may not meet all local zoning and building code requirements for construction. Before beginning any major project, consult with local authorities or see a structural architect. WORK SAFELY WITH HAND AND POWER TOOLS. WEAR EYE PROTECTION. READ MANUFACTURER'S INSTRUCTIONS AND WARNINGS FOR ALL PRODUCTS.

# Contents

**1** First mark the straight cutlines for the sides on your stock. Then, using a compass, mark the circular cutlines.

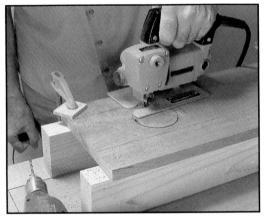

**2** Bore a blade-entry hole in the waste area, then cut along the line to form cutout for the clock movement.

# Mantel clock

This simple mantel clock is easy and inexpensive to build, giving beginning woodworkers a worthwhile project without putting too much at risk. This piece is not, however, without its challenges. The rounded top looks easy to shape but actually requires a steady hand when cutting and sanding. The clever approach to thinning stock—by using a router instead of a hand plane or power planer—can open up a whole new world of uses for this most versatile tool.

The clock shown is made of mahogany, but you can opt for any species of wood. Because so little is required, you can come by your raw materials just about anywhere.

## Stock Preparation

Begin by laying out the circular cutting lines on the face using a compass (Fig. 1). Then bore a hole on the waste side of the clock movement hole line to allow blade entry for the internal cut. Using a sabre saw, cut on the inside of this line to drop out the waste (Fig. 2). Once the cut is complete, chuck a sanding drum in your drill and sand the wall of the opening until the clock movement fits snugly in the hole (Fig. 3).

Next, rip the stock to finished width, allowing a bit extra for final smoothing with a hand plane. Use a straight piece of wood to act as a guide while sawing (Fig. 4). Then make a freehand cut to shape the top curve. With the front board completed, make an identical back piece, but this time without the hole cutout. Then put these pieces aside while you work on the center piece.

*Mantel Clock* was written by Rosario Capotosto. Lead photo by J.R. Rost with how-to photos by Rosario Capotosto. Technical art by Eugene Thompson. The finish used on the clock shown is McCloskey's Satin Finish polyurethane. The clock movement is available from Armor Products, Box 445, East Northport, NY 11731. Model No. D-23016 requires one AA battery.

## Planing with a Router

Because this piece is made from a front and back piece that are both $\frac{3}{4}$ in. thick and a middle piece that is $\frac{1}{2}$ in. thick, some thickness planing is required. Normally, one would use a band saw, planer, hand plane or even a portable power planer to reduce the thickness of the middle board from $\frac{3}{4}$ in. to $\frac{1}{2}$ in. But you also can use a router.

All you have to do is fabricate the oversize subbase shown in the drawing. Simply cut the plywood stock to size and bore a 1-in.-dia. bit clearance hole through the center. Then remove your router's baseplate and attach this panel in its place. Its long base will bridge the area being routed, thus keeping the machine—and cutter—on one consistent plane.

To reduce the thickness of the board, make repeated passes across the grain to remove the bulk of the waste (Fig. 5). You should stop these cuts about $\frac{1}{16}$ in. above the finished thickness. Then readjust the router so it will cut to the finished dimension. These final shallow passes should give the board a smooth, glass-like surface.

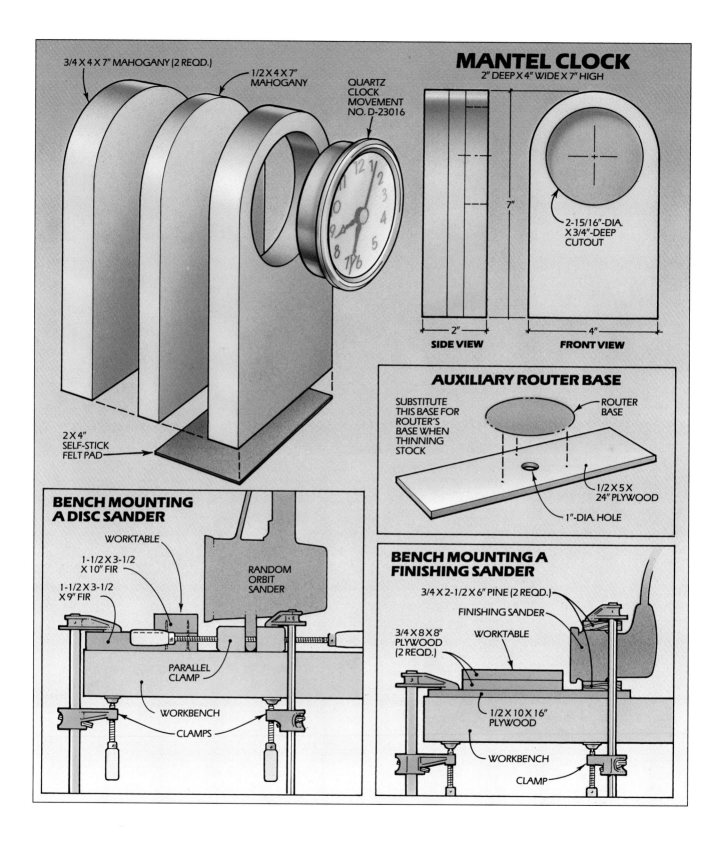

3/4 X 4 X 7" MAHOGANY (2 REQD.)

1/2 X 4 X 7" MAHOGANY

QUARTZ CLOCK MOVEMENT NO. D-23016

2 X 4" SELF-STICK FELT PAD

## MANTEL CLOCK
2" DEEP X 4" WIDE X 7" HIGH

7"

2"

2-15/16"-DIA. X 3/4"-DEEP CUTOUT

4"

**SIDE VIEW**

**FRONT VIEW**

### AUXILIARY ROUTER BASE

SUBSTITUTE THIS BASE FOR ROUTER'S BASE WHEN THINNING STOCK

ROUTER BASE

1/2 X 5 X 24" PLYWOOD

1"-DIA. HOLE

### BENCH MOUNTING A DISC SANDER

WORKTABLE

1-1/2 X 3-1/2 X 10" FIR

1-1/2 X 3-1/2 X 9" FIR

RANDOM ORBIT SANDER

PARALLEL CLAMP

WORKBENCH

CLAMPS

### BENCH MOUNTING A FINISHING SANDER

3/4 X 2-1/2 X 6" PINE (2 REQD.)

FINISHING SANDER

3/4 X 8 X 8" PLYWOOD (2 REQD.)

WORKTABLE

1/2 X 10 X 16" PLYWOOD

WORKBENCH

CLAMP

**3** Use a sanding drum to smooth the wall of the cutout. Test fit the movement.

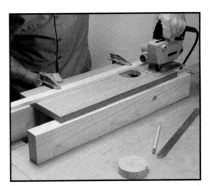

**4** Cut the stock to width using a wood straightedge to guide the saw.

**5** Attach an oversize base to a router and rout the middle board to thickness.

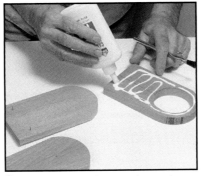

**6** Apply glue evenly to mating surfaces, then install clamps until glue is dry.

**7** Use a bench-mounted sander to shape the top curve of the workpiece.

Once the routing is finished, cut the stock to match the exact size and shape of the other two boards. Then glue and clamp together all three. You'll need three or four C-clamps and a couple of scrap boards to protect the surface of the relatively soft mahogany stock. First, apply a thin coat of glue to the mating surfaces (Fig. 6), and then drive a couple of 1-in. brads through the back of the center board and into the back of the front board. Attach the back board in the same way. Then cover the assembly with scrap wood and clamp securely. The brads will keep the pieces from sliding out of place during the clamping process.

Once the glue has dried, scrape off any excess squeeze-out and then plane the straight edges smooth.

**Finish Sanding**

To sand the broad, semicircular top of the clock assembly, you can use a jig—shown in the drawing—to hold a portable disc sander. All that's required are a few clamps and a couple of pieces of scrap 2 × 4. Just tighten the sander until it is firmly in place, turn it on and hold the workpiece on the 2 × 4 table (Fig. 7). Just about any sander can be used in this jig. Make sure that when the tool is clamped in place it is absolutely stable and won't move when you push a workpiece up against it.

Start with 120-grit, followed by 180- and 220-grit sandpaper. If you don't have this kind of sander, you can do the same thing with a finishing sander clamped firmly to your workbench.

To complete the project, apply two coats of polyurethane, sanding lightly between coats. Once the piece is dry, apply a self-sticking felt pad to the bottom to avoid scratching furniture tops. These pads are commonly available at hardware and craft stores. Then, slide the clock movement in place.

# Traditional clothes tree

This attractive and easy-to-build clothes tree is based on a design that was common in homes and offices during the first half of this century. Like those pieces of the past, this one is made of solid white oak—stained a dark color to bring out its dramatic grain—and is outfitted with black iron hooks that can accommodate the heaviest of coats.

## Getting Started

The basic, straight cutting chores are handled with a portable circular saw mounted in a shop-built table. (See page 18 for building plans.) For controlled sanding operations, you might want to build one of the simple jigs for portable power sanders shown on page 6.

## Post Construction

Begin construction by ripping the post stock to size. Use the shop-built table for this job after clamping a straightedge guide to its surface and the extension table to its outfeed side (Fig. 1). Once these boards are ripped to width, cut them to rough length (Fig. 2). Apply glue to the mating surfaces, clamp the boards together and set them aside until dry.

Next, scrape off any hard glue beads. Then plane one of the laminated sides of this post assembly until it's flat, smooth and square to its adjacent sides. Place this planed side against the table saw's straightedge guide and rip the opposite side to finished width. Remove any saw marks or imperfections with a hand plane, always working in the same direction as the grain. If your saw can't cut through the full thickness of the assembly, just rip one side as deep as you can. Then, flip over the board, end for end, and cut it again. Cut the post to finished length, making sure to square up both ends, then turn to the base.

## Base Construction

The large dadoes that comprise the middle half lap joint featured on the crossed base members are not cut out of solid wood. Instead they are formed by gluing up several layers of blocks—selectively spaced—to create the overall thickness required.

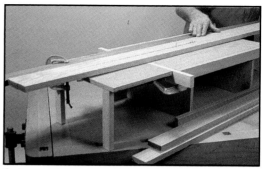

**1** Rip post stock to width on a table saw or a table-mounted circular saw with extension table.

**2** This shop-built table works well for crosscuts using a fixed-angle miter gauge and an extension table.

Start by cutting the 5/4 stock to size. Then plane the edges smooth if necessary, being careful to maintain consistent widths on all the pieces. Accurate spacing of the piggybacked blocks that form the dado is essential for a well-fitted joint. To get it right, dry assemble the base, good faces down, using spring clamps to hold the components together. Next, bore pilot holes for the finishing nails in each block and code each piece before disassembly to avoid mismatching the parts during the gluing process. Apply glue to each surface, drive in the nails to keep the parts in proper alignment and clamp securely. Wipe off any glue that squeezes into the dado.

While the glue is drying, cut the stock for the pads (Fig. 3). These are made by hand sawing and planing, or by cutting with a bandsaw, if you have one. Then, nail and glue them in place on the base arms (Fig. 4) and clamp securely. The stock also can be thinned by using a router fitted with an oversize base, as shown in the drawing on page 6.

Next, using a crosscut saw, cut the broad, angled faces on the top surface of each base arm (Fig. 5). Then plane the surface smooth and square. Use a router with a $\frac{1}{4}$-in.-rad. rounding-over bit to ease the corners. The larger radii shown in the plans are formed by hand sanding or using a bench-mounted finishing sander, as shown on page 6. Finish sand the base parts. Assemble them with glue and screws. Check for square and then put them aside while the post supports are made.

*Traditional Clothes Tree* was written by Rosario Capotosto. How-to photos by Rosario Capotosto with lead photo by J.R. Rost. Technical art by Eugene Thompson. Finish used on the project shown was Minwax Jacobean stain followed by two coats of Minwax Semi-Gloss Polyurethane. The cast-iron hooks (Hallway Hook No. SHF 15) are available from Van Dyke's, P.O. Box 278, Woonsocket, SD 57385.

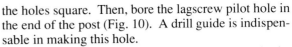

## Post Supports

Cut the post support blanks from 5/4 stock. Lay out and cut the curved outlines using a sabre saw (Fig. 6). Smooth the curved edges with a spokeshave (Fig. 7), using the curved-base type to work the concave portions and the flat-base type for the convex sections. Finish up the supports by rounding over the edges with a router (Fig. 8).

Because the supports are attached to the post with dowel pins, a doweling jig is essential for achieving perfectly aligned perpendicular holes. Draw matching centerlines on the post and supports. Then bore $5/16$-in.-dia. holes to a depth of $11/16$ in. for each member (Fig. 9).

Next, bore the holes for the lagscrew that joins the post to the assembled base using a drill guide to keep the holes square. Then, bore the lagscrew pilot hole in the end of the post (Fig. 10). A drill guide is indispensable in making this hole.

Final assembly is done in two stages. First, join the supports to the post with glue, dowels and clamps (Fig. 11). Then, once this glue has cured, dry assemble the base and post and bore the pilot holes for the screws that join the two. Remove the base from the post, then bore and countersink the screwholes in the base. Once these holes are complete, join the two assemblies with glue, screws and the center lagscrew.

Next, bore the holes for the hook screws. Sand the entire project using 120-grit, followed by 220-grit sandpaper. Remove all the dust, then stain and finish the piece.

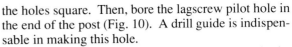

**3** Use a sharp rip saw—or band saw—to resaw stock to a $3/8$-in. thickness. Make the cut on the waste side of the line.

**4** Once the base pads are resawed and planed smooth, cut them to length. Then glue and nail them to the base members.

**5** Use a crosscut saw to cut inclines on the top surface of the base members. Remove any cut marks by hand planing.

**6** Carefully lay out the profile of the post supports, and then make the curved cuts with a sabre saw and sharp blade.

**7** Smooth the post support edges with a spokeshave. Use the type with a curved base and always cut with the grain.

**8** Ease sharp edges using a router with a rounding-over bit. Hold small pieces to a clamped scrap piece with masking tape.

**9** Bore dowel holes in post and post supports using a doweling jig. Attach tape to drill bit to act as depth gauge.

**10** Bore a lagscrew clearance hole in the base assembly. Then bore a pilot hole in the post using a drill guide.

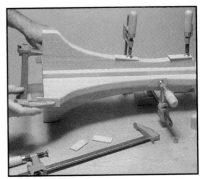

**11** Glue and clamp the post supports to the post and when the assembly is dry, join it to the base with its lagscrew.

This simple pine cabinet has three deep shelves for holding all kinds of wide or tall items.

# Linen cupboard

There are few things more versatile than a simple pine cupboard, especially like this that was inspired by old Shaker designs. The original versions of this venerable piece were used for storing vegetable and fruit preserves. But its traditional bearings have long since been obscured and now cabinets like this are used for just about anything, from pots and pans to toys and linens.

Constructed of solid pine, this cabinet features three roomy shelves and a frame-and-panel door that swings on self-closing hinges. No. 2 pine was used because it's still affordable, but lumber of this grade can be twisted and usually features large knots, some of which are loose. To avoid, or at least minimize, these imperfections be sure to plan your work to cut around the bad areas. Another solution is simply to buy No. 1 or Select, pine. This grade is more expensive, but it's also much straighter and has fewer knots.

Linen Cupboard was written and photographed by Rosario Capotosto. Lead photo by J.R. Rost. Technical art by Eugene Thompson. The chest shown was finished first with Minwax Wood Conditioner to promote even staining, then Minwax Golden Oak Stain followed by two coats of Minwax Satin Polyurethane.

## Sides and Top

Once you've selected the best arrangement of boards, cut them to size, joint the mating edges and arrange them flat on your workbench. Hold them together with masking tape while you mark the circular cutout at the bottom with a compass (Fig. 1). Next, mark the locations for your joining plates, or biscuits, which should be about 8 in. apart (Fig. 2). Be sure to avoid placing a plate where the circular cutout falls.

Apply glue to the slots (Fig. 3), the plates and the edges of the boards. Then insert the plates, slide the boards together and clamp securely. Use cross cauls (Fig. 4) to keep the panel from bowing. When the glue has set, scrape off any squeeze-out and use a belt sander, if necessary, to smooth the surface. Assemble the top panel in the same way.

Cut the top and side panels to width and length. If you're using a table saw, place the miter gauge in the reverse position—against the leading edge of the panel—to start the cut (Fig. 5). These panels are so wide that if the miter gauge is behind the back edge, it can't reach its table groove. When the trailing edge clears the front of the table, shut off the power and, without moving the panel, put the miter gauge in its regular position and then complete the cut.

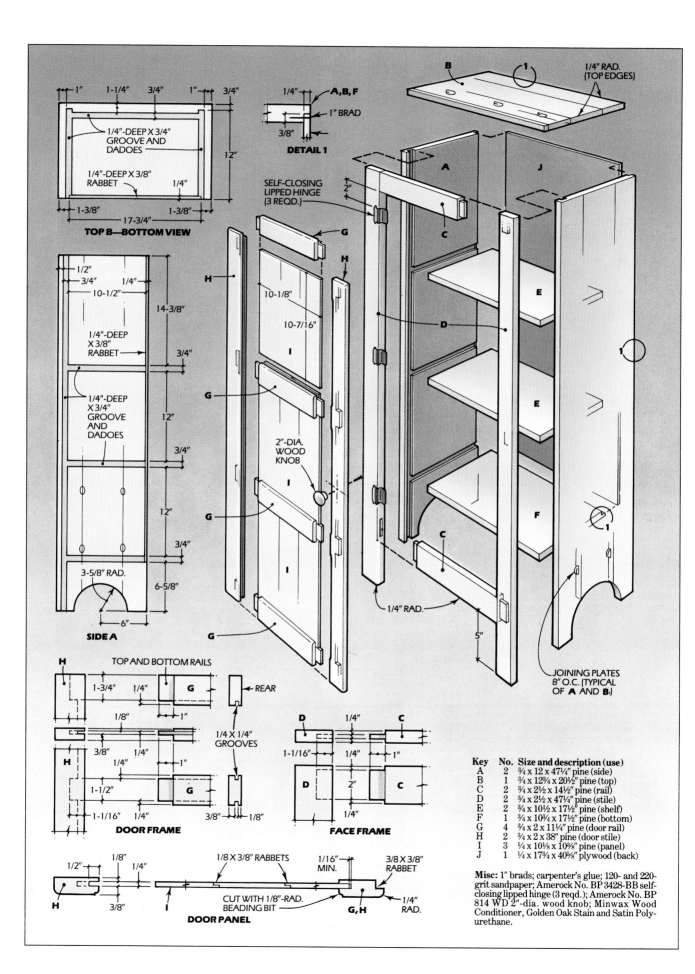

1/4" RAD. (TOP EDGES)

1"  1-1/4"  3/4"  1"  3/4"

1/4"-DEEP X 3/4" GROOVE AND DADOES

12"

1/4"-DEEP X 3/8" RABBET

1/4"

1-3/8"  1-3/8"

17-3/4"

**TOP B—BOTTOM VIEW**

1/4"  A, B, F

1" BRAD

3/8"

**DETAIL 1**

B

1'

A

J

SELF-CLOSING LIPPED HINGE (3 REQD.)

2"

C

G

H

1/2"

3/4"  1/4"

10-1/2"

14-3/8"

1/4"-DEEP X 3/8" RABBET

3/4"

10-1/8"

10-7/16"

I

D

H

E

G

1/4"-DEEP X 3/4" GROOVE AND DADOES

12"

3/4"

2"-DIA. WOOD KNOB

I

G

E

12"

3/4"

I

F

C

3-5/8" RAD.

6-5/8"

G

1/4" RAD.

C

6"

**SIDE A**

5"

1'

JOINING PLATES 8" O.C. (TYPICAL OF A AND B)

1/4" RAD.

H

TOP AND BOTTOM RAILS

1-3/4"  1/4"  G

REAR

1/8"  1"

1/4 X 1/4" GROOVES

D  1/4"  C

3/8"  1/4"

H

1/4"

1-1/2"  G

1-1/16"  1/4"  1"

D  2"  C

1-1/16"  1/4"  3/8"  1/8"

1/4"

**DOOR FRAME**

**FACE FRAME**

| Key | No. | Size and description (use) |
|---|---|---|
| A | 2 | ¾ x 12 x 47¼" pine (side) |
| B | 1 | ¾ x 12¾ x 20½" pine (top) |
| C | 2 | ¾ x 2½ x 14½" pine (rail) |
| D | 2 | ¾ x 2½ x 47¼" pine (stile) |
| E | 2 | ¾ x 10½ x 17½" pine (shelf) |
| F | 1 | ¾ x 10¾ x 17½" pine (bottom) |
| G | 4 | ¾ x 2 x 11¼" pine (door rail) |
| H | 2 | ¾ x 2 x 38" pine (door stile) |
| I | 3 | ¼ x 10⅛ x 10⅝" pine (panel) |
| J | 1 | ¼ x 17¾ x 40⅝" plywood (back) |

**Misc:** 1" brads; carpenter's glue; 120- and 220-grit sandpaper; Amerock No. BP 3428-BB self-closing lipped hinge (3 reqd.); Amerock No. BP 814 WD 2"-dia. wood knob; Minwax Wood Conditioner, Golden Oak Stain and Satin Polyurethane.

1/2"  1/8"  1/4"

1/8 X 3/8" RABBETS

1/16" MIN.

3/8 X 3/8" RABBET

H  3/8"  I

CUT WITH 1/8"-RAD. BEADING BIT

G, H

1/4" RAD.

**DOOR PANEL**

Use a band saw, a sabre saw with a pivot guide or careful freehand cutting to make the curved cutout (Fig. 6). Next, using a ¾-in. straight bit and a router with an edge guide, cut the lengthwise grooves for the face frame in the sides and the top. Use the same bit to cut the rabbet along the back edge of each panel to receive the case back (Fig. 7). Also, cut the crossgrain dadoes on the sides with the same bit. But this time, use wood strips tack-nailed to the surface to act as a routing guide (Fig. 8).

## Face Frame

The face frame is assembled with mortise-and-tenon joints. Begin by cutting the rails and stiles to size, then lay out the mortises in the stiles and the tenons on the rails. Using a drill press—or a portable drill and drill guide—and a ¼-in. bit, bore a series of overlapping holes in the stiles to form the mortises. Use a chisel to square the corners and trim the walls of each mortise smooth. Then, cut the rail tenons with a dado head in your table saw and assemble the frame with glue and clamps. Make sure the assembly is square.

While the glue is drying on the face frame, use a router to round over the edges on the top and side panels. Then cut the shelves to size and sand them and the other panels smooth. Once the face frame is sanded,

remove all the dust from the parts and assemble the case in this order: First, lay one side panel on the bench and apply glue to its groove and dadoes. Then, spread glue on the end grain of all the shelves and place them in the dadoes on the side panel (Fig. 9). Apply glue to the edge of the face frame and squeeze it into place. Then, apply glue to the joints on the second side and push it into place.

Once everything is together, carefully lay the assembly on its back, install the clamps and check for square. When the glue has set, remove the clamps, glue the top in place and reinstall the clamps.

## Door Construction

Cut the stock for the rails and stiles to size and mark the parts for the mortises and tenons that will join them. Cut these joints the same way you cut them on the face frame, using the drill press for the mortises and the table saw for the tenons (Fig. 10).

Fabricate each door panel by lap joining three pieces of pine lattice. The lattice is ¼ in. thick and 3⅝ in. wide, and the lap joints are formed by rabbets cut in the edges of the lattice boards. Cut these using a dado head in your table saw, making sure to clamp an auxiliary fence and a featherboard to your saw's fence (Fig. 11).

**1** Align the stock for the sides, and lay out the circular cutout for the feet and the location of the joining plates.

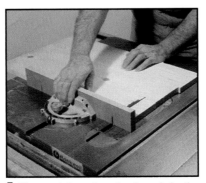

**2** Using a plate joiner, cut the plate slots in the board edges. Work on a flat surface or the slots will not align.

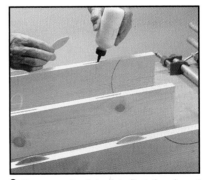

**3** Squeeze glue into slots first, then insert plates. Once the plates are installed, apply glue to the board edges.

**4** Join the boards with bar or pipe clamps first. Then clamp wood cauls across the surface to keep the panel flat.

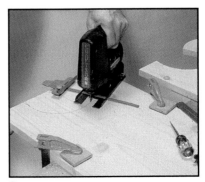

**5** Glue and clamp together boards for the top panel. Once the glue has dried, cut the panel to size on the table saw.

**6** Use a sabre saw with a pivot guide, or work freehand, to cut the legs to shape. Cut from the back side of the panel.

Once the cutting is done, glue the lattice pieces together using masking tape as clamps (Fig. 12). Use a piece of wax paper under this assembly to keep it from sticking to your workbench. When the glue is dry, sand all the panels smooth and set them aside.

Next, dry assemble the door frame with clamps to check for fit and square. Then rout the inside edges of the doorframe to give them shape (Fig. 13).

Disassemble the pieces, apply glue to the mortises and tenons and push the parts together. Slide the door panels into their grooves—but don't use any glue to hold them (Fig. 14). They should float so they can move with changes in temperature and humidity. Clamp the whole assembly and set it aside until it's dry. Then remove the clamps and rout the rabbet around the back edge of the door using a straight bit and an edge guide.

Finish sand the door and case with 120-grit, followed by 220-grit sandpaper. Bore the hinge holes and temporarily mount the door to check for proper fit. Also, attach the back panel at this point. Then remove the door and apply your finish.

**7** Cut a stopped rabbet for the back panel in the case sides, using a router with an edge guide and a straight cutting bit.

**8** Cut shelf dadoes using an L-shaped guide. Place the short leg into the long dado and tack the other leg to the side.

**9** Assemble piece on its side. First glue the face frame and shelves to one side, then add second side and clamp.

**10** Use a dado head in a table saw to cut the tenons on the ends of the door rails.

**11** Cut lattice stock to size for door panels. Then cut rabbets on mating edges.

**12** Join panels with glue and tape. Wax paper keeps assembly from sticking.

**13** Dry assemble door frame. Then make bead cuts on inside edges.

**14** Join door parts by gluing rails to stiles. Do not glue door panels in place.

# Folding card table

The common folding table—or card table as many of us grew up calling it—is the height of simplicity and versatility in furniture design. Its sturdy and spacious top can comfortably accommodate four adults with full table service, and when the need for it passes, it can easily fold up and fit in almost any closet.

### Top Frame
Because a project like this requires cutting stock into relatively narrow strips, the work is best done on a table saw. But if you have only a portable circular saw, you can still tackle this job with ease if you install your saw in the simple shop-made table shown in Fig. 1. The version shown is made for a relatively small, 5½-in. saw. But if your saw is bigger, simply alter the dimensions to suit your needs.

The accessories include a straight wood strip—which must be clamped in place—to serve as a rip fence and a one-position miter gauge with a fixed fence that aids in making right-angle crosscuts. Finally, for safety purposes, there's a see-through saw-blade guard.

Begin construction by ripping the stock to width for the top frame pieces (Fig. 2) and crosscutting them to length. If the saw leaves rough edges, use a hand plane to remove them. Next, mark the ends of each board for the half lap joints as shown in Fig. 3. It's best to stack the actual pieces in their final overlapped position to ensure accuracy in marking. Note that the joint lines alternate on the board ends as you move around the frame.

Cut the rabbets for these half lap joints using a router with a straight bit and the jig shown in Fig. 4. (Building instructions appear in the plans on page 18.) To use the jig, clamp the work in place and make the passes required to shave away the waste. The depth of cut should equal half the thickness of the stock.

To assemble the frame, you'll need four C-clamps and eight scrap wood pads. Apply glue to the mating surfaces of each joint and drive a pair of ⅝-in. brads into the back of each to keep the members from shifting around during the clamping (Fig. 5). Install the clamps

*Folding Card Table* was written by Rosario Capotosto. Lead photo by J.R. Rost. How-to photographs by Rosario Capotosto. Technical art by Eugene Thompson. Stain used on the table shown is Minwax Colonial Walnut Wood-Sheen Stain and Finish. The folding leg hardware is available from The Woodworker's Store, 21801 Industrial Blvd., Rogers Minnesota 55374. A pair is part No. 63198.

This sturdy card table is made of white oak and has heavy-duty folding hardware to make storage a breeze.

and protective pads and then set the whole assembly aside until dry. Once the glue has cured, remove any squeeze-out by using a sharp chisel or cabinet scraper.

Next, using a router, cut the rabbet on the inside edge of the frame that will receive the top panel (Fig. 6). The plan calls for a 5⁄16-in.-deep rabbet, which represents the combined thickness of the plywood and the vinyl fabric. Since product sizes can vary so much, it's best to check the thickness of the materials you have and adjust your router depth accordingly.

To complete the top frame, use a sabre saw or a coping saw to cut the radii on the four corners. Sand away any saw ripples, then use a router to round over all the outside edges. Finish sand the entire assembly with 120-grit, followed by 220-grit sandpaper.

### Apron
Cut the four apron pieces to length and width. Rout a rabbet on one end of each piece as shown in the plans. Apply glue and drive two 1-in. brads in each corner joint. Lay the frame edge down on the workbench, check the assembly for square with a triangle or square. Use masking tape to keep the assembly from moving until the glue sets (Fig. 7). Once the glue is dry, round over the bottom corners, sand the faces smooth, then put the assembly aside. Remember to handle the apron with care. It won't be structurally sound until it's attached to the bottom of the top frame.

## Legs

Cut the $1\frac{1}{4}$-in.-sq. legs from a blank made by gluing together two $\frac{3}{4}$-in. × 6-in. boards. Spread the glue on the surface of both boards (Fig. 8) and use at least six C-clamps to distribute the pressure evenly.

When the glue has set, hand plane one edge of the slab so it's straight, flat and smooth. Then set the fence on the circular saw table to rip the four legs. If the blade projection is too shallow on your table to make a through cut, just flip over the stock and make a second pass (Fig. 9).

Mark the hole locations for the leg brace rivets as indicated on the template that comes with the hardware. Cut to shape and sand smooth the round top of each leg. Then bore the rivet clearance holes. These holes must be perfectly perpendicular to the surface of the leg, so some form of drill guide should be used for this job (Fig. 10). Finish sand the legs with 120-grit, followed by 220-grit sandpaper before attaching the hardware. Be sure to round over the outside corner edges of the legs.

Because the upper screwholes for this brace are located close to the top edge where drill access would be impossible after assembly, mark and bore the pilot holes now (Fig. 11).

Next, clamp the apron in place and bore screw pilot holes through the apron and into the underside of the top frame. Remove the apron and enlarge the holes to match the screw shank size. Then counterbore for the screwheads and reattach the top.

**1** A shopmade table for your circular saw will yield easier, more accurate cuts. See drawing for building directions.

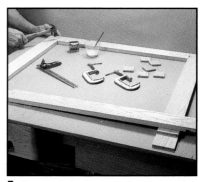

**2** Using shop-built table, rip top frame members to width. Clamp blade guard in place and use pushstick for safety.

**3** Align the top frame members as shown, then mark cutting lines for corner half lap joints directly on the boards.

**4** Use this easy-to-build router jig for cutting the half lap joints. Just slide in the stock, clamp in place and rout.

**5** Assemble frame parts facedown. Apply glue, then drive two alignment brads through both pieces and clamp.

**6** Use a router and a rabbet bit to make the recess cut in the top frame for the top panel. Make cut in several passes.

**7** Fabricate the apron pieces, then join them with glue and brads. Hold the joint in square alignment using masking tape.

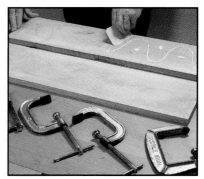

**8** Obtain the stock for the legs by gluing up two 4/4 boards. Spread the glue evenly and clamp boards securely.

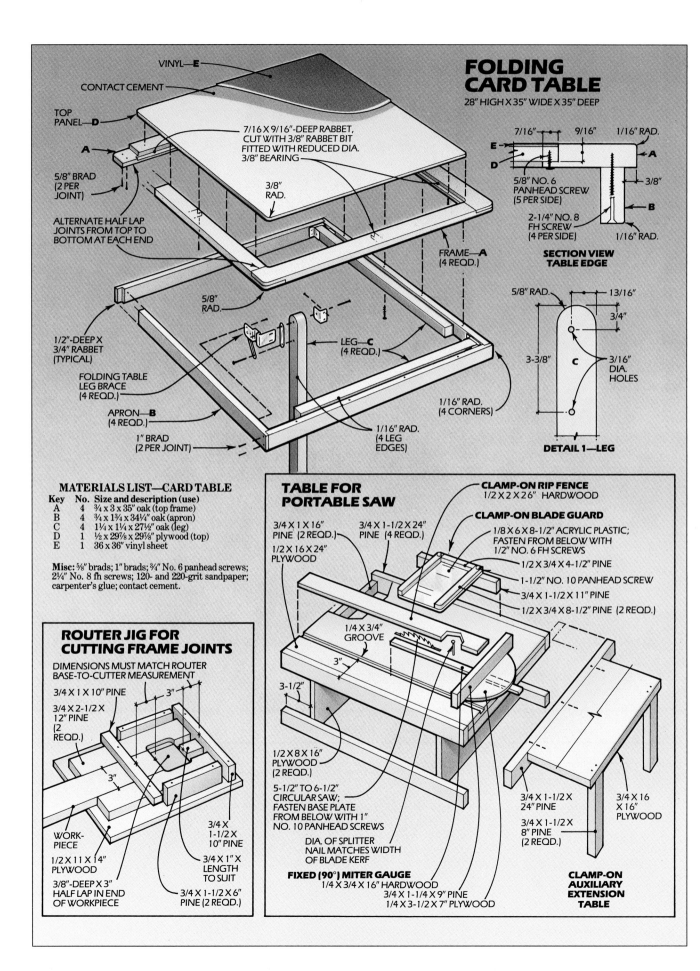

**FOLDING CARD TABLE**
28" HIGH X 35" WIDE X 35" DEEP

VINYL—E

CONTACT CEMENT

TOP PANEL—D

A

5/8" BRAD (2 PER JOINT)

7/16 X 9/16"-DEEP RABBET, CUT WITH 3/8" RABBET BIT FITTED WITH REDUCED DIA. 3/8" BEARING

3/8" RAD.

ALTERNATE HALF LAP JOINTS FROM TOP TO BOTTOM AT EACH END

FRAME—A (4 REQD.)

5/8" RAD.

1/2"-DEEP X 3/4" RABBET (TYPICAL)

FOLDING TABLE LEG BRACE (4 REQD.)

LEG—C (4 REQD.)

APRON—B (4 REQD.)

1" BRAD (2 PER JOINT)

1/16" RAD. (4 CORNERS)

1/16" RAD. (4 LEG EDGES)

7/16"   9/16"   1/16" RAD.

E
D
A

5/8" NO. 6 PANHEAD SCREW (5 PER SIDE)

3/8"

B

2-1/4" NO. 8 FH SCREW (4 PER SIDE)

1/16" RAD.

**SECTION VIEW TABLE EDGE**

5/8" RAD.   13/16"
3/4"

3-3/8"   C   3/16" DIA. HOLES

**DETAIL 1—LEG**

## MATERIALS LIST—CARD TABLE

| Key | No. | Size and description (use) |
|-----|-----|----------------------------|
| A | 4 | ¾ x 3 x 35" oak (top frame) |
| B | 4 | ¾ x 1¾ x 34¼" oak (apron) |
| C | 4 | 1¼ x 1¼ x 27½" oak (leg) |
| D | 1 | ½ x 29⅞ x 29⅞" plywood (top) |
| E | 1 | 36 x 36" vinyl sheet |

**Misc:** ⅝" brads; 1" brads; ¾" No. 6 panhead screws; 2¼" No. 8 fh screws; 120- and 220-grit sandpaper; carpenter's glue; contact cement.

## ROUTER JIG FOR CUTTING FRAME JOINTS

DIMENSIONS MUST MATCH ROUTER BASE-TO-CUTTER MEASUREMENT

3/4 X 1 X 10" PINE   3"

3/4 X 2-1/2 X 12" PINE (2 REQD.)

3"

WORK-PIECE

1/2 X 11 X 14" PLYWOOD

3/8"-DEEP X 3" HALF LAP IN END OF WORKPIECE

3/4 X 1-1/2 X 10" PINE

3/4 X 1" X LENGTH TO SUIT

3/4 X 1-1/2 X 6" PINE (2 REQD.)

## TABLE FOR PORTABLE SAW

3/4 X 1 X 16" PINE (2 REQD.)

1/2 X 16 X 24" PLYWOOD

3/4 X 1-1/2 X 24" PINE (4 REQD.)

**CLAMP-ON RIP FENCE**
1/2 X 2 X 26" HARDWOOD

**CLAMP-ON BLADE GUARD**

1/8 X 6 X 8-1/2" ACRYLIC PLASTIC; FASTEN FROM BELOW WITH 1/2" NO. 6 FH SCREWS

1/2 X 3/4 X 4-1/2" PINE

1-1/2" NO. 10 PANHEAD SCREW

3/4 X 1-1/2 X 11" PINE

1/2 X 3/4 X 8-1/2" PINE (2 REQD.)

1/4 X 3/4" GROOVE

3"

3-1/2"

1/2 X 8 X 16" PLYWOOD (2 REQD.)

5-1/2" TO 6-1/2" CIRCULAR SAW; FASTEN BASE PLATE FROM BELOW WITH 1" NO. 10 PANHEAD SCREWS

DIA. OF SPLITTER NAIL MATCHES WIDTH OF BLADE KERF

**FIXED (90°) MITER GAUGE**
1/4 X 3/4 X 16" HARDWOOD
3/4 X 1-1/4 X 9" PINE
1/4 X 3-1/2 X 7" PLYWOOD

3/4 X 1-1/2 X 24" PINE

3/4 X 1-1/2 X 8" PINE (2 REQD.)

3/4 X 16 X 16" PLYWOOD

**CLAMP-ON AUXILIARY EXTENSION TABLE**

## Top Panel

Use a clamped straightedge strip to guide the circular saw, and once the panel is cut, round the corners to match the inside corners of the top frame. When the panel fits exactly, turn over the assembly and bore pilot holes for the screws that join the two.

Next, cut the vinyl fabric about 2 in. larger than the top panel in both directions. Apply a coat of contact cement to the back of the vinyl (Fig. 12). Also apply a coat of cement to the top side of the panel. Allow the cement to dry.

The cement-coated surfaces will bond immediately and permanently when contact is made, so you must take precautions against misalignment. You can use a technique called the slip-sheet method. Just cut two pieces of kraft paper slightly bigger than half the size of the panel. Then lay the paper on the panel (Fig. 13), slightly overlapping the pieces in the middle. Position the vinyl so it overhangs the panel on all sides, too. Then slide out one paper sheet and allow the cement surfaces to make contact. While holding up the other end of the vinyl, slide out the remaining sheet (Fig. 14) and carefully lower the rest of the vinyl into place. Allow it to make contact slowly as the other hand sweeps across the surface to press it into place. Exert final pressure with a roller. Turn over the panel and use a sharp knife to trim off the excess (Fig. 15).

While the top panel is still separate from the top frame, apply the finish of your choice (Fig. 16). Seal the back of the panel with two coats of shellac. When everything is dry, attach the legs and top (Fig. 17).

**9** If you use the table to rip the legs, its shallow blade projection requires cutting in two passes, one on each side.

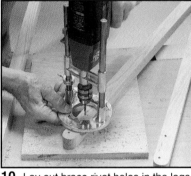

**10** Lay out brace rivet holes in the legs. Then bore them using a drill with a guide to keep holes perpendicular.

**11** Temporarily place all the folding hardware on the legs and aprons. Then mark all the bracket screwholes.

**12** Cut the sheet vinyl to rough size. Then, using a short bristle brush, apply contact cement to its bottom side.

**13** Cut the top plywood panel to size and shape. Then sand it smooth and cover it with two pieces of kraft paper.

**14** Carefully align the vinyl over the kraft paper, then lower it into place. Slip out the paper sheets one at a time.

**15** Use a roller to smooth the vinyl in place. Then turn over the panel and trim off the excess with a sharp utility knife.

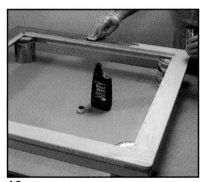

**16** Check the top panel for fit. Finish sand the frame and apply finish before installing the top.

**17** Attach the legs to the fame assembly and slide the top panel into place. Attach the panel with screws from below.

# Ｈigh-boy chest

Most dressers are basically horizontal furniture pieces, and with good reason. This shape allows for plenty of drawer space and yields a broad flat surface on top that is always handy in a bedroom. Of course, a substantial dresser can occupy quite a bit of floor space, which is a real problem in a smaller bedroom.

The obvious way to cope with such tight quarters is to create a piece that is predominately vertical. It should occupy a smaller footprint and achieve its large storage volume by extending up much higher. Its only shortcoming would be a lack of a large, open top.

The piece shown here is just such a problem solver, and it is by no means a new idea. Such pieces have been around for centuries and have borne many different names—from the traditional high-boy chest description to the enticing appellation of lingerie chest (one drawer for each day of the week), to the more prosaic description of tall chest. No matter what the name, the virtues of this piece remain unchanged: It has a lot of storage space and can fit just about anywhere.

The unit shown is made of solid mahogany, with a little poplar thrown in for the drawer and divider-frame parts. Mahogany was chosen to impart a traditional feel to the piece. But you can use any wood species you'd like—the construction details remain the same.

## Case Sides and Top

Begin by joining narrower boards to make up the top and sides. Cut the boards about 1 in. longer than the finished size to allow for trimming after gluing. Add a bit extra in width for the same reason. Keep in mind that if you don't have a jointer, you can effectively joint your edges on a table saw. Just tack-nail a metal straightedge guide to one side of a board, letting it extend just over the edge. Then make your rip cut, keeping the metal guide against the fence for the entire cut (Fig. 1). This will create one straight edge. To straighten the other, simply turn over the board and rip the rough edge.

*High-Boy Chest* was written by Rosario Capotosto. Lead photo by J.R.Rost with how-to photos by Rosario Capotosto. Technical art by Eugene Thompson. The cove-and-bead bit shown is Bosch No. 85604M; the ogee fillet bit is Sears No. 21257.

**1** To straighten stock on table saw, tack-nail metal rule to one edge, then rip. Remove rule and rip the other edge.

**2** Because pencil marks are hard to see on darker woods, apply tape to edge then lay out the frame dadoes.

Once all your stock is prepared, glue and clamp the boards together, let them dry and then use a cabinet scraper or belt sander to smooth the surfaces. Finish the edge-joining process by cutting the panels to finished size.

Next, mark the side panels for the dadoes and rabbets. If you want your pencil marks to be more visible, make them on a strip of masking tape—applied along the edge—rather than on the surface of the dark mahogany (Fig. 2). Then set up a dado blade in your radial saw and cut all the dadoes (Fig. 3). When these are done, readjust the blade to make the rabbet cuts on the top edges of the sides and the end edges of the top. Next, using a router with a rabbet or straight bit, cut the stopped rabbets on the sides and top for the case back. Use a sharp chisel to square the corners.

To join the narrow strips to the front of the sides and top, begin by marking the location of the joining plates. Then use the joiner to cut slots for No.0 plates (Fig. 4). Spread glue in the slots, on the plates and on the edge, then push the boards together. Install clamps and set the assembly aside to dry (Fig. 5).

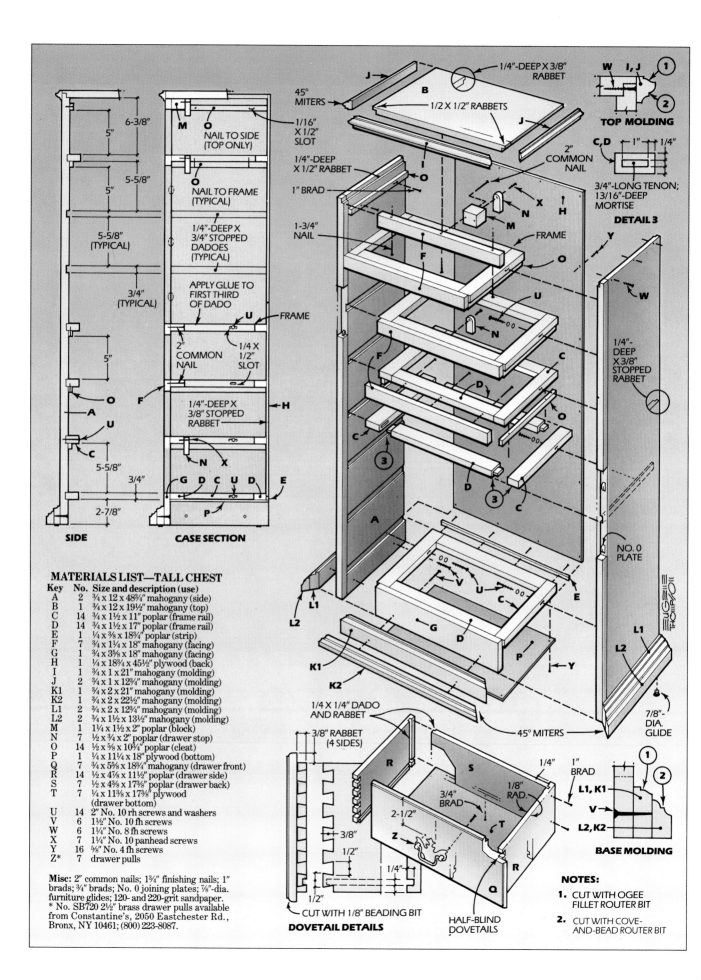

**SIDE**

6-3/8"
5"
5"
5-5/8"
5-5/8" (TYPICAL)
3/4" (TYPICAL)
5"
5-5/8"
3/4"
2-7/8"

O
M
O
O
U
A
U
C

**CASE SECTION**

M  O
NAIL TO SIDE (TOP ONLY)
1/16" X 1/2" SLOT
O
NAIL TO FRAME (TYPICAL)
1/4"-DEEP X 3/4" STOPPED DADOES (TYPICAL)
APPLY GLUE TO FIRST THIRD OF DADO
U
FRAME
2" COMMON NAIL
1/4 X 1/2" SLOT
1/4"-DEEP X 3/8" STOPPED RABBET
H
N  X
G  D  C  U  D  E
F
P

J
45° MITERS
1/16" X 1/2" SLOT
1/4"-DEEP X 1/2" RABBET
1" BRAD
1-3/4" NAIL
B
1/4"-DEEP X 3/8" RABBET
1/2 X 1/2" RABBETS
J
I
O
X  H
N
M
F
FRAME
O
U
C
F
D
O
C
D
C
3
3
A

2" COMMON NAIL

**TOP MOLDING**
W  I, J
1
2

**DETAIL 3**
C,D  1"  1/4"
3/4"-LONG TENON; 13/16"-DEEP MORTISE

Y
W
1/4"-DEEP X 3/8" STOPPED RABBET

NO. 0 PLATE

V  U  C
E
L1
L2
G
D
P
Y
K1
K2
45° MITERS
L1
L2
7/8"-DIA. GLIDE

EUGENE THOMPSON

## MATERIALS LIST—TALL CHEST

| Key | No. | Size and description (use) |
|---|---|---|
| A | 2 | 3/4 x 12 x 48-3/4" mahogany (side) |
| B | 1 | 3/4 x 12 x 19-1/2" mahogany (top) |
| C | 14 | 3/4 x 1-1/2 x 11" poplar (frame rail) |
| D | 14 | 3/4 x 1-1/2 x 17" poplar (frame rail) |
| E | 1 | 1/4 x 3/8 x 18-3/4" poplar (strip) |
| F | 7 | 3/4 x 1-1/4 x 18" mahogany (facing) |
| G | 1 | 3/4 x 3-3/8 x 18" mahogany (facing) |
| H | 1 | 1/4 x 18-3/4 x 45-1/2" plywood (back) |
| I | 1 | 3/4 x 1 x 21" mahogany (molding) |
| J | 2 | 3/4 x 1 x 12-3/4" mahogany (molding) |
| K1 | 1 | 3/4 x 2 x 21" mahogany (molding) |
| K2 | 1 | 3/4 x 2 x 22-1/2" mahogany (molding) |
| L1 | 2 | 3/4 x 2 x 12-3/4" mahogany (molding) |
| L2 | 2 | 3/4 x 1-1/2 x 13-1/2" mahogany (molding) |
| M | 1 | 1-1/4 x 1-1/2 x 2" poplar (block) |
| N | 7 | 1/2 x 3/4 x 2" poplar (drawer stop) |
| O | 14 | 1/2 x 5/8 x 10-3/4" poplar (cleat) |
| P | 1 | 1/4 x 11-1/4 x 18" plywood (bottom) |
| Q | 7 | 3/4 x 5-5/8 x 18-3/4" mahogany (drawer front) |
| R | 14 | 1/2 x 4-7/8 x 11-1/2" poplar (drawer side) |
| S | 7 | 1/2 x 4-3/8 x 17-7/8" poplar (drawer back) |
| T | 7 | 1/4 x 11-3/8 x 17-7/8" plywood (drawer bottom) |
| U | 14 | 2" No. 10 rh screws and washers |
| V | 6 | 1-1/2" No. 10 fh screws |
| W | 6 | 1-1/4" No. 8 fh screws |
| X | 7 | 1-1/4" No. 10 panhead screws |
| Y | 16 | 5/8" No. 4 fh screws |
| Z* | 7 | drawer pulls |

**Misc:** 2" common nails; 1-3/4" finishing nails; 1" brads; 3/4" brads; No. 0 joining plates; 7/8"-dia. furniture glides; 120- and 220-grit sandpaper.
* No. SB720 2-1/2" brass drawer pulls available from Constantine's, 2050 Eastchester Rd., Bronx, NY 10461; (800) 223-8087.

1/4 X 1/4" DADO AND RABBET
3/8" RABBET (4 SIDES)
R
S
1/4"  1" BRAD
1/8" RAD.
3/4" BRAD
2-1/2"
T
Z
3/8"
1/2"
1/4"
1/2"
Q
R
CUT WITH 1/8" BEADING BIT
**DOVETAIL DETAILS**
HALF-BLIND DOVETAILS

**BASE MOLDING**
1
2
L1, K1
V
L2, K2

## NOTES:
**1.** CUT WITH OGEE FILLET ROUTER BIT
**2.** CUT WITH COVE-AND-BEAD ROUTER BIT

## Support Frames

Rip poplar stock to width for the drawer support frames and crosscut the frame members to length. Mark the short pieces for mortises and the long pieces for tenons. Then mount a dado blade in a radial-arm or table saw and cut the tenons (Fig. 6). Be sure to clamp a stopblock in place on the fence so that all the repetitive cuts will be exactly the same.

Begin cutting the mortises by boring a series of overlapping holes in the stock (Fig. 7). Once the holes are bored, use a chisel to pare the walls of the mortises smooth (Fig. 8). Before joining the frame members, several specialized holes must be bored. First are the slotted holes near the back of each side frame member. These holes are for the screws that help hold the frames to the sides.

Next, bore three clearance holes in each front frame member for three alignment nails. These nails are used to position the mahogany facing strips that will cover the front of the frames later. Finally, bore the holes for the drawer stopblocks. Then apply glue to the mortise and tenon joints, push the parts together and clamp securely (Fig. 9). Check for square and put the assemblies aside to dry.

## Case Assembly

Begin by laying one side panel face down on your bench. Then slide a frame into each dado and check for fit. On the edge of each front frame, mark the corner formed by the frame and the dado (Fig. 10). Remove the frames and install them in the other side panel and mark the dado joints again. The distance between these two marks on each frame represents the length of the facing strip. Next, cut these mahogany strips to length. Glue, clamp and nail them to the frames (Fig. 11).

Once all the facing strips are in place, dry assemble the case to check for proper fit (Fig. 12). Then bore pilot holes for the three flathead screws in the top rabbets on each side. Measure for the back plywood panel, cut it to size and set it aside.

Because the final case assembly can take awhile, you should use slow-setting hide glue for this phase of the work. Begin by gluing and screwing the top to one side panel. Apply glue to the entire rabbet joint because the grain runs the same way in the top and side and therefore wood movement will not be a problem. On the frame assemblies, however, glue is applied only to the front third of the dado and frame. The back of the frame is held to the side with screws.

**3** Adjust radial-arm saw for proper dado depth then test cut a scrap block. When satisfied, cut dadoes in both case sides.

**4** Clean out mortises in frame members using sharp chisel. Mortise walls should be exactly perpendicular to stock edge.

**5** Apply glue to frame mortises and tenons, then clamp securely. Check for square and readjust clamps if necessary.

**6** Cut to size narrow stock that closes front of the dadoes. Use plate joiner to cut matching slots in side and strip.

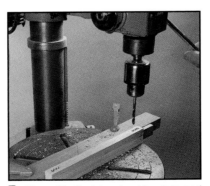

**7** Place No.0 plates in side slots and push strip onto plates. Check for fit, and when satisfied, glue and clamp.

**8** Use radial saw and dado blades to cut tenons on frame members. Clamp stopblock to fence to ensure identical cuts.

When all the frames have been installed, apply glue to all the joints on the second side panel. Then, with a helper, carefully position this panel over the frame assemblies and push the joints together, working from one end of the case to the other. Install clamps and check for square.

While the glue dries on the case, fabricate the top and bottom moldings using a table-mounted router. Form the top molding—on a 1-in.-wide strip—with two passes over two different bits: first a 1⁵⁄₁₆-in. cove-and-bead bit, and then an ogee fillet bit. On the first pass, hold the board face down. When you switch to the ogee bit, run the work on its edge.

Form the base moldings with the same bits but on separate strips of stock. First, run a 2-in. wide strip—on edge—over the ogee bit. Then switch bits and run a 1¹⁄₂-in.-wide strip—broad face down—over the cove-and-bead bit (Fig. 13). Glue these pieces together—back to face—and hold them with masking tape.

Next, cut the molding pieces to length and miter their outside corners. Glue and clamp the top molding in place. Then glue, clamp and screw the bottom molding to the case (Fig. 14). Once the moldings are installed, attach the drawer stopblocks to each frame and install the spacer cleats that keep the drawers from tipping downward when opened (Fig. 15). Note that the cleats are nailed to the bottom of the side frame members, not to the side panels, except at the top. The top cleats do get nailed to the side because the wood movement problem is avoided by making slotted expansion holes for the nails.

**Drawers**

These drawers feature overlapping fronts, joined to the drawer sides with dovetails. The backs are secured to the sides with corner dado joints. The bottoms fit into simple grooves. These rabbets, dadoes and grooves are cut on a table or radial-arm saw with a dado blade installed.

Cut the stock for the drawer fronts to size. Cut a rabbet completely around the inside surface of each piece. Cut the ¹⁄₂-in.-thick stock to size for the sides and the backs. Cut the rabbets on the ends of the back pieces and the dadoes on the ends of the side members.

The dovetails shown were cut using a router jig that is comprised of a template and a dovetail router bit (Fig. 16). Setup and cutting procedures will vary depending on the jig you use, so refer to your operating manual for instructions on cutting these joints.

**9** Bore mortise holes in frame parts on drill press. Clamp fence with stopblocks in place to limit board travel.

**10** Slide all drawer frames into their dadoes. Then mark on frame edge exactly where frame facing boards should stop.

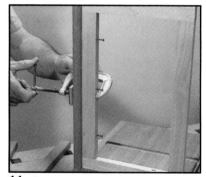

**11** Cut frame facing to length and clamp in place. Then tap frame nails into back of facing to create alignment dimples.

**12** Join frames to sides with hide glue. Apply glue to front third of joint. Back is held with screws in slotted holes.

**13** Use a router table, or a table saw with a molding cutter head, to cut the base and top moldings for the case.

**14** Cut base molding to size. Bore pilot holes for screws that join molding and case. Clamp together and drive screws.

When the dovetails are complete, cut the grooves for the bottom panel in the front and sides of each drawer. Then cut the bottom panels to size and bore the clearance holes for the drawer pulls through the drawer fronts. Next, install a ⅛-in.-rad. beading bit in your router table and shape the edges of the drawer fronts. Make the crossgrain passes on the ends first, holding a backup block against the trailing edge to prevent any tearout (Fig. 17). Use the same bit to round over the top edges of the drawer sides.

Sand all the parts smooth and remove the dust. Then assemble the drawers with glue (Fig. 18) in this order: Fit one side onto the front, then the back onto the side, followed by the second side onto the back and then onto the front. Slide the bottom panel in place, then attach it with nails driven into the bottom edge of the back piece. Also drive a couple of brads into the box dado joints at the rear of all drawers.

## Finishing

Finish sand the entire cabinet with 220-grit sandpaper and ease all sharp corners. To obtain the rich, deep mahogany tone, the cabinet was first given a coat of Behlen's Solar Lux Medium Red Stain (Fig. 19). This is a nongrain-raising stain formulated for spray application. If you're brushing by hand, it must be mixed with a retarder to slow the drying rate. You can try 1-part retarder to 6-parts stain.

Next, seal the stain with a wash coat of shellac—mix 6 parts alcohol with 1 part 3-pound-cut, white shellac. Apply full-strength shellac to the inside of the cabinet and to all the surfaces of the drawers except, of course, the outside of the drawer front.

Then mix a natural paste wood filler with burnt umber Japan color, to match the color of the stained piece, and spread on the filler (Fig. 20). Let this filler dry until it starts to become dull, then wipe it off—working across the grain—using burlap cloth. Once the bulk of the filler is removed, wipe lightly in the direction of the grain with a clean, soft cloth.

After letting the piece dry, apply a wash coat of shellac. Then let the shellac dry and lightly sand the surface to remove any small imperfections. Finish by applying two coats of Behlen's Clear Gloss Brushing Lacquer. When the finish is complete, install the back panel and drawer pulls and you're done.

**15** Cut drawer spacer cleats to size. Nail them to bottom edge of frame members, not to the case sides.

**16** Cut dovetails by hand or use router template. Just align template, according to maker's directions, and rout.

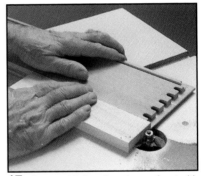

**17** Cut outside bead on drawer front with router table. Hold backup board against workpiece to prevent tearout.

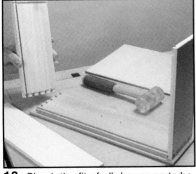

**18** Check the fit of all drawer parts before assembly. Then apply glue to the joints, slide the parts together and clamp.

**19** Apply stain to drawer fronts with clean, soft cloth. Retarder is added to stain to keep lap marks from showing.

**20** Apply filler to stained surfaces. When filler reflection begins to dull, wipe off across the grain with a coarse cloth.

# C lothes press TV cabinet

When cabinet is closed, it reveals the tasteful lines of a traditional clothes press. But inside, it has room for a full-size TV and two VCRs.

It's difficult to think of a home appliance that has made—and continues to make—a bigger impact on our lives than television. The myriad sensibilities that come through this electronic eye may entice or irritate, but usually—in one way or another—they do compel. The box itself—especially many of today's flat-screen, flat-black models—is another story. Many people consider the tube unattractive or, at the very least, not something they want staring back at them 24 hours a day. While most of us may have come to grips with this Orwellian box in the family room or den, it can still seem out of place in the bedroom.

This traditional clothes press was designed to put a better face on your bedroom TV. It can accommodate a full-size TV and VCR while boasting plenty of room for tape storage. Plus, it has three spacious drawers for clothes or linens. The special cranked hinges used swing 250° instead of the usual 180°, so the doors can open almost flat against the cabinet sides.

Clothes Press TV Cabinet written and photographed by Rosario Capotosto. Lead photo by J.R. Rost. Technical art by Eugene Thompson.

The joinery techniques required for this piece run the gamut from mortise-and-tenons, to dowels and plate joints, to traditional dovetails and dadoes. So you'll have a chance to hone many different skills before you apply the finish.

Just a word of caution before you begin: This piece was dimensioned to hold the basic 20-in. television. Recent RCA, Sony and Hitachi models should all fit well. But no matter which brand or model TV you have, be sure to measure it before you start building—and, if necessary, alter these dimensions to suit your particular model.

This cabinet not only hides the TV, it also features two false drawers with drop-down lids, which can house a single VCR and plenty of tapes or two VCRs.

**1** Cut stock to size. Then cut panel grooves in cabinet and door rails and stiles using dado blade in table saw.

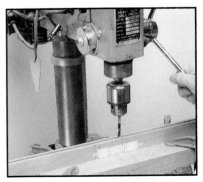

**2** Cut joint mortises in stiles by boring overlapping holes with drill press. Marked tape on surface guides spacing.

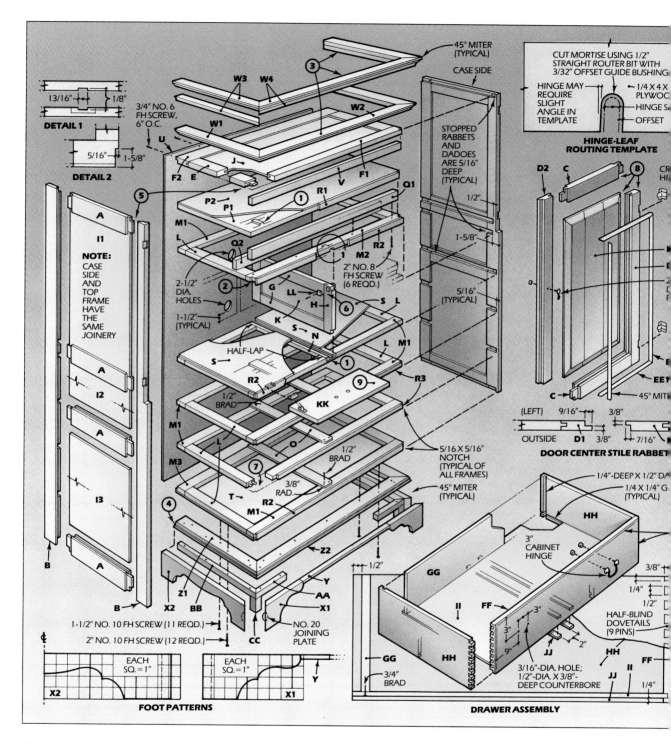

## Case Construction

Start by cutting the stock to size for the door, side and top rails and stiles. Note that one door stile is slightly wider than the others to allow for a rear overlap where the two doors meet. Use a dado blade in a table saw to cut the panel grooves in the rails and stiles (Fig. 1). Be sure to fabricate the door and case members separately because the grooves in the case members are centered while those in the door members are off-center and of a different dimension. Since the top frame members are grooved the same as the side frames, cut these grooves

with the same dado setup. You also should be aware that the plans show 1/4-in.-wide grooves used to seat the plywood panels in the case sides and top frame. Hardwood plywood commonly measures slightly less than 1/4 in. thick, so check the thickness of your plywood and size the grooves accordingly.

After the grooves are cut, lay the door rails and stiles face down on the table saw and cut a 1/4-in.-wide setback on the face of the grooved edges. This allows space for the bead molding that will be applied later.

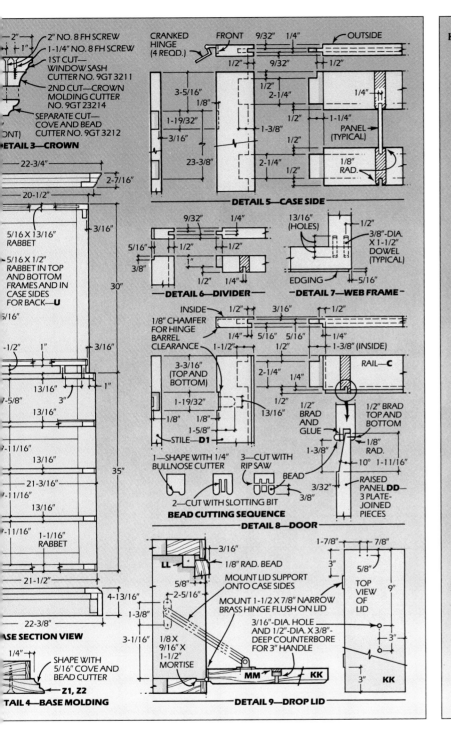

**MATERIALS LIST**

| Key | No. | Size and description (use) |
|---|---|---|
| A | 8 | $^{13}/_{16}$ x $3^{1}/_{4}$ x $17^{1}/_{2}$" cherry (rail) |
| B | 4 | $^{13}/_{16}$ x $3^{1}/_{4}$ x 65" cherry (stile) |
| C | 4 | $^{13}/_{16}$ x $3^{1}/_{4}$ x $18^{1}/_{2}$" cherry (rail) |
| D1 | 3 | $^{13}/_{16}$ x $3^{1}/_{4}$ x $29^{3}/_{4}$" cherry (stile) |
| D2 | 1 | $^{13}/_{16}$ x $3^{5}/_{8}$ x $29^{3}/_{4}$" cherry (stile) |
| E | 2 | $^{13}/_{16}$ x $3^{1}/_{4}$ x $17^{1}/_{2}$" cherry (rail) |
| F1 | 1 | $^{13}/_{16}$ x $2^{1}/_{4}$ x $43^{3}/_{4}$" cherry (stile) |
| F2 | 1 | $^{13}/_{16}$ x $3^{1}/_{4}$ x $43^{3}/_{4}$" cherry (stile) |
| G | 2 | $^{13}/_{16}$ x $1^{1}/_{2}$ x $18^{3}/_{4}$" cherry (rail) |
| H | 2 | $^{13}/_{16}$ x 2 x $7^{1}/_{8}$" cherry (stile) |
| I1 | 2 | $^{1}/_{4}$ x 16 x $24^{1}/_{2}$" cherry plywood (panel) |
| I2 | 2 | $^{1}/_{4}$ x $9^{1}/_{2}$ x 16" cherry plywood (panel) |
| I3 | 2 | $^{1}/_{4}$ x 16 x 21" cherry plywood (panel) |
| J | 1 | $^{1}/_{4}$ x 16 x $38^{1}/_{4}$" cherry plywood (panel) |
| K | 1 | $^{1}/_{4}$ x $5^{5}/_{8}$ x $18^{1}/_{4}$" cherry plywood (panel) |
| L | 10 | $^{13}/_{16}$ x 2 x $16^{7}/_{8}$" maple (rail) |
| M1 | 8 | $^{13}/_{16}$ x 2 x $43^{3}/_{4}$" maple (stile) |
| M2 | 1 | $^{13}/_{16}$ x 2 x $43^{3}/_{4}$" cherry (stile) |
| M3 | 1 | $^{13}/_{16}$ x $2^{5}/_{8}$ x $43^{3}/_{4}$" maple (stile) |
| N | 1 | $^{13}/_{16}$ x 2 x $20^{7}/_{8}$" maple (crossmember) |
| O | 3 | $^{1}/_{4}$ x $1^{3}/_{4}$ x $20^{1}/_{2}$" maple (guide) |
| P1 | 1 | $^{3}/_{4}$ x $19^{3}/_{4}$ x $43^{3}/_{4}$" fir plywood (shelf) |
| P2 | 1 | $^{1}/_{4}$ x $19^{3}/_{4}$ x $43^{3}/_{4}$" cherry plywood (veneer) |
| Q1 | 1 | $^{13}/_{16}$ x $1^{1}/_{2}$ x $43^{1}/_{8}$" cherry (support) |
| Q2 | 1 | $^{13}/_{16}$ x $1^{1}/_{2}$ x $43^{1}/_{8}$" maple (support) |
| R1 | 1 | $^{5}/_{16}$ x 1 x $43^{1}/_{8}$" cherry (edge band) |
| R2 | 3 | $^{5}/_{16}$ x $1^{1}/_{16}$ x $43^{1}/_{8}$" cherry (edge band) |
| R3 | 1 | $^{5}/_{16}$ x $^{13}/_{16}$ x $43^{1}/_{8}$" cherry (edge band) |
| S | 2 | $^{1}/_{4}$ x $20^{5}/_{8}$ x $21^{1}/_{8}$" cherry plywood (platform) |
| T | 1 | $^{1}/_{4}$ x $21^{1}/_{4}$ x $43^{1}/_{8}$" plywood (panel) |
| U | 1 | $^{1}/_{4}$ x 44 x 64" cherry plywood (back) |
| V | 1 | $^{13}/_{16}$ x $1^{1}/_{2}$ x $43^{1}/_{8}$" cherry (rail) |
| W1 | 2 | $^{13}/_{16}$ x $2^{3}/_{4}$ x $22^{1}/_{8}$" cherry (molding) |
| W2 | 1 | $^{13}/_{16}$ x $2^{3}/_{4}$ x $46^{1}/_{2}$" cherry (molding) |
| W3 | 4 | $^{13}/_{16}$ x $2^{3}/_{4}$ x $22^{3}/_{4}$" cherry (molding) |
| W4 | 2 | $^{13}/_{16}$ x $2^{3}/_{4}$ x 48" cherry (molding) |
| X1 | 2 | $^{13}/_{16}$ x 4 x $8^{3}/_{4}$" cherry (foot) |
| X2 | 2 | $^{13}/_{16}$ x 4 x $22^{5}/_{8}$" cherry (foot) |
| Y | 1 | $^{5}/_{16}$ x $^{13}/_{16}$ x 29" cherry (filler strip) |
| Z1 | 2 | $^{13}/_{16}$ x 3 x $22^{5}/_{8}$" cherry (molding) |
| Z2 | 1 | $^{13}/_{16}$ x 3 x $46^{1}/_{2}$" cherry (molding) |
| AA | 2 | $1^{1}/_{8}$ x $1^{1}/_{8}$ x $8^{1}/_{2}$" maple (cleat) |
| BB | 2 | $1^{1}/_{8}$ x $1^{1}/_{8}$ x $21^{1}/_{4}$" maple (cleat) |
| CC | 2 | $1^{1}/_{2}$ x $1^{1}/_{2}$ x $2^{1}/_{2}$" maple (corner block) |
| DD | 2 | $^{5}/_{8}$ x $16^{11}/_{16}$ x $24^{3}/_{16}$" cherry (panel) |
| EE1 | 4 | $^{1}/_{4}$ x $^{3}/_{8}$ x $16^{9}/_{16}$" cherry (bead) |
| EE2 | 4 | $^{1}/_{4}$ x $^{3}/_{8}$ x $23^{3}/_{4}$" cherry (bead) |
| FF | 3 | $^{13}/_{16}$ x $7^{1}/_{2}$ x 43" cherry (drawer front) |
| GG | 3 | $^{3}/_{4}$ x 7 x $42^{1}/_{2}$" poplar (drawer back) |
| HH | 6 | $^{1}/_{2}$ x $7^{1}/_{2}$ x $20^{1}/_{2}$" poplar (drawer side) |
| II | 3 | $^{1}/_{4}$ x $20^{5}/_{8}$ x $42^{1}/_{2}$" lauan plywood (drawer bottom) |
| JJ | 6 | $^{1}/_{4}$ x $^{13}/_{16}$ x $20^{1}/_{4}$" maple (guide) |
| KK | 2 | $^{13}/_{16}$ x 7 x $21^{1}/_{16}$" cherry (drop-down front) |
| LL | 2 | $^{3}/_{8}$ x $^{5}/_{8}$ x $^{5}/_{8}$" cherry (stop) |
| MM | 4 | $^{1}/_{8}$ x $^{1}/_{2}$-dia. cherry (plug) |

**Misc.:** $1^{1}/_{4}$" No. 8 fh screws; 2" No. 8 fh screws; $1^{1}/_{2}$" No. 10 fh screws; 2" No. 10 fh screws; $^{3}/_{4}$" No. 6 fh screws; $^{1}/_{2}$" brads; $^{3}/_{4}$" brads; No. 20 joining plates; 2 Brainerd No. 1085 $5^{3}/_{4}$" lid supports; 8 Garrett Wade (161 Avenue of the Americas, New York, NY 10013) No. A 34.02 C 3" cabinet handles and 2 No. A 48.02 2" teardrop pulls; 4 Stanley No. CD 5300 $1^{1}/_{2}$ x $^{7}/_{8}$" brass hinges; 4 Armor Products (Box 445, East Northport, NY 11731) No. 78090 cranked hinges; 120- and 220-grit sandpaper; glue; stain; sanding sealer and polyurethane.

Next, mark the mortise locations on the stiles and use a drill press to bore overlapping holes to remove most of the mortise waste (Fig. 2). Then follow up with a sharp chisel to square the corners and smooth the walls (Fig. 3).

To cut the tenons, adjust the dado blade to make equal depth cuts on both faces of the side frame rails. Be sure to clamp a stopblock on the miter gauge fence to ensure identical repetitive cuts (Fig. 4) and to form a haunch on all the tenons to fill the groove holes (Fig. 5). Readjust the cutter height, as required, to make the tenon cuts on the ends of the door frame rails.

Temporarily dry assemble the case side frames and use a $^{1}/_{8}$-in.-rad. rounding-over bit to ease the corners that will be visible (Fig. 6). Also, hand sand the groove edges with a felt-lined sanding block. Disassemble the frame, and then cut a rabbet in the rear stiles to recess the back panel. Cut the 1-in. setback for the doors in the front stiles.

Next, cut the plywood insert panels to size and sand the faces. Dry assemble the frames again, to check the fit of the panels (Fig. 7). When satisfied, use hide glue and clamps to assemble the side frame parts. Then,

**3** Clean out all mortises with sharp chisels. Make sure that mortise walls are pared smooth and square to edge.

**4** Cut rail tenons using dado blade on table saw. Wood fence and stopblock on miter gauge ensure identical repeat cuts.

**5** Closeup shows configuration of joints. Haunch on tenon is required to fill gap in the groove above mortise.

**6** Temporarily dry assemble side frame, making sure parts are square. Then round over inside edges with router and bit.

**7** Assemble frame and panels using slow-setting hide glue. Add second stile only after all other parts are joined.

**8** Cut shelf dadoes using a router and simple jig made of scrap lumber. Block at end of jig stops router travel.

make a simple jig to guide your router and cut the stopped dadoes and rabbets in the case sides (Fig. 8). A stopblock nailed at one end of the jig will control the router's travel. Square the ends of the dadoes with a chisel.

Fabricate the maple frames inside the cabinet. Begin by cutting the stock to size, and use a doweling jig to bore the holes for the dowel pins (Fig. 9). Note that the VCR compartment frame receives a half-lapped cross-member that supports a vertical dividing panel. When all the parts are cut, glue and clamp them together. Check each assembly for square, then set them aside to dry. After the glue is set on the VCR shelf, cut a groove in the crossmember—and a dado in the frame parts above—for the compartment divider panel. Assemble the frame and panel that form the top of the case and the TV support slab.

Dry assemble all the cross-frames with one case side lying on the bench. Add the other side and check everything for fit. When satisfied, cut the plywood back panel to size and temporarily tack-nail it in place. Then, measure the length of the cherry edge banding at each crossframe location. (In theory, they should all be identical, but discrepancies do creep in, so it's best to measure and cut each to fit its space.) Disassemble the case. Glue and clamp the strips in place on the frames and the TV slab.

Assembly of the case is best handled in two stages. You'll need eight bar or pipe clamps, two 7-ft. cauls and

four more cauls that are about 1 ft. longer than the width of your workbench. Begin by laying one side of the case on your bench. Apply hide glue to all the rabbets and dadoes. Then coat the mating edges of the cross-frames with hide glue as well. Slide all the frames into position and lift the second case side into place. Do not glue the second side to the frames. Install the cauls and clamps, check for square and let the glue dry (Fig. 10). When the glue has set, invert the assembly and apply glue to all the joints on the second side. Then reinstall the clamps.

Cut the parts for the VCR-compartment divider to size and assemble them. Then, slide this assembly into place and secure it with glue and screws. Also, at this time, add the horizontal rails that help to stiffen the TV shelf, and tack-nail the back panel in place so you can bore pilot holes for the screws used to attach it permanently. Bore these holes at 6-in. intervals around the perimeter and into each crossframe. Then remove the back, countersink these screwholes, apply glue and attach the back with the case lying flat down on your workbench.

## Case Doors and Drawers

Cut three pieces of stock—slightly oversized—for the door panels, and mark the correct planing direction (with the grain) on each board. Then, using a plate joiner, cut the joining slots—three per edge—in all the mating boards. When this is done, glue and clamp the

**9** Lay out dowel locations in support frame members. Bore dowel holes using portable drill and doweling jig.

**10** Glue and clamp case together. Clamps can bear directly on case, or be attached to cauls and workbench as shown.

**11** Use plates or dowels to join stock for door panels. Locate plates or dowels clear of area that will be beveled.

**12** Apply glue to slots, plates and mating edges, then clamp. When dry, smooth panel surface with hand plane.

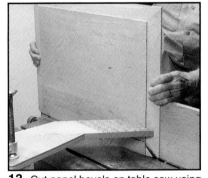

**13** Cut panel bevels on table saw using high auxiliary fence and elevated featherboard as safety precautions.

**14** Cut bead molding on router table with two different bits: a bullnose bit first, followed by a slotting bit.

boards together, keeping all the grain lines pointing in the same direction (Fig. 11). Once the glue is dry, use a sharp hand plane to reduce the thickness of the panels to approximately $\frac{5}{8}$ in. (Fig. 12).

Dry assemble the door frame members and measure the space between the grooves to establish the size for the door panel. Reduce the height dimension by $\frac{1}{16}$ in. and the width by about $\frac{1}{4}$ in. to allow for expansion. Cut the panel to size. Then set up a high auxiliary wood fence on your saw's rip fence. Tilt the blade to 10° for making the bevel cuts that create the raised-panel effect (Fig. 13). Also use an elevated featherboard to steady the panel. Be sure to make the crossgrain cuts first to prevent tearing out the wood fibers at the panel corners.

The next step is to cut the bead molding that surrounds the door panels. Use a $\frac{1}{4}$-in. bullnose bit in a table-mounted router. First, make a pass on the edge of both board faces. Then use a $\frac{1}{16}$-in. slotting bit to extend the width of the bead (Fig. 14). Rip the finished $\frac{5}{16}$-in.-wide beads on the table saw and miter their ends to fit the door frames.

Use a 20-gauge brad, with a clipped-off head, to bore pilot holes in the bead molding. Then install the bead, while the door is still dry assembled, with a slight amount of glue and some $\frac{1}{2}$-in. 20-gauge brads. Do not apply glue to the mitered ends of the bead molding

because the frame members must still be taken apart. You don't have to countersink the brad heads. A 20-gauge brad is so fine that once the piece is stained and finished, the brad heads are nearly invisible. You should be careful, however, not to nick or dent the molding when hammering the brads flush.

Disassemble, finish sand and wipe off the dust from all the door parts. Then apply glue to a stile and two rails. Insert the panel and add the second stile (Fig. 15), being careful to avoid getting glue on the panel. It must be allowed to float so it can expand. You can, however, drive a small brad near the edge of the upper and lower rails. Locate the brad in the center of the length of the rail. With the panel fastened this way, its expansion will be equalized on both sides of the brad.

Clamp the parts together and when dry install the cranked hinges. To do this, it's necessary to cut mortises on the edge of the rear of each door. Use a simple plywood template and a router with a guide bushing to make these cuts (Fig. 16). Note that the long leaf on the cranked hinge used was slightly angled relative to the barrel. This didn't affect its performance, but did require a matching angle in the template cutout. Be sure to check the hinges you buy—before you make the mortises—and follow suit if necessary. Always make some test cuts in scrap stock before you cut the finished mortise on the doors.

**15** Attach bead to frame members, then glue and clamp frame together. Do not glue panel into groove—it should float.

**16** Cut hinge mortises using router with guide bushing and two scrap wood jigs— one for door surface, one for door edge.

**17** Cut drawer stock to size. Lay out and cut dovetails using router and jig. Code mating pieces to avoid mismatches.

**18** Cut crown with molding head in table saw. Use featherboard and pushstick to keep stock firmly against fence.

**19** Join crown molding parts with glue and screws. Then support back side of assembly with scrap block. Cut miters.

**20** Cut case feet to shape and join to mounting cleat. Then glue and screw to bottom, using plate to reinforce corner.

To make the drawers, first cut the stock to size. Then set up a router dovetail template and cut the half-blind dovetails in the drawer sides and front (Fig. 17). Follow these by cutting dadoes in the side members for the back boards and by cutting the grooves for the bottom panel in the sides and front boards. Next, shape the bead around the front with a router, bore the holes for the handle hardware and sand the inside surface of all parts. Assemble the pieces with glue and clamps, check for square and set aside to dry. Complete the drawers by attaching the guide strips to the bottom panels.

### Case Moldings

The crown molding is fabricated from three narrow boards shaped on a table saw fitted with a molding cutter. To build it, glue together the top and middle strips with a ⅜-in. offset. Then attach an auxiliary wood fence to the rip fence on your table saw. This will allow you to adjust the fence properly when making the cove cut. You also should use a raised featherboard to keep the work on a true course (Fig 18).

Cut the first profile with the window-sash cutter, then switch to the cover cutter. Adjust the fence and cut the second shape. The bottom member is shaped with a cove-and-bead cutter, and then is glued and screwed to the top assembly. To obtain smooth, non-forced molding cuts, make several incremental passes. Don't try to cut the whole profile in one pass. Miter the corners (Fig. 19) and attach the crown to the case top with screws and glue.

Cut the stock for the case feet to size and miter the ends. Then, cut the curved profiles on a band or scroll saw. Lay out the miter faces to receive a single joining plate and cut the slot using a plate joiner. If you don't have a plate joiner, use a spline set into a saw kerf groove.

Cut the backing cleats for the feet to size and attach them to the case with glue and screws. Then attach the feet, beginning with the front ones. When both front feet are installed, apply glue to the side feet, miter joints and the plate slots. Then insert the joining plates and slide the side feet in place (Fig. 20). Clamp to the cleats until dry.

The cabinet shown was finished with a coat of Behlen's Virginia Cherry Master-Gel Stain, followed with three coats of Minwax Semi-Gloss Polyurethane. The drawers are finished with a single coat of sanding sealer.

# Ash corner cabinet

For many of us, the quest for adequate storage space consumes quite a bit of our energy and time. One particularly nice solution to this problem is the corner cabinet. By combining areas for both display and enclosed storage, the corner cabinet offers a lot without sacrificing much valuable wall space. Because it's built to fit a corner, the cabinet uses its space efficiently.

Another nice feature of this simple ash cabinet is that it complements many design schemes. If you prefer a cabinet that looks a little more contemporary, you can change the scrolled headpiece to something a little more austere.

The project is easy to build even if you don't have an elaborately equipped shop. Although full-size shop machines were used for much of the work, you could use power and hand tools. A circular saw, router, hand plane and an electric drill would do nicely.

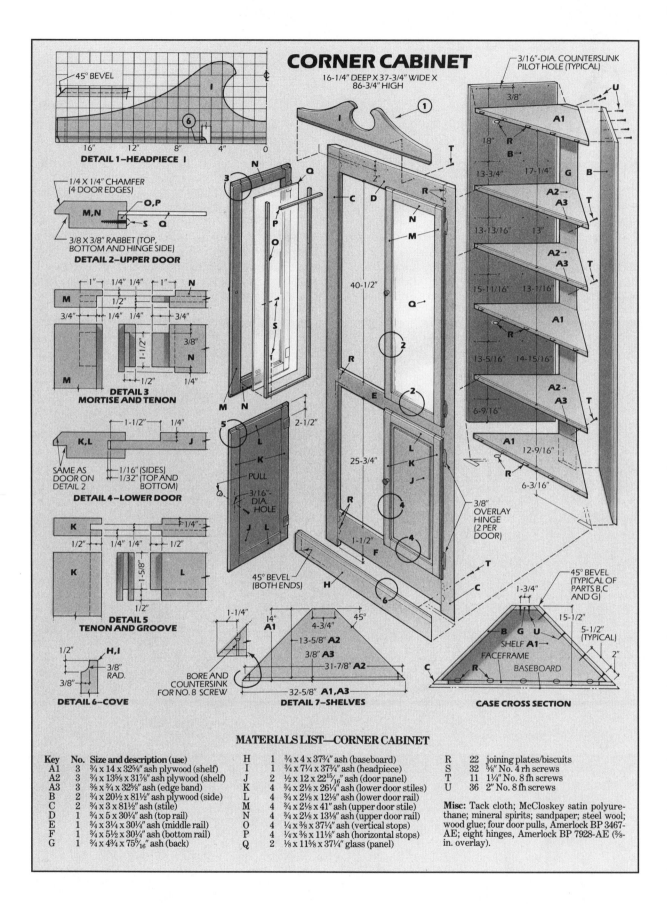

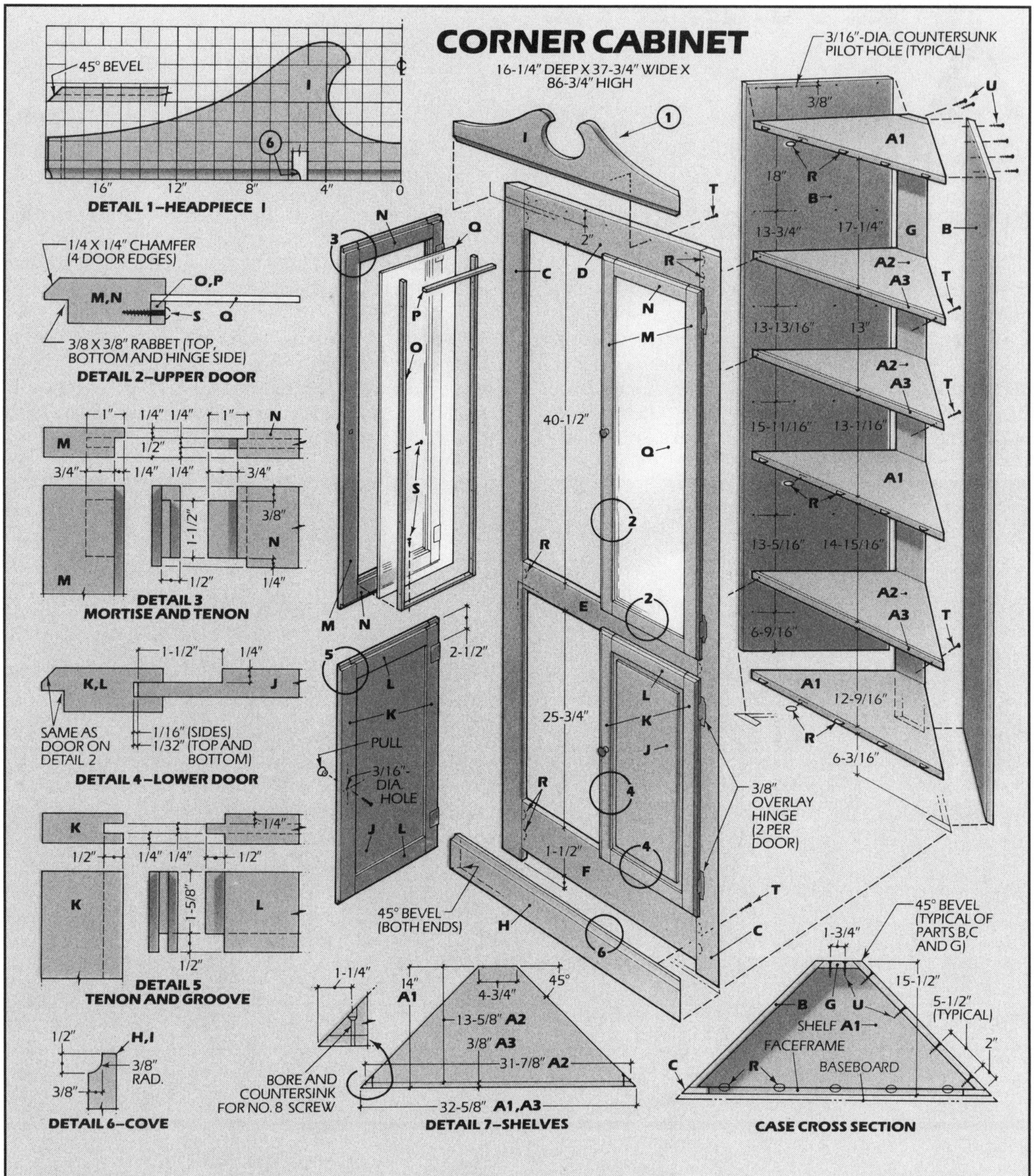
CORNER CABINET
16-1/4″ DEEP X 37-3/4″ WIDE X 86-3/4″ HIGH
45° BEVEL
16″ 12″ 8″ 4″ 0
DETAIL 1–HEADPIECE I
1/4 X 1/4″ CHAMFER (4 DOOR EDGES)
O,P
M,N
S Q
3/8 X 3/8″ RABBET (TOP, BOTTOM AND HINGE SIDE)
DETAIL 2–UPPER DOOR
DETAIL 3 MORTISE AND TENON
SAME AS DOOR ON DETAIL 2
1/16″ (SIDES)
1/32″ (TOP AND BOTTOM)
DETAIL 4–LOWER DOOR
DETAIL 5 TENON AND GROOVE
3/8″ RAD.
DETAIL 6–COVE
BORE AND COUNTERSINK FOR NO. 8 SCREW
DETAIL 7–SHELVES
32-5/8″ A1,A3
31-7/8″ A2
13-5/8″ A2
3/8″ A3
3/16″-DIA. COUNTERSUNK PILOT HOLE (TYPICAL)
PULL
3/16″-DIA. HOLE
3/8″ OVERLAY HINGE (2 PER DOOR)
45° BEVEL (BOTH ENDS)
45° BEVEL (TYPICAL OF PARTS B,C AND G)
SHELF A1
FACEFRAME
BASEBOARD
5-1/2″ (TYPICAL)
CASE CROSS SECTION

## MATERIALS LIST—CORNER CABINET

| Key | No. | Size and description (use) |
|---|---|---|
| A1 | 3 | ¾ x 14 x 32⅝″ ash plywood (shelf) |
| A2 | 3 | ¾ x 13⅝ x 31⅞″ ash plywood (shelf) |
| A3 | 3 | ⅜ x ¾ x 32⅝″ ash (edge band) |
| B | 2 | ¾ x 20½ x 81½″ ash plywood (side) |
| C | 2 | ¾ x 3 x 81½″ ash (stile) |
| D | 1 | ¾ x 5 x 30¼″ ash (top rail) |
| E | 1 | ¾ x 3¼ x 30¼″ ash (middle rail) |
| F | 1 | ¾ x 5½ x 30¼″ ash (bottom rail) |
| G | 1 | ¾ x 4¾ x 75 5/16″ ash (back) |
| H | 1 | ¾ x 4 x 37¾″ ash (baseboard) |
| I | 1 | ¾ x 7¼ x 37¾″ ash (headpiece) |
| J | 2 | ½ x 12 x 22 15/16″ ash (door panel) |
| K | 4 | ¾ x 2⅛ x 26¼″ ash (lower door stiles) |
| L | 4 | ¾ x 2⅛ x 12⅛″ ash (lower door rail) |
| M | 4 | ¾ x 2⅛ x 41″ ash (upper door stile) |
| N | 4 | ¾ x 2⅛ x 13⅛″ ash (upper door rail) |
| O | 4 | ¼ x ⅜ x 37¼″ ash (vertical stops) |
| P | 4 | ¼ x ⅜ x 11⅛″ ash (horizontal stops) |
| Q | 2 | ⅛ x 11⅝ x 37¼″ glass (panel) |
| R | 22 | joining plates/biscuits |
| S | 32 | ⅝″ No. 4 rh screws |
| T | 11 | 1¼″ No. 8 fh screws |
| U | 36 | 2″ No. 8 fh screws |

**Misc:** Tack cloth; McCloskey satin polyurethane; mineral spirits; sandpaper; steel wool; wood glue; four door pulls, Amerlock BP 3467-AE; eight hinges, Amerlock BP 7928-AE (⅜-in. overlay).

## Making Case Parts

Begin by ripping slightly overwidth pieces of ¾-in.-thick ash plywood for the cabinet shelves. Due to the triangular shape of the shelves, you can get the best yield from your materials by nesting the shelf cutouts along the length of the plywood panel. Lay out the shelves, leaving about 1 in. between each.

Next, cut strips for edge banding the exposed shelf edges and glue them to the front edge of the shelves (Fig. 1). When the glue has set, plane and sand the edge banding flush to the panel faces, then cut out the rough shape of each shelf.

The shelves will be cut to finish size with a template and a flush trimming bit in a router. Make the template from a piece of ¼-in. hardboard and screw it to the bottom of a shelf (Fig. 2). Next, clamp the shelf firmly to the worktable and cut around the template with a flush trimming bit in the router (Fig. 3).

Using the table saw, rip the panels for the case sides to rough width. Crosscut the pieces to finished length using a portable circular saw, guided by a straightedge clamped to the workpiece. Tilt the table saw blade to 45° and rip the long edges of the sides to finished dimension. Lay out the position of the shelves on each side, then bore pilot holes for attaching the sides to the shelves. Counterbore these holes on the outside surface of the sides.

Cut out the parts for the cabinet face frame from 4/4 ash. Note that the face frame is assembled using joining plates, though other methods, such as dowels or mortise-and-tenon construction, will work as well. If you use mortise-and-tenon construction, you'll need to increase the length of the rails to accommodate the tenons.

Lay out the face frame parts on an assembly table and mark the position of the joining plates at each stile-rail joint. Note that the wider rails at the top and bottom of the frame can accommodate two plates per joint. Use the plate joiner to cut the slots in stiles and rails for the plates. Hold the workpiece and plate joiner firmly on the work surface while cutting the slots (Figs. 4 and 5).

Apply glue to the joining plate slots and plates, and assemble the face frame. Use bar clamps to bring the joints tight. Then, compare opposite diagonal measurements to check that the face frame is square (Fig. 6). If the frame is out of square, readjust the clamps to bring it into square.

Set the table saw blade to 45° and then rip the long edges of the face frame. The case top, bottom and middle shelf are joined to the face frame with joining plates. Mark the position of these joining plates on the shelves and the face frame (Fig. 7). Cut the required slots with a straightedge clamped to the frame to position the plate joiner (Fig. 8).

**1** Lay out the shelves so they nest along the length of a piece of plywood. Then glue and clamp on the edge band.

**2** Cut out oversize shelf blanks. Make a hardboard template the shape of the shelf and screw it to the blank.

**3** Clamp the shelf-blank template to the workbench. Use a flush trimming bit in the router to cut the blank to size.

**4** Lay out the position of the joining plates on face frame parts. The top and bottom rails have two plates per joint.

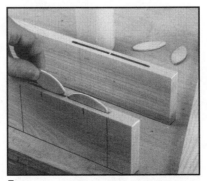

**5** Spread glue in the plate joint slot, insert the plates and spread a little glue on the plates as well.

**6** Clamp the face frame parts on a flat surface. Check diagonal measurements to be sure the face frame is square.

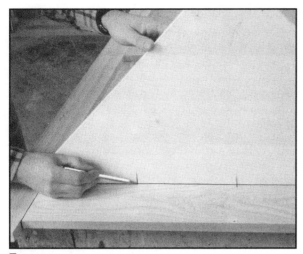

**7** Mark the location of the joining plates on the face frame and on the top, middle and bottom shelves.

**8** Cut joining plate slots on the back of the face frame using a straightedge to guide the plate joiner.

### Case Assembly

Cut the case back from solid 4/4 ash or ¾-in. ash plywood, and rip both edges at 45° on the table saw. Lay out the position of each shelf on the case back and use the drill press to bore and counterbore two pilot holes through the back for attaching each shelf.

Cut small triangular blocks from scrap stock and attach them with hot glue along the back edges of the top, bottom and middle shelves to act as clamping ears (Fig. 9). These ears make assembly easy. They are attached with just a dot of hot glue and are removed with a chisel after the shelves are joined to the cabinet face. Presand all interior cabinet parts with 120- and 220-grit sandpaper, dust off and wipe with a tack cloth.

Apply glue to the joining plate slots and clamp the top, bottom and middle shelves to the face frame (Fig. 10). Check that the shelves are square to the frame and let the glue set. While the glue sets, bore pilot holes through the edges of the remaining three shelves and

attach them to the face frame with 1¼-in. No.8 fh screws.

Position the case back and screw it to the backs of the shelves through the previously bored pilot holes (Fig. 11). Before driving the screws, remember to check that the shelves are perpendicular to the cabinet face.

Remove the clamping ears from the shelf edges by prying gently under their edges with a sharp chisel. Cut the pieces for the baseboard trim and decorative headpiece to rough length and width. Then, crosscut to finish dimension using the miter gauge on the table saw with the blade tipped to 45°.

Reset the blade to 90°, and rip the baseboard to finished width. Trace the outline of the headpiece on the blank, and cut out the piece on the bandsaw (Fig. 12). Stay on the waste side of the line as you cut. Then, use a drum sander in the drill press to remove the saw marks (Fig. 13). If you don't have a drill press, care-

**9** Use hot glue to attach small triangular clamping ears to the edges of the top, middle and bottom shelves.

**10** Use joining plates and glue to attach the shelves to the face frame. Remove clamping ears later with a chisel.

fully remove the saw marks using files and rasps. Finish by sanding the edge smooth. Use a cove bit in the router table to shape the molding on the bottom edge of the headpiece and the top edge of the baseboard (Fig. 14).

Drill and countersink pilot holes through the back of the face frame for attaching the baseboard and headpiece. Attach both pieces using 1¼-in. No.8 fh screws (Fig. 15).

Place one of the case sides in its proper position and attach it with 2-in. No.8 fh screws. Bore a pilot hole for each screw and drive four evenly spaced screws along the length of each shelf (Fig. 16). This job is completed quickly with a power screwdriver tip chucked in an electric drill. Attach the remaining side in the same way. When both sides are attached, stand the case up.

## Door Construction

Rip and crosscut the door parts. Cut the mortises in the upper door stiles with a ¼-in.-dia. straight bit in a plunge router. Clamp some scrap pieces of the same width as the stile next to the stile to serve as a base for the router (Fig. 17). Use a sharp chisel to square the mortise ends. You also can bore out the bulk of the mortise on the drill press, then pare its sides and ends flat using a chisel.

Cut the rabbet on the upper door stiles and rails with dado blades in the table saw (Fig. 18). Readjust the

dado blade height and use the miter gauge in combination with the rip fence to cut the tenons on the upper door rails (Figs. 19 and 20). It's safe to use the miter gauge and rip fence together in this operation, where normally it is not. In this case, cutting the tenon does not produce a scrap piece that can get wedged between the miter gauge and the fence.

Readjust the saw fence to cut the tenons on the lower door rails. Change the dado blades to cut the groove in the lower door stiles and rails.

Rip, crosscut and joint the stock for the lower door panels. Glue and clamp together two panels. After the glue has set, scrape and plane the panels smooth. Cut the panels to finished size. Then, using a straight bit in the router table, cut the wide rabbet around each panel.

Next, seal the panels with a coat of finish, thinned 50% with its proper solvent. Let the finish dry, and sand the panels lightly with 220-grit sandpaper before installing them.

Apply glue to the mortises and tenons on the upper door and clamp the parts. Check the assembly for square and let the glue dry (Fig. 21).

Glue and press together three pieces of each lower door, and slide the panel in place (Fig. 22). Glue and press the stile in place. Clamp the door until the glue is dry. Cut the rabbet on three sides of each door on the router table.

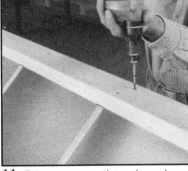

**11** Drive screws—through prebored and counterbored holes—from case back into the back of each shelf.

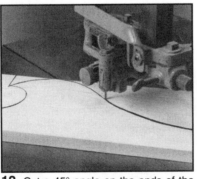

**12** Cut a 45° angle on the ends of the headpiece. Trace the profile on the workpiece and cut it to shape.

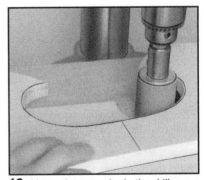

**13** Use a drum sander in the drill press to remove saw marks and refine the profile of the cabinet's headpiece.

**14** Use a cove molding bit in a router table to cut the cove on the headpiece and on the baseboard.

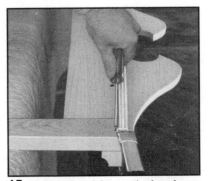

**15** Hold the headpiece to the face frame with spring clamps. Bore pilot holes and screw the headpiece in place.

**16** Bore pilot holes through the case sides, and attach the case sides by screwing them into the shelf edges.

**17** To support the plunge router while cutting a mortise in an upper door stile, clamp scrap next to the stile.

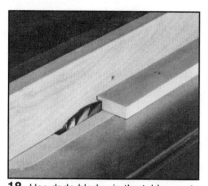

**18** Use dado blades in the table saw to cut the rabbet on the inner edges of the upper door stiles and rails.

**19** Use the miter gauge and the rip fence to cut tenons on the upper door rails. Make the cheek cuts first.

**20** Tip the rails on edge, butt them against the fence and cut the shoulder on each upper door rail tenon.

**21** Glue and clamp the upper doors. Check the assembly for square by comparing diagonal measurements.

**22** Slide the panel into the stile-rail assembly on a lower door. Then clamp the assembly with the remaining stile.

**23** Clamp a straight board to the front of the cabinet to support the doors as you screw their hinges to the face frame.

Use a chamfer bit in the router table to cut the molded edge around the face of each door. Mount the hinges to the back of each door. Next, clamp a board across the cabinet to support the doors during installation. Bore the pilot holes in the face frame and screw the door hinges in place (Fig. 23).

Bore holes for the door pulls, but do not install them. Remove the doors from the cabinet. Fit the glass panels in the upper doors and cut the stops to hold them. Bore pilot holes for screws, then install the stops to test their fit. Remove the stops and glass, then finish sand the case and doors. Dust off thoroughly, then wipe the case with a tack cloth before finishing.

Apply a coat of satin polyurethane to the cabinet, thinned 20% with mineral spirits, and let it dry overnight. Then sand the cabinet lightly with 220-grit sandpaper. Dust off the workpiece again and apply the next coat unthinned. Let it dry overnight, sand it lightly with 220-grit paper and apply the final coat. After it's dry, rub it out with 4/0 steel wool.

Install the glass in the upper doors, and reinstall the hinges and door pulls. Rehang the doors and the cabinet is done. For the neatest fit, remove and miter the baseboard along the walls where you will install the cabinet. Screw through the case sides into a stud to install the cabinet.

*Ash Corner Cabinet* was written by Neal Barrett. Lead photo by J.R. Rost with other photos by Neal Barrett. Technical art by Eugene Thompson.

# Continuous-arm chair

■ Throughout the history of civilization, there are instances when the design of household objects rises above the mundane and enters the category of things we call "art."

The best of these objects display a sense of proportion, balance and grace of line that make them timeless in their visual appeal while maintaining the function that defines their existence.

An example of such an object is the Ming Dynasty continuous-arm chair. To build the chair, you will use a combination of machines and power tools, but you also must explore your hand tool skills. This is not a project for a beginner, but it is within reach for the accomplished enthusiast.

Traditionally these chairs were constructed of rosewood. To keep costs within reason, however, the piece shown can be built of mahogany and given an ebonized finish.

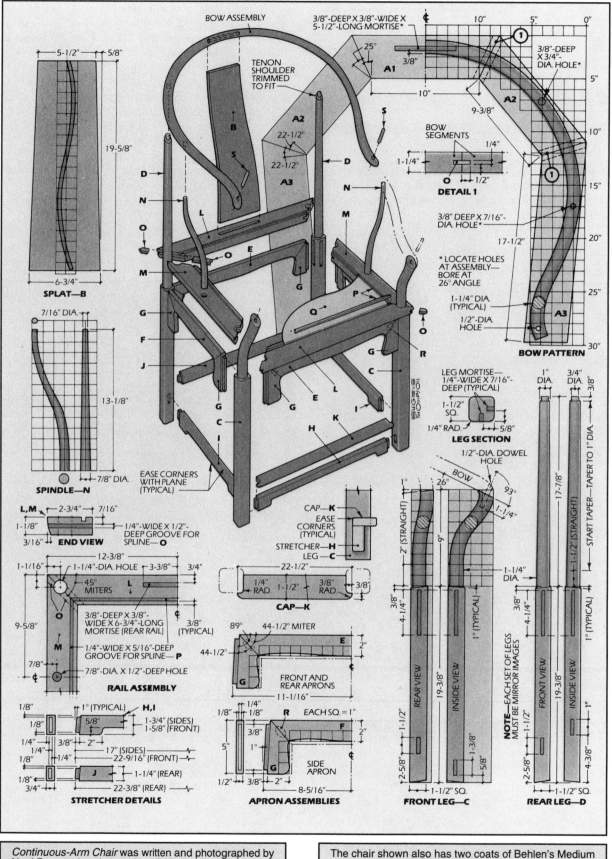

BOW ASSEMBLY

3/8"-DEEP X 3/8"-WIDE X 5-1/2"-LONG MORTISE*

TENON SHOULDER TRIMMED TO FIT

SPLAT—B

5-1/2" 5/8"
19-5/8"
6-3/4"

25°
A1
3/8"
10"

3/8"-DEEP X 3/4"-DIA. HOLE*

A2
9-3/8"

22-1/2"
22-1/2"
A3

BOW SEGMENTS

1-1/4"  1/4"

DETAIL 1
O  1/2"

3/8" DEEP X 7/16"-DIA. HOLE*

17-1/2"

* LOCATE HOLES AT ASSEMBLY—BORE AT 26° ANGLE

1-1/4" DIA. (TYPICAL)

1/2"-DIA. HOLE

A3

BOW PATTERN

SPINDLE—N

7/16" DIA.
13-1/8"
7/8" DIA.

EASE CORNERS WITH PLANE (TYPICAL)

LEG MORTISE—1/4"-WIDE X 7/16"-DEEP (TYPICAL)

1-1/2" SQ.
1/4" RAD.
5/8"
LEG SECTION

1"
DIA.
3/4"
DIA.
3/8"

START TAPER—TAPER TO 1" DIA

1/2"-DIA. DOWEL HOLE

BOW
26°
93°
1-1/4"

1° (STRAIGHT)

2" (STRAIGHT)

9"

1-1/4" DIA.

17-7/8"

1-1/2" (STRAIGHT)

NOTE—EACH SET OF LEGS MUST BE MIRROR IMAGES

END VIEW
L,M
2-3/4"  7/16"
1-1/8"
3/16"

1/4"-WIDE X 1/2"-DEEP GROOVE FOR SPLINE—O

RAIL ASSEMBLY
12-3/8"
1-1/16"
1-1/4"-DIA. HOLE  3-3/8"  3/4"
45° MITERS
L
3/8"-DEEP X 3/8"-WIDE X 6-3/4"-LONG MORTISE (REAR RAIL)
3/8" (TYPICAL)
1/4"-WIDE X 5/16"-DEEP GROOVE FOR SPLINE—P
9-5/8"
7/8"
7/8"-DIA. X 1/2"-DEEP HOLE

CAP—K
EASE CORNERS (TYPICAL)
STRETCHER—H
LEG—C

CAP—K
22-1/2"
1/4" RAD.  1-1/2"  3/8" RAD.
3/8"

APRON ASSEMBLIES
89°  44-1/2° MITER
44-1/2°
E  2"
G
FRONT AND REAR APRONS
11-1/16"

EACH SQ. = 1"
1/4"
1/8"  1/8"
R
3/8"
5"  1°
F  2"
G
SIDE APRON
8-5/16"

STRETCHER DETAILS
1/8"  1° (TYPICAL)  H,I
1/8"  5/8"  1-3/4" (SIDES)  1-5/8" (FRONT)
1/4"  3/8"  2"
1/4"  17" (SIDES)
1/8"  1/4"  22-9/16" (FRONT)
1/8"  J  1-1/4" (REAR)
3/4"  22-3/8" (REAR)

FRONT LEG—C
REAR VIEW
INSIDE VIEW
1°
3/8"
4-1/4"
19-3/8"
1-1/2"
2-5/8"
1-3/8"
5/8"
1-1/2" SQ.
1° (TYPICAL)

REAR LEG—D
FRONT VIEW
INSIDE VIEW
3/8"
4-1/4"
19-3/8"
1-1/2"
2-5/8"
4-3/8"
1"
1-1/2" SQ.
1° (TYPICAL)

*Continuous-Arm Chair* was written and photographed by Neal Barrett. Lead photo by J.R. Rost. Technical art by Eugene Thompson. The wood filler used on the chair shown was Behlen's Medium Brown Mahogany Filler.

The chair shown also has two coats of Behlen's Medium Brown Mahogany Solar Lux stain. A sealer of 80% varnish and 20% paint thinner was also applied.

**1** Cut the bow blanks on the table saw. Use a miter gauge with an extended fence to ensure an accurate cut.

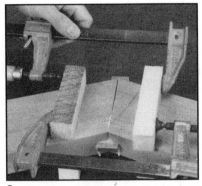

**2** Hot glue clamping ears to the bow blanks. Clamp the blanks with glue and splines at each joint.

**3** Trace the outer profile of the bow on the glued-up blank and cut just outside the line using a band saw.

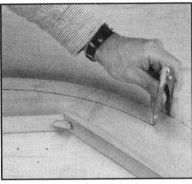

**4** Use a pencil compass or pair of scribers to mark the inner edge of the bow. Cut just outside this line also.

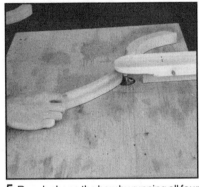

**5** Rough shape the bow by running all four corners over a ⅝-in.-rad. rounding-over bit on the router table.

**6** Clamp the bow upright and smooth it with a spokeshave. Check your progress often by sighting along its curve.

## Making the Bow

Clearly the most distinctive feature of this chair is the arched bow-arm which joins with the front legs in a sweeping curve. Although the bow looks difficult to make, it isn't. You don't have to resort to steam bending or complicated procedures since it is built of glued-together segments. The important thing is to get a good glue joint where the segments join. Be sure to dry fit the bow segments with splines before you try to glue them together.

The bow is your introduction to the gradual shaping process that is necessary to build other parts for this chair. By making the bow, you'll develop your techniques for making the parts that come later. A few words of advice: you can remove wood, but you can't put it back. Shape the chair parts carefully, removing small amounts of wood at a time. Stop frequently to check your progress. Work with razor-sharp cutting tools, and when you use a rasp, stop and clean it

frequently. As you remove wood, you're liable to encounter changes in grain direction. Sharp tools reduce the possibility of tearout, which could destroy the graceful curves that give this piece its distinctive character.

Begin bow construction by making a template of ¼-in. plywood or hardboard for the shape of the outside profile of the bow. Using 6/4 stock, planed to 1¼ in. thick, cut the five segments of the bow to size using the miter gauge with an extended fence or the table saw (Fig. 1). The segments are joined with splines and glue. Use a ¼-in. slotting cutter in the router to cut the spline grooves in the ends of each segment of the bow. Cut spline stock from solid mahogany so that the grain of the wood will run across the joint. Temporarily hot glue clamping blocks to the surfaces of the segments, then apply glue to the joints and splines and clamp them together (Fig. 2).

| MATERIALS LIST | | | | | | | | | |
|---|---|---|---|---|---|---|---|---|---|
| Key | No. | Size and description (use) | | | | | | | |
| A1 | 1 | 1¼ x 4 x 10″ mahogany (bow segment) | H | 1 | ¾ x 1⅝ x 22⅝″ mahogany (stretcher) | S | 2 | ½″-dia. x 2¾″ mahogany (dowel, see misc.) | |
| A2 | 2 | 1¼ x 4 x 9⅜″ mahogany (bow segment) | I | 2 | ¾ x 1¾ x 17″ mahogany (stretcher) | | | | |
| A3 | 2 | 1¼ x 4 x 17½″ mahogany (bow segment) | J | 1 | ¾ x 1¼ x 22½″ mahogany (stretcher) | * Cut pieces oversize, then pare to fit joint. | | | |
| B | 1 | ⅜ x 6¾ x 19⅝″ mahogany (splat) | K | 1 | ⅜ x 1½ x 22⅝″ mahogany (cap) | **Misc.:** Mahogany dowel, part No. MDW7: Constantine's, Eastchester Rd., Bronx, NY 10461; Behlen stain and wood filler: Woodworker's Supply, 5604 Alameda Pl. NE, Albuquerque, NM 87113, (800) 645-9292; Cane and spline: VanDyke's, Box 278, Woonsocket, SD 57385. Epoxy, wood glue, varnish. | | | |
| C | 2 | 1½ x 1½ x 28⅜″ mahogany (front leg) | L | 2 | 1⅛ x 2¾ x 24¾″ mahogany (seat rail) | | | | |
| D | 2 | 1½ x 1½ x 37¼″ mahogany (rear leg) | M | 2 | 1⅛ x 2¾ x 19¼″ mahogany (seat rail) | | | | |
| E | 2 | ½ x 2 x 21⅜″ mahogany (apron) | N | 2 | ⅞ x 13⅛″ mahogany (spindle) | | | | |
| F | 2 | ½ x 2 x 15⅛″ mahogany (side apron) | O* | 2 | ¼ x 1 x 24″ mahogany (spline) | | | | |
| G | 8 | ½ x 2⅜ x 5″ mahogany (apron ends) | P | 1 | 8-ft. piece of cane spline | | | | |
| | | | Q | 1 | 24″ x 24″ sheet of cane | | | | |
| | | | R | 8 | No. 10 plates | | | | |

Let the assembly set overnight. Remove the clamping blocks with a chisel, and trace the outer profile of the bow from the template. Cut the outer bow shape on the band saw, staying on the waste side of the line (Fig. 3). Refine the profile with a plane and spokeshave, then trace the inner profile with a pair of scribers set to 1¼ in. wide (Fig. 4).

Cut the inner profile on a band saw and smooth it with a spokeshave. Rough out the circular shape of the bow by rounding over both faces on the router table. Use a ⅝-in.-rad. rounding-over bit (Fig. 5). Don't round the last 6 in. of each bow end. The ends are left square to form the joint at the front legs, and this section will be carved to shape later.

Clamp the bow in the vise and use a spokeshave and scraper to smooth for a uniform round profile (Fig. 6).

### Making the Splat and Legs

Rip and crosscut the splat blank, then cut it out on the band saw, staying on the waste side of the line (Fig. 7). Clamp the splat to the bench and scrape its faces smooth. Cut its taper on the band saw.

Rip and crosscut blanks for the front legs from 8/4 stock. Trace the profile of the legs onto each blank. Note that the legs are angled inward 1°. All leg bottoms, tops and shoulder cuts must reflect that angle.

Cut the compound angle on the bottom of each leg blank using the table saw and miter gauge. Transfer the side and front leg profiles to the blank.

Cut the straight section of each leg on the table saw. Mark on the leg where to stop the cut. Mark the outer edge of the saw blade on the fence—when the marks line up, stop the cut (Fig. 8). Use a backsaw to make a ⅛-in.-deep kerf, around the leg where the cut stops. Cut the compound angle on the top of each leg with the table saw and miter gauge (Fig. 9).

Next, cut the front profile of the upper leg section on the band saw. Temporarily hot glue the cutoff piece back on the leg to cut the other profile (Figs. 10 and 11). Leave a square step of wood at the back of the leg top to facilitate clamping later (the square step is visible in Fig. 24).

Shape the first 2 in. of the round portion of each leg before assembly. Clamp each leg in the vise, and use rasps, chisels and a spokeshave to shape the leg (Fig. 12). Check your work with gauge blocks (Fig. 13).

Rip the remaining leg blanks. Lay out the angled shoulder cuts at seat height, then use a backsaw to make the ⅛-in.-deep cuts around the legs.

Turning the back legs on a lathe requires a ball-bearing steady rest to support the blank as it spins (Fig. 14). You can make this device from plywood. Otherwise, shape the legs with hand tools.

**7** Mark the back splat's outline on the edge of the blank. Cut just beyond the lines on a band saw.

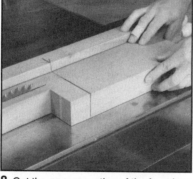

**8** Cut the square portion of the front legs on the table saw. Mark where to stop the cut on the fence and the leg.

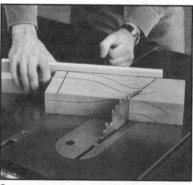

**9** Use the miter gauge and extension fence on the table saw to make the compound angle cut on each front leg.

**10** Cut the front profile of the legs on the band saw. Keep the blade to the waste side of the layout line.

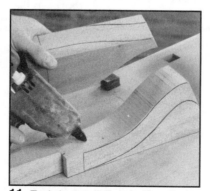

**11** Tack the cutoff piece back on the leg blank with hot glue to provide a guide for cutting the side profile.

**12** Clamp the front leg in a vise and shape the round section of the front legs using chisels and rasps.

**13** Use gauge blocks to check the round section. Work slowly and check the leg shape frequently.

**14** Turn the round section of the rear legs by first using a gouge. The legs also can be shaped with a spokeshave.

Use a chisel and rasp to shape the leg where it meets the square section. Crosscut the legs, and use the miter gauge on the table saw to cut the compound angle at the leg bottom.

Cut the mortises in each leg using a plunge router equipped with a ¼-in.-dia. straight bit and edge guide. Chop the ends of the mortise square with a chisel.

## Building the Base

Rip and crosscut the seat aprons. Since the legs are splayed 1°, the angle of the miter joint at each apron is 44½° (not the usual 45°). Also, the aprons are cut to shape after they are assembled, so each one is slightly oversized when glued together.

Cut joining plate slots in each miter joint (Fig. 15). Apply glue to each miter, the slot and the biscuit, then clamp it until the glue sets. Trace the aprons' shape on

each blank, and use the band saw to cut them out. Smooth the apron curve with a drum sander on a drill press (Fig. 16).

Rip and crosscut the stretchers. Next, use the dado blades in the table saw to cut the tenon cheeks on them, and readjust the saw to make the cheek cuts on the apron tenons. Use a backsaw to make the shoulder cuts at the top and bottom of each tenon.

Mark the profile on the stretchers and use the band saw to cut them. Scrape or sand the cuts smooth. Rip and crosscut the cap for the front stretcher, and lay out its end cuts. Saw the cap to shape on a band saw.

Rip and crosscut the seat frames and cut their miters with a table saw and miter gauge. Use a router with a slotting cutter to cut the spline groove in the end of each piece. Clamp the pieces to the drill-press table and bore the 1¼-in.-dia. hole through each miter (Fig. 17).

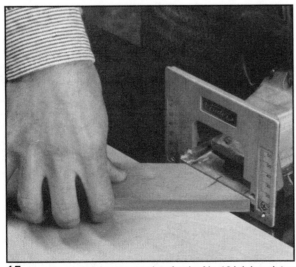

**15** Use the plate joiner to cut slots for the No.10 joining plates in the mitered aprons. Then, glue and clamp the aprons.

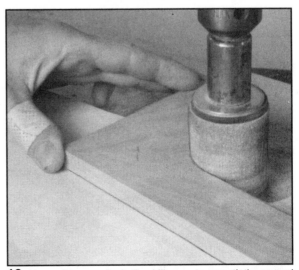

**16** Use a drum sander in the drill press to smooth the curved inside edge of the aprons and remove saw marks.

**17** Clamp the seat frame pieces to the drill-press table. Then bore 1¼-in.-dia. holes through the miter.

**18** Hold a seat frame to the workbench and use the plunge router and a straight bit to cut the splat mortise.

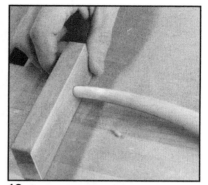

**19** Test the spindle end diameters with gauge blocks. They should be snug in the hole but not too tight.

**20** Make a plywood holding jig to keep the bow at the correct angle for boring spindle and leg mortises.

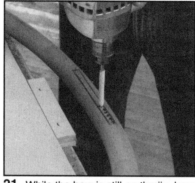

**21** While the bow is still on the jig, bore a series of ⅜-in.-dia. holes to remove the bulk of the splat mortise.

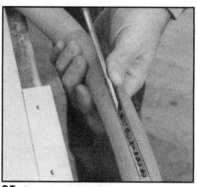

**22** Pare the sides of the splat mortise flat and its ends square using a chisel. Work down to the knife line.

Cut the splat mortise in the rear frame using a ⅜-in.-dia. straight bit and router (Fig. 18), and square the mortise ends with a chisel.

Cut the spline groove in each seat frame piece with a router and ¼-in.-dia. straight bit. Then bore the ⅞-in.-dia. × ½-in.-deep holes for the side spindles in the side members.

Use a block plane to round slightly the top outside and inside edges of all seat frame pieces.

Rip and crosscut blanks for the side spindles. Trace the outline onto the blanks and cut to shape on the band saw. Hold each spindle in the vise and use a spokeshave and rasp for the tapering profile. Use gauge blocks to check the spindle ends (Fig. 19).

Construct an angled plywood jig to hold the inverted bow in position for boring the holes for the spindles and the back legs (Fig. 20). Use a hand-held drill to bore the holes and have an assistant help you sight the drill.

Next, using the jig, mark and bore out the bulk of the splat mortise. Pare the mortise into a rectangle using a sharp chisel (Figs. 21 and 22).

## Finish and Assembly

Sand all chair parts with 120-grit sandpaper. Glue and clamp the two rear legs, back stretcher and seat apron. The seat frame is positioned, but not glued, between the legs (Fig. 23). Glue and clamp together the subassembly for the front legs.

Glue and clamp the subassemblies spanned by the side seat frames, aprons and stretchers (put glue on the seat-frame miters). Complete the base by driving glue-covered splines on the inside and outside of the miter joints. The spline face is curved to match the chair leg. Trim the splines flush after the glue has set.

Clamp the bow to the base, and trace along the bow with dividers to mark the tenon shoulders on the back legs. Remove the bow and carve the tenons down to the scribed line. Next, clamp the bow and bore a hole through the bow into each front leg (Fig. 24).

Apply glue to all mortises and tenons, but use epoxy where the front legs and bow are joined (Fig. 25). Clamp the chair until the glue sets.

Shape the transition between the bow and front legs using gouges and rasps. Check your progress with a gauge block (Figs. 26 and 27). When you are finished, sand the chair with 120- and 220-grit sandpaper.

To avoid getting sealer in the seat's spline groove, cut and temporarily install four ¼-in.-thick × ½-in.-wide strips in the groove.

Next, apply wood filler and when the filler is dry, sand the chair with 220-grit paper. Wipe off the sanding dust, and apply the stain of your choice.

The chair shown has a closed-weave cane for the seat because it is more durable than the more common open-weave type. Soak the cane in water for 4 hours before proceeding. About 20 minutes before caning the seat, soak the spline too. Use a chisel to cut and miter a piece of spline for each side of the seat and guide the cut with a mitered hardwood block. Use heavy shears to cut the cane so it overhangs the spline groove by 1 in. on all sides.

Cut 10 wedges about 2 in. long from the extra spline. Partially drive the wedging blocks into the cane groove. Start at the center of the front and back grooves and work around (Fig. 28). Keep the cane square to the seat. Use a knife to trim off the excess cane, and apply a water-soluble glue to the cane over the groove.

Remove the wedges from one side and tap the spline into the groove with a wooden block under the hammer (Fig. 29). Repeat this for each side. Keep the cane moist—until the glue on the spline has set—by placing a damp sponge in the center of the seat.

When the seat is dry, scuff the sealer with 320-grit sandpaper, dust off and apply two coats of undiluted varnish to the chair and cane.

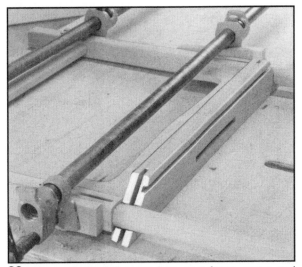

**23** Glue and clamp the rear legs, seat frame, apron and stretcher. Follow the same procedure for the front legs.

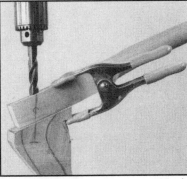

**24** Clamp the bow to the front legs and bore the dowel hole into the leg. Note the clamping ear on the leg's top.

**25** Apply epoxy where the bow front and legs meet and on the dowel. Clamp until the epoxy has cured.

**26** With the chair well supported on a padded surface, use gouges, chisels and rasps to shape the bow-leg joint.

**27** Shape the joint removing small amounts of wood in many passes. Check the joint's shape with a guide block.

**28** Cut the soaked cane oversize and tack it in place using small spline wedges. Keep the cane square to the seat.

**29** Trim off excess cane and drive the spline into its groove. Protect the cane from hammer blows with a block.

# Table for four

■ This versatile gateleg table and chair set is a marvel of compactness. It seats four people comfortably yet, when folded, it needs a space only 14 in. wide and 34 in. long. That includes the four folding chairs stored underneath.

It's ideally suited for apartments and other confined quarters, but this handsome dining set will be an asset even if you have lots of space. Just unfold the table and chairs when company arrives. The chairs are solid mahogany, and the table has a mahogany base with a mahogany plywood top. The deep rich color was achieved with a mahogany stain topped by three coats of gloss polyurethane.

*Table for Four* was written by Rosario Capotosto. Lead photo by J.R. Rost with how-to photos by Rosario Capotosto. Technical art by Eugene Thompson. For the finish, use Behlen's Solar-Lux stain, Medium Red Mahogany, altered with 1 part Solar-Lux retarder to 6 parts stain. This nongrain-raising stain is very fast-drying and must be retarded to avoid leaving lap marks. A source for the cornering tool is Garrett Wade, 161 Avenue of the Americas, New York, NY 10013.

**1** Bore the dowel holes in the top rail. Offset a self-centering doweling jig using a thin piece of wood.

**2** Use alignment nails to prevent the two pieces of the top rail from sliding while you are gluing and clamping them.

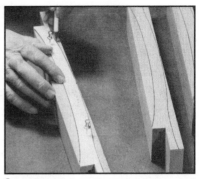

**3** Make a cardboard pattern of the top rail and pin it to the blanks. Carefully trace the pattern with a pen.

**4** To mark the dowel holes in the legs, insert dowel centers in the top rail and press the rail against the leg.

**5** Tip the band saw table to 7°. Cut just to the waste side of the line and save the cutoff pieces.

**6** Clamp a panel to the drill-press table elevated at 7°. Use a drum sander to smooth the top rail.

## The Chair

Rip and crosscut the pieces for the rails and stiles from 4/4 stock. Also rip and crosscut two pieces of stock to be face glued for the top rail. The top rail uses a combination dowel and lap joint. Remember to bore the dowel holes in the front piece of the top rail before you glue and clamp it to the back piece.

Use a doweling jig to bore the dowel holes in the rail ends. If you have a self-centering jig, insert a wood spacer to position the dowel holes off-center (Fig. 1).

Next, center the front rail section over the rear section. Tape the two pieces together and bore a pair of pilot holes for alignment nails near the ends of the back. Apply glue to the pieces, partially drive $1\frac{1}{2}$-in. finishing nails into the holes and clamp the assembly (Fig. 2). When the glue is dry, pull out the nails.

Cut a thin cardboard template that matches the bottom outline of the rail. Trace the outline on each top, and put the pieces aside (Fig. 3).

Mark the stiles and lower rails for mortises and tenons. Use a dado head on a table saw to cut the tenons on the rails. To form the mortises, bore a series of overlapping holes then chisel the mortise sides parallel and the ends square. Next, insert dowel centers in the upper rail and press the rail and stiles together so the dowel centers make indents (Fig. 4). Bore dowel holes on the marks in the stile using a drill press.

Now cut the contour in the upper rail. Adjust the band saw for a 7° bevel and make the cuts with the bottom edge of the rail facing up (Fig. 5). Be sure to save the cutoff pieces.

To sand out the saw marks, clamp a scrap board to the drill-press table so the table is propped up at 7°. This puts the face of the workpiece parallel to the sanding drum (Fig. 6). Also, cut a $3\frac{1}{4}$-in.-dia. hole in the baseboard so the end of the drum is below the edge of the workpiece. This allows the drum to make full contact with the workpiece.

Use a $\frac{3}{16}$-in.-rad. rounding-over bit in a router to round the edges on the top rail. Clamp the rail, front face down, onto the workbench with scrap blocks under the end laps while rounding the corners. Next, hold the rail in a vise with its bottom edge facing up. Use the curved cutoffs as clamping pads (Fig. 7).

Next, tape the rear cutoffs to the rail to hold the workpiece level, and cut the front profile on the rail with a band saw.

Cut the tenons on the lower rail using a dado head in a table saw. Attach a fence and stopblock to the miter gauge. Butt the workpiece to the block and run it over the blade (Fig. 8). Bore the mortises in the legs on the drill press, then pare their sides flat and their ends square with a chisel (Fig. 9).

Tilt the blade on the table saw, and cut the angle on the bottom of the legs. Use a stopblock clamped to the miter-gauge fence to ensure consistency among all legs.

Rip and crosscut the stock for the rear frame and cut mortises and tenons where called for. Cut the seat pivot

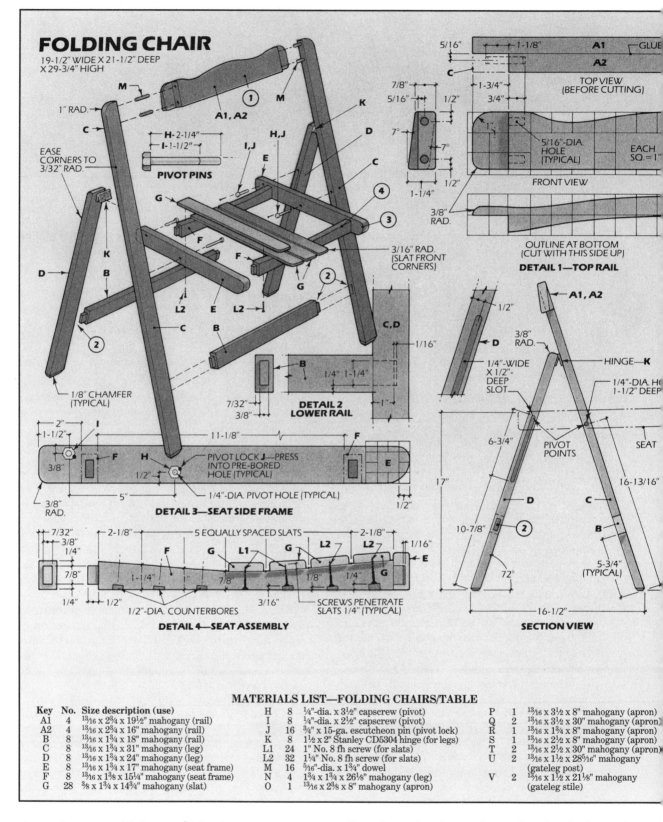

# FOLDING CHAIR
19-1/2" WIDE X 21-1/2" DEEP X 29-3/4" HIGH

## MATERIALS LIST—FOLDING CHAIRS/TABLE

| Key | No. | Size description (use) | Key | No. | Size description (use) | Key | No. | Size description (use) |
|---|---|---|---|---|---|---|---|---|
| A1 | 4 | $^{13}/_{16}$ x $2^{3}/_{4}$ x $19^{1}/_{2}$" mahogany (rail) | H | 8 | $^{1}/_{4}$"-dia. x $3^{1}/_{2}$" capscrew (pivot) | P | 1 | $^{13}/_{16}$ x $3^{1}/_{2}$ x 8" mahogany (apron) |
| A2 | 4 | $^{13}/_{16}$ x $2^{3}/_{4}$ x 16" mahogany (rail) | I | 8 | $^{1}/_{4}$"-dia. x $2^{1}/_{2}$" capscrew (pivot) | Q | 2 | $^{13}/_{16}$ x $3^{1}/_{2}$ x 30" mahogany (apron) |
| B | 8 | $^{13}/_{16}$ x $1^{3}/_{4}$ x 18" mahogany (rail) | J | 16 | $^{3}/_{4}$" x $2^{1}/_{2}$" escutcheon pin (pivot lock) | R | 1 | $^{13}/_{16}$ x $1^{3}/_{4}$ x 8" mahogany (apron) |
| C | 8 | $^{13}/_{16}$ x $1^{3}/_{4}$ x 31" mahogany (leg) | K | 8 | $1^{1}/_{2}$ x 2" Stanley CD5304 hinge (for legs) | S | 1 | $^{13}/_{16}$ x $2^{1}/_{2}$ x 8" mahogany (apron) |
| D | 8 | $^{13}/_{16}$ x $1^{3}/_{4}$ x 24" mahogany (leg) | L1 | 24 | 1" No. 8 fh screw (for slats) | T | 2 | $^{13}/_{16}$ x $2^{1}/_{2}$ x 30" mahogany (apron) |
| E | 8 | $^{13}/_{16}$ x $1^{3}/_{4}$ x 17" mahogany (seat frame) | L2 | 32 | $1^{1}/_{4}$" No. 8 fh screw (for slats) | U | 2 | $^{13}/_{16}$ x $1^{1}/_{2}$ x $28^{5}/_{16}$" mahogany (gateleg post) |
| F | 8 | $^{13}/_{16}$ x $1^{3}/_{8}$ x $15^{1}/_{4}$" mahogany (seat frame) | M | 16 | $^{5}/_{16}$"-dia. x $1^{3}/_{4}$" dowel | V | 2 | $^{13}/_{16}$ x $1^{1}/_{2}$ x $21^{1}/_{8}$" mahogany (gateleg stile) |
| G | 28 | $^{3}/_{8}$ x $1^{3}/_{4}$ x $14^{3}/_{4}$" mahogany (slat) | N | 4 | $1^{3}/_{4}$ x $1^{3}/_{4}$ x $26^{1}/_{8}$" mahogany (leg) | | | |
| | | | O | 1 | $^{13}/_{16}$ x $2^{3}/_{8}$ x 8" mahogany (apron) | | | |

slot on the router table in three $^{1}/_{4}$-in.-deep passes with a $^{1}/_{4}$-in.-dia. straight bit. Clamp stopblocks on the router-table fence, and tilt the workpiece down onto the straight bit, then advance it to the stop (Fig. 10). Hold the workpiece against the fence with a featherboard.

Round over the edges on the rear legs, but don't round the section where the leg and stile meet. Use a cornering tool to round the corners here (Fig. 11). Next, glue and clamp the front frame. Attach the upper and lower rails to a leg and add the second leg. Clamp the assem-

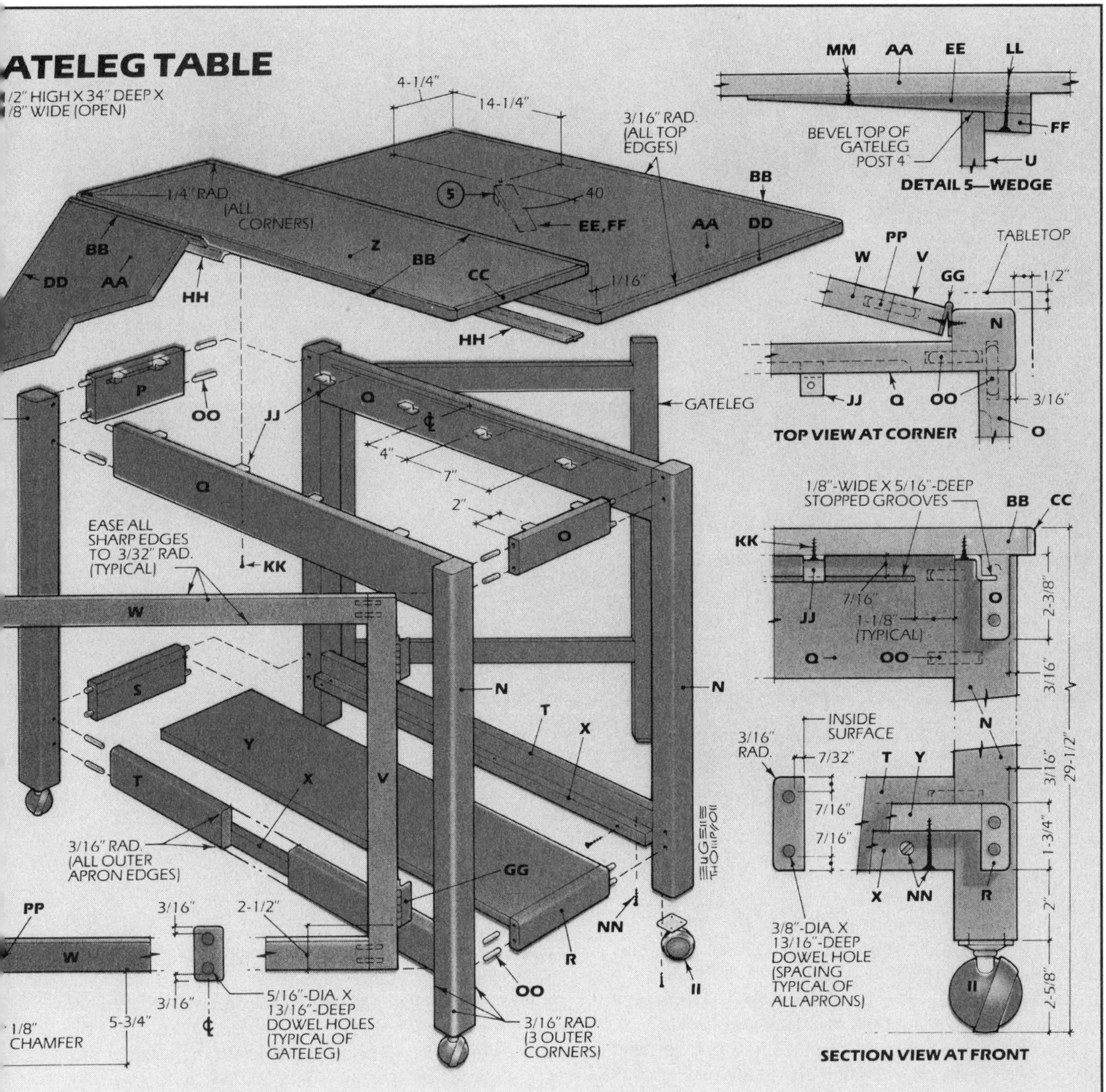
ATELEG TABLE
/2" HIGH X 34" DEEP X
/8" WIDE (OPEN)
4-1/4"
14-1/4"
3/16" RAD. (ALL TOP EDGES)
1/4" RAD. (ALL CORNERS)
40
EE, FF
BB
DD
AA
Z
CC
HH
1/16"
P
OO
JJ
Q
GATELEG
4"
7"
2"
O
EASE ALL SHARP EDGES TO 3/32" RAD. (TYPICAL)
KK
W
S
N
T
X
Y
V
3/16" RAD. (ALL OUTER APRON EDGES)
GG
R
NN
II
PP
3/16"
2-1/2"
5/16"-DIA. X 13/16"-DEEP DOWEL HOLES (TYPICAL OF GATELEG)
3/16" RAD. (3 OUTER CORNERS)
1/8" CHAMFER
5-3/4"
MM
LL
BEVEL TOP OF GATELEG POST 4°
FF
U
DETAIL 5—WEDGE
TABLETOP
1/2"
TOP VIEW AT CORNER
1/8"-WIDE X 5/16"-DEEP STOPPED GROOVES
7/16"
1-1/8" (TYPICAL)
2-3/8"
29-1/2"
INSIDE SURFACE
3/16" RAD.
7/32"
1-3/4"
2-5/8"
3/8"-DIA. X 13/16"-DEEP DOWEL HOLE (SPACING TYPICAL OF ALL APRONS)
SECTION VIEW AT FRONT

| | | |
|---|---|---|
| W | 4 | 13/16 x 1½ x 20" mahogany (gateleg rail) |
| X | 2 | 13/16 x 1 x 30" mahogany (shelf cleat) |
| Y | 1 | ¾ x 8 x 31½" mahogany plywood (shelf) |
| Z | 1 | ¾ x 12 x 34" mahogany plywood (top) |
| AA | 2 | ¾ x 24½ x 34" mahogany plywood (leaf) |
| BB | 6 | ¼ x 13/16 x 34½" mahogany (top/leaf trim) |
| CC | 2 | ¼ x 13/16 x 12" mahogany (top trim) |
| DD | 4 | ¼ x 13/16 x 24½" mahogany (leaf trim) |
| EE | 2 | ¾ x 1¾ x 10¾" mahogany (stop wedge) |
| FF | 2 | ¾ x 1¾ x 1¾" mahogany (stopblock) |
| GG | 4 | 1⅜ x 2" Stanley CD 5302 hinge (for gatelegs) |
| HH | 2 | 1½ x 30" Stanley SC 311 continuous hinge (for top and leaves) |
| II | 4 | 2¼"-dia. Shepherd ball casters |
| JJ | 12 | Tabletop fasteners |
| KK | 12 | ½" No. 8 rh screws |
| LL | 2 | 2" No. 10 fh screws |
| MM | 2 | ¾" No. 6 fh screws |
| NN | 12 | 1¼" No. 8 fh screws |
| OO | 16 | ⅜"-dia. x 1½" dowel |
| PP | 16 | 5/16"-dia. x 1½" dowel |

**Misc.:** Source for stain, retarder and cornering tool: Garrett Wade, 161 Avenue of the Americas, New York, NY 10013. Stain: Behlen's Solar-Lux Stain, Medium Red Mahogany No. B5033A116; Behlen's Solar-Lux Retarder No. B500-00A25; Minwax Clear Gloss Polyurethane.

bly with two bar clamps and two C-clamps (Fig. 12). Don't use the router to round the top edge of the rail, since the edge is curved in two planes. Instead, use a cornering tool. Finish sand the front and rear frames. Then temporarily attach the hinges.

Next, rip and crosscut the stock for the seat sides and crossmembers. Mark the pivot pinholes in the side members, then bore the holes. Next, mark and cut the mortise and tenons in the seat sides and crossmembers.

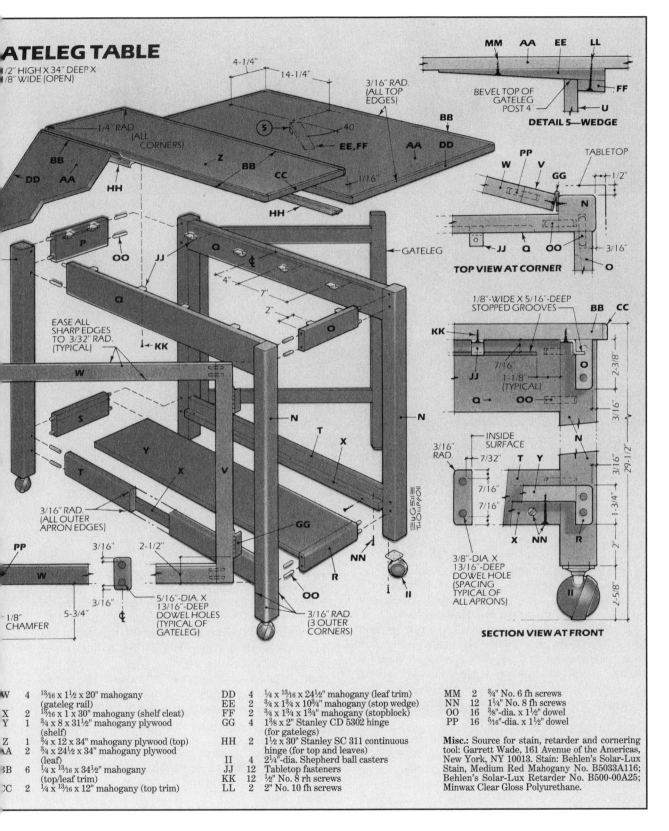

**7** Clamp the top rail in a vise using cutoffs as clamp pads. Round its front edge with a router and rounding-over bit.

**8** Cut the tenons on the rails using a dado head in a table saw. Use an auxiliary fence and stopblock in this step.

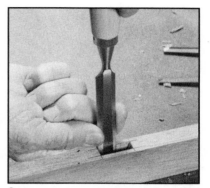

**9** Bore overlapping holes in a leg to form a mortise. Pare the mortise sides flat and parallel, and pare the ends square.

**10** Cut the slots in the legs with a straight bit in a router table. Cut the slot in three progressively deeper passes.

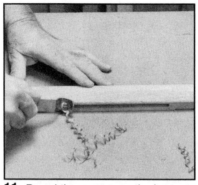

**11** Round the corners on the legs, except where they meet the rails. This is done quickly with a cornering tool.

**12** Using two bar clamps and two C-clamps, glue and clamp together a pair of legs spanned by a top rail and lower rail.

The top edge of the crossmembers is a series of flats. Cut a cardboard template of the shape and trace the outline onto each piece (Fig. 13). Cut the facets on a band saw, then clean up the saw cuts with files.

The seat slats are screwed to the crossmember, and the screws are driven perpendicular to the face of each facet. Mark layout lines perpendicular to each facet for the pilot holes and use the lines as a guide while boring the pilot holes with a $3/32$-in.-dia. bit. Next, counterbore each hole with a $1/2$-in.-dia. bit then glue and clamp the seat frames together (Fig. 14).

Make the $3/8$-in.-thick seat slat stock by resawing 5/4 stock on a band saw or table saw. Crosscut the slats to length and rip them to width. Clamp them to the crossmembers using the shaped cutoffs from the crossmembers. Bore the pilot holes into the slats with a $3/32$-in. bit (Figs. 15 and 16). Use a piece of tape on the drill bit to serve as a depth indicator, and code each slat to avoid mix-ups during later reassembly.

The pivot pins are hexhead capscrews with the threaded section cut off. Cut these to length from $1/4$-in.-dia. × $2 1/2$-in. and $3 1/2$-in.-long capscrews. Bore

$1/4$-in.-dia. holes in the seat frames and chair legs to accept the pivot pins.

Drive oval-head nails (escutcheon pins) next to the capscrew heads to serve as retainer pins to hold the screws in place. To bore the hole for the retainer pin, insert the capscrew then position a $1/16$-in.-dia. drill bit against the flat of the hexhead (Fig. 17). The nail should fit the hole snugly, and its head will prevent the capscrew from creeping out. Just make sure to bore these holes before installing the slats.

### The Table

Rip and crosscut the upper and lower aprons and the components for the gatelegs. Glue up the stock for the legs, then rip, crosscut and joint the legs to shape and dimension.

Use a doweling jig to bore dowel holes in the ends of the aprons. Place two thin pieces of stock under the apron to align it correctly with the legs, and use guide blocks clamped to the legs to locate the apron position on the leg. Insert dowel centers in the dowel holes, and press the parts together to mark the location of the dowel joints (Fig. 18). Bore matching holes in the legs.

**13** After you cut the tenons, make a cardboard pattern of the seat crossmember and trace it onto the workpiece.

**14** Bore the pilot holes in the crossmembers, then glue and clamp them to the seat sides.

**15** Hold the seat slats to the seat frame using the curved cutoffs from the crossmembers and clamps.

**16** Bore pilot holes into the seat slats. Use a piece of tape wrapped around the drill bit as a depth guide.

**17** Bore a hole for the escutcheon nail that fastens the hinge pin. Position the drill bit against the hinge pin.

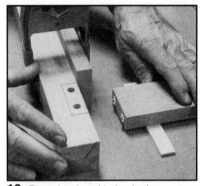

**18** Bore the dowel holes in the aprons, and mark hole positions on the legs using dowel centers and guide blocks.

Next, cut the stopped grooves in the aprons. To do this, tape markers on the table-saw fence and the workpiece to guide the length of the cuts. Then make the cuts (Fig. 19).

Use a router to round over the corners of the aprons and legs, then sand the aprons and legs. Glue and clamp the long aprons to the legs. Then glue and clamp these subassemblies to the short aprons (Fig. 20).

Temporarily attach the casters to the legs, then glue and clamp the gateleg assemblies and attach the hinges to them. Mark the hinge locations on the table legs so the bottom of the gateleg coincides with the bottom of the casters (Fig. 21).

Next, attach the cleats to the lower aprons. Cut a plywood panel to fit, and glue and screw it to the cleats.

Cut the plywood panels for the top to rough dimension. Then attach a strip of wood to each panel that fits snugly in the miter-gauge slot in the saw table. Mark the desired cutting line on the back of the panel, then tack nail the strip to it. Offset the strip on the panel by the distance from the inside edge of the blade to the inside edge of the table groove (Fig. 22).

Rip $\frac{1}{4}$-in.-thick $\times$ $1\frac{13}{16}$-in.-wide strips and glue them to two opposite edges in two stages. When the glue has set, plane the banding flush to the surface (Fig. 23).

Lay the three tabletop panels on the workbench, bottom face up. Insert $\frac{1}{16}$-in. shims between them for edge clearance. Mark the hinge screwhole centers along the drop leaves and the center top piece (Fig. 24). Screw the hinges in place.

Secure the table base to the top with the tabletop fasteners installed in the apron grooves. Cut and install the gateleg stop wedges. Then, partially disassemble the chairs and the table.

Stain the chair and table components. Finish the project by applying three coats of polyurethane, such as Minwax's Clear Gloss Polyurethane. Sand lightly between coats with 220-grit sandpaper.

**19** Saw the slots in the aprons. Put tape on the fence and workpiece to mark where the cut starts and stops.

**20** Glue and clamp the legs to the long aprons. Then glue and clamp these subassemblies to the short aprons.

**21** Clamp the gatelegs to the table base and mark their hinge locations. Remember to install casters for this step.

**22** Cut the top on a table saw. Guide the workpiece with a strip tacked to the panel's back.

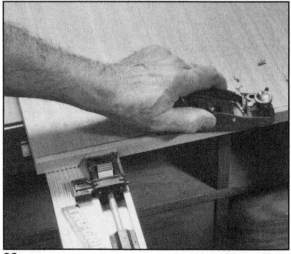

**23** Glue edge banding to the plywood. Banding is slightly thicker than plywood and is planed flush after glue sets.

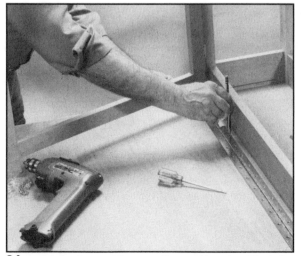

**24** Invert the top and base on the workbench. Attach the center top to the aprons and mark the hinge screwholes.

# Redwood table and bench set

■ One of life's simple pleasures is to dine outdoors on a beautiful warm day, and whether your tastes run to hot dogs on the grill or chilled strawberry soup, it is always nice to have a pleasant place to sit and enjoy your repast.

This redwood table and bench set is very functional and extremely attractive, while not being that difficult to build. It's a good project for moderately experienced woodworkers. Its construction is straight forward and requires mostly mortise-and-tenon joints. Because the project requires so many joints and slots, however, it does require that you prepare your stock uniformly and accurately.

The table is large enough to seat six to eight adults, and the benches can be used either in combination with the table, or as casual seating on their own.

*Redwood Table and Bench* was written by Neal Barrett. Photos by Neal Barrett with lead photo by J.R. Rost. Technical artist Eugene Thompson. A supplier of redwood is M.L. Condon Co. Inc., 250 Ferris Ave., White Plains, New York 10603. System Epoxy was used for gluing up the leg stock, and Titebond II, a new waterproof glue by Franklin, was used for the remainder of the assembly. The penetrating finish used was Cabot's Decking Stain No. 1400 Clear.

## Materials

Heart redwood was chosen as the material for this furniture because of the natural resistance to rot and insect damage (other grades of redwood are not rot and insect resistant). Although redwood is generally available from lumberyards around the country, should you have trouble locating suitable stock, there are suppliers that will ship nationwide.

On the model shown, 5/4 stock was used for the table and bench tops, aprons and center rails, and 8/4 stock for the table and bench legs. If you can get rough 8/4 stock, cut the bench legs from a single piece—however, if you can only buy surfaced lumber (normally 1½ in. thick), you will have to glue up the leg stock from two pieces.

Throughout the construction of these pieces, use glue that has a waterproof rating. Titebond II is suitable for any application that will not be left submersed in water. This adhesive offers good weather resistance in combination with low toxicity and a relatively fast setup. An epoxy seemed a better choice for the legs because the table and bench legs may often be standing in water long after the rest of the pieces have dried off.

## Legs and Aprons

Begin by gluing up stock for the table legs and bench legs. You can save time by gluing up blanks that are wide enough to provide two legs each. Mix the resin and hardener for the leg blanks in the proportions suggested by the manufacturer, then spread liberally on both mating surfaces. Clamp the pieces together and then let set overnight (Fig. 1). Be sure to wear gloves when working with the epoxy, as the hardener can be irritating to your skin. Also, ensure good ventilation when using epoxy, and place some old newspapers under where you are gluing up the legs.

Since the table and benches have many similar parts, cut out all the parts at one time. First rip and crosscut the leg stock for both the table and benches. Next, rip and crosscut all the slats for the table and bench tops. Then rip and crosscut the pieces for the top frames. Finally, rip and crosscut the aprons and crossrails. To keep from confusing the groups of workpieces, identify them with a masking-tape label or print on them with a piece of white chalk.

Install dado blades in the table saw to cut the tenons on aprons, slats, top end rails and cross support rails. Study the plans carefully, noting how the tenons differ on the various parts. Even though all tenons in this project are ⅜ in. wide, the length, shoulders and offsets

**4** Clamp a rail to the bench top with a scrap block next to it, and cut the mortises in the rail with a router.

**2** Clamp a stopblock to the saw table. Butt each workpiece that will have a tenon to the block and cut the tenon.

**3** Tip the workpiece on edge, butt it to the stopblock and move the piece over the dado head to finish the tenon.

**1** Unless you can get very thick redwood stock, use epoxy and clamp the leg blanks from two pieces.

**5** Finish each mortise by chopping its ends square with a chisel. Be sure to clear out waste chips before assembly.

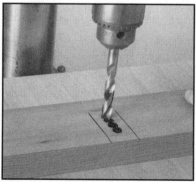

**6** Mark out the apron mortises with pencil lines, and remove the bulk of the mortise by boring on a drill press.

change from piece to piece. Cut all like parts with a single setup on the table saw, using a stopblock clamped to the saw table for repeat cuts (Figs. 2 and 3). Readjust the saw and block as necessary for each different part.

As usual, since the dado blades leave small ridges on the surface of the cuts, it is good practice to cut the tenons just a bit oversize and pare them to fit with a sharp chisel.

Next, lay out the mortises, bench legs and top frame pieces. Since there are quite a few mortises required, the most expedient method of cutting these joints is to use a plunge router with a straight bit and edge guide.

Use a scrap block to test the router setup for each different joint. Then clamp the workpiece between bench dogs to cut the mortises. When working on the narrow top frame members, clamp a scrap block to the side of the workpiece to help support the router base (Fig. 4). Complete each mortise by squaring the ends with a sharp chisel (Fig. 5).

Lay out the mortises in the aprons to house the center support rails. Use the drill press to remove waste from these mortises and finish them with a chisel (Figs. 6 and 7).

The table and bench tops are fastened to the base by driving long screws up through the aprons into the tops. Use the drill press and a long $13/64$-in.-dia. bit to bore the pilot holes through the aprons. Then counterbore the holes from the bottom with a $7/16$-in.-dia. bit (Figs. 8 and 9).

Note in the plans that all exposed edges are rounded to a $3/16$-in. radius. Use the router table and rounding-over bit to cut this radius on all legs, slats, and apron bottom edges (Fig. 10). The inside edges of the long sides of the table and bench top frames also can be rounded over, although you must stop just short of the joint with the end rails.

**7** Finish the apron mortises with a sharp chisel. Pare down to flatten the mortise sides and square the mortise ends.

**8** Bore the pilot holes through the width of the aprons using a long bit chucked into the drill press.

**9** Counterbore the apron pilot holes. The counterbored hole will hide the screwheads from view.

**10** Cut a radius on the leg, slat and lower apron corners using a rounding-over bit in the router table.

**11** Use a small brush to apply glue to the apron tenons. Also apply a little glue to the mortise walls.

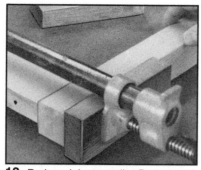

**12** Redwood dents easily. Protect work surfaces during assembly by positioning a scrap block under the clamp jaws.

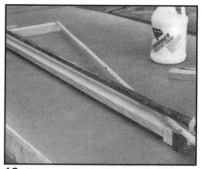

**13** Compare diagonal measurements of each leg-apron assembly to check it for square. Adjust the clamps if necessary.

## Base Assembly

Start assembling the base for both the table and the bench by joining a long apron to a pair of legs. Apply glue to the tenons and mortises with a small brush, then use a long clamp to pull the joint tight (Figs. 11 and 12). Use scrap blocks between the clamp jaws and the work because the redwood is a soft material and can be easily dented or scratched. Compare opposite diagonal measurements of the leg-apron assembly to be sure it is square before leaving the glue to set (Fig. 13). If the diagonal measurements differ slightly, shift the clamps and remeasure.

**14** Glue and clamp together the leg-apron assemblies spanned by the short aprons and center support rails.

**15** Place a long scrap block against the top frame while gluing and clamping the slats to the rails.

Complete the bases by joining the short aprons and center support rails to the long side assemblies (Fig. 14). Apply glue to the joints, slide the pieces together and clamp firmly. Be sure to assemble the bases on a flat, even surface, checking that all legs sit firmly and that the base does not rock. Readjust the clamps if required to eliminate any twist in the base. Check the assembly for square as before, then let the glue set.

Rip, crosscut and miter the table's corner blocks. Bore and counterbore pilot holes and screw the blocks to the aprons.

**16** Glue and clamp the stiles to the rails to complete the top assembly. Again, use a block under the clamp jaws.

**17** Cut the radius on each top corner using a sabre saw, staying just to the waste side of the line.

**18** Use a rounding-over bit in the router to put a curved edge along the top and bottom edges of each top.

## Top Assembly

Begin assembling the tops by joining the slats to the end rails. Position the glue, scrap blocks and clamps within easy reach of each other. Begin by applying glue to the mortises in the end rails and the slat tenons. Slide the parts together. If the joints have been cut accurately, the proper spacing between slats will be automatic.

Place a scrap block across the ends of the rails to distribute the clamping pressure, Then pull the joints tight with long clamps (Fig. 15). After the glue has set, apply glue to the end rail tenons and the mortises on the long side, and complete the top assembly (Fig. 16). Glue will squeeze out of the joints, but don't wipe it off. Wait until the glue gets rubbery, then cut it off with a chisel.

Trace the radius on the corners of the tops and use a sabre saw to make the cuts (Fig. 17). Remove saw marks with a file or belt sander. Next, use the $\frac{3}{16}$-in.-rad. rounding-over bit in a router to shape the curved top and bottom edges of each top (Fig. 18).

## Finishing

Since it is likely that these pieces will be exposed to wet grass or a wet patio or deck surface, it's a good idea to seal the bottom ends of the table and bench legs. If left unsealed, these end-grain surfaces will readily absorb water, with stains, mildew and rot all possible consequences. To seal the legs, paint on two coats of West System Epoxy, letting the first coat harden completely before applying the second (Fig. 19). The epoxy actually absorbs into the end grain of the wood, effectively sealing the surface from moisture penetration.

Sand the tops and bases with 120- and 150-grit paper, then dust off thoroughly.

Although heart redwood is naturally resistant to rot, if it is left untreated, the wood weathers and changes color. In addition, the glue in the joints—as well as the epoxy—degrades with exposure to the sun's ultraviolet rays. To protect the pieces, yet preserve their natural appearance, apply a penetrating finish (Fig. 20).

Complete assembly of the pieces by joining the tops to the bases. Invert a top on a padded surface and place the appropriate base over it. Adjust the base for equal overhang on all sides and attach the top by driving screws through the apron holes into the top frame.

Next, cut $\frac{3}{16}$-in.-thick spacers from scrap stock and place them between the slats—near the center of their span—to maintain proper spacing. Bore pilot holes and screw through the center support rail into each slat, again using 3-in. No.10 fh screws (Fig. 21). Remove the spacer blocks and the pieces are now complete.

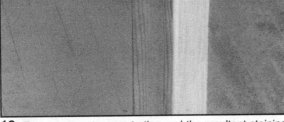

**19** To prevent water penetration and the resultant staining, apply two coats of epoxy on the bottom of each leg.

**20** Protect the table and benches by applying a penetrating finish stain, like Cabot Decking Stain No. 1400 Clear.

**21** Insert small thin blocks between the slats, and drive screws through the rails and into the slats.

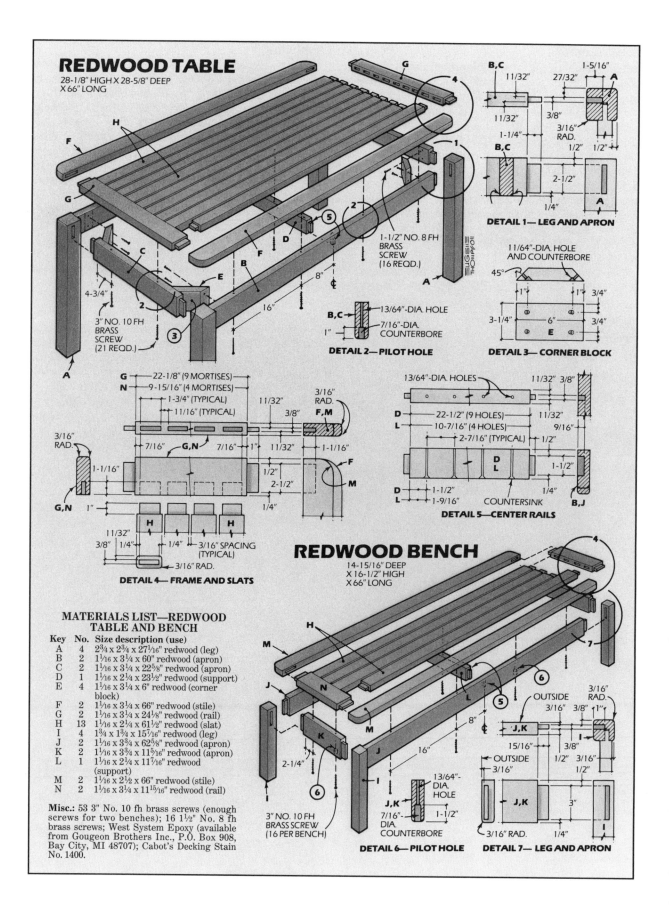

# REDWOOD TABLE

28-1/8" HIGH X 28-5/8" DEEP X 66" LONG

DETAIL 1— LEG AND APRON

DETAIL 2— PILOT HOLE

DETAIL 3— CORNER BLOCK

DETAIL 4— FRAME AND SLATS

DETAIL 5—CENTER RAILS

# REDWOOD BENCH

14-15/16" DEEP X 16-1/2" HIGH X 66" LONG

DETAIL 6— PILOT HOLE

DETAIL 7— LEG AND APRON

## MATERIALS LIST—REDWOOD TABLE AND BENCH

| Key | No. | Size description (use) |
|-----|-----|------------------------|
| A | 4 | 2¾ x 2¾ x 27⁷⁄₁₆" redwood (leg) |
| B | 2 | 1¹⁄₁₆ x 3¼ x 60" redwood (apron) |
| C | 2 | 1¹⁄₁₆ x 3¼ x 22⅝" redwood (apron) |
| D | 1 | 1¹⁄₁₆ x 2¼ x 23½" redwood (support) |
| E | 4 | 1¹⁄₁₆ x 3¼ x 6" redwood (corner block) |
| F | 2 | 1¹⁄₁₆ x 3¼ x 66" redwood (stile) |
| G | 2 | 1¹⁄₁₆ x 3¼ x 24⅛" redwood (rail) |
| H | 13 | 1¹⁄₁₆ x 2¼ x 61½" redwood (slat) |
| I | 4 | 1¾ x 1¾ x 15⁷⁄₁₆" redwood (leg) |
| J | 2 | 1¹⁄₁₆ x 3¾ x 62⅝" redwood (apron) |
| K | 2 | 1¹⁄₁₆ x 3¾ x 11⁵⁄₁₆" redwood (apron) |
| L | 1 | 1¹⁄₁₆ x 2¼ x 11⁷⁄₁₆" redwood (support) |
| M | 2 | 1¹⁄₁₆ x 2½ x 66" redwood (stile) |
| N | 2 | 1¹⁄₁₆ x 3¼ x 11¹⁵⁄₁₆" redwood (rail) |

**Misc.:** 53 3" No. 10 fh brass screws (enough screws for two benches); 16 1½" No. 8 fh brass screws; West System Epoxy (available from Gougeon Brothers Inc., P.O. Box 908, Bay City, MI 48707); Cabot's Decking Stain No. 1400.

# Coffee table

■ The design of this coffee table has its roots in the Arts-and-Crafts tradition. With its strong yet simple lines, this table of curly maple complements a variety of furniture styles.

Should you need an end table, kitchen table or worktable, the dimensions of the legs, aprons and top can be modified easily to suit different needs.

Because the table is a reasonably simple design, it is an ideal project for a woodworker with intermediate-level skill, who has a well-equipped workshop that includes a table saw.

The table's top is glued-up and forms a solid panel. Its legs are cut from thick slabs of curly maple. The finish has three coats of hand-rubbed Waterlox Transparent finish. This oil finish builds up to a thin coating. It produces an invitingly soft sheen and brings out the figure in the curly maple without having to use stain. The finish imparts a slightly amber tone to the wood.

*Coffee Table* was written by Neal Barrett. Technical art by Eugene Thompson. Lead photo by John Griebsch, how-to photos by Neal Barrett. For a supplier of the extra-thick curly maple, contact Sandy Pond Hardwoods, 921-A Lancaster Pike, Quarryville, PA 17566.

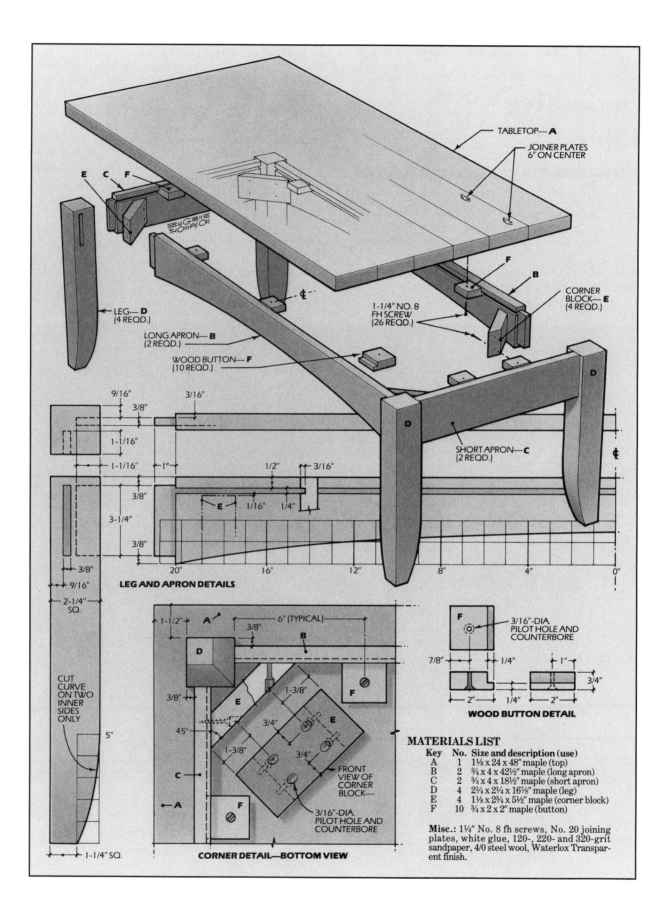

TABLETOP—**A**

JOINER PLATES
6" ON CENTER

**E  C  F**

LEG—**D**
(4 REQD.)

LONG APRON—**B**
(2 REQD.)

WOOD BUTTON—**F**
(10 REQD.)

1-1/4" NO. 8
FH SCREW
(26 REQD.)

**F**

**B**

CORNER
BLOCK—**E**
(4 REQD.)

**D**

**D**

SHORT APRON—**C**
(2 REQD.)

9/16"
3/8"
3/16"
1-1/16"
1-1/16"   1"
3/8"
3-1/4"
3/8"
1/2"   3/16"
**E**   1/16"   1/4"
3/8"
9/16"
2-1/4"
SQ.

20"        16"        12"        8"        4"        0"

**LEG AND APRON DETAILS**

CUT
CURVE
ON TWO
INNER
SIDES
ONLY

5"

1-1/4" SQ.

1-1/2"   **A**
3/8"
6" (TYPICAL)
**B**
**D**
3/8"
**E**
45°
1-3/8"
1-3/8"
3/4"
3/4"
**E**
**C**
**A**
**F**
**F**
FRONT
VIEW OF
CORNER
BLOCK—

3/16"-DIA.
PILOT HOLE AND
COUNTERBORE

**CORNER DETAIL—BOTTOM VIEW**

**F**
3/16"-DIA.
PILOT HOLE AND
COUNTERBORE
7/8"   1/4"   1"
2"   1/4"   2"   3/4"

**WOOD BUTTON DETAIL**

## MATERIALS LIST

| Key | No. | Size and description (use) |
|-----|-----|----------------------------|
| A | 1 | 1⅛ x 24 x 48" maple (top) |
| B | 2 | ¾ x 4 x 42½" maple (long apron) |
| C | 2 | ¾ x 4 x 18½" maple (short apron) |
| D | 4 | 2¼ x 2¼ x 16⅞" maple (leg) |
| E | 4 | 1⅛ x 2¾ x 5½" maple (corner block) |
| F | 10 | ¾ x 2 x 2" maple (button) |

**Misc.:** 1¼" No. 8 fh screws, No. 20 joining plates, white glue, 120-, 220- and 320-grit sandpaper, 4/0 steel wool, Waterlox Transparent finish.

**1** Joint one edge of each board used in the top. Rip the board slightly over width. Joint the sawn edge smooth and straight.

**2** Cut the joining plate slots in the edge of each board. Work on the table saw or another clean, flat surface.

**3** After glue-up, use a razor-sharp plane to remove irregularities in the top. Work diagonally or across the top.

**4** Before sanding the top, use a cabinet scraper to remove small areas of tearout left from the hand plane.

## Making the Top

Begin by selecting the 5/4 stock for the tabletop. Note that the top is glued-up from six 4-in.-wide strips. In selecting the wood for the top, try to match the pieces for color and grain pattern so the piece will have a uniform appearance.

Joint the edge of each board. Rip each to about $4\frac{1}{8}$ in. Then joint the boards again to remove the saw marks. Crosscut them about 2 in. longer than the finished dimension (Fig. 1). Check to be sure that each joint is tight and square along its entire length. Mark the stock for joining plates spaced about 6 to 8 in. on center. Cut the slots with the plate joiner (Fig. 2). Use a flat tabletop or a saw table as a work surface. Be sure to hold both the workpiece and joiner tightly to the table as you cut the slots.

Spread glue on the board edges and in the plate grooves, insert the joining plates and assemble the top.

Use bar clamps to push the joints tight. After about 20 to 30 minutes, scrape off any excess glue squeeze-out from the surfaces of the panel, then let the glue cure completely.

Trim the tabletop to length, using either a sliding table jig on the table saw or a circular saw with a straightedge clamped to the top.

Next, hold the top between the bench dogs and lightly plane the top to remove any small irregularities left from gluing the stock together (Fig. 3). Use a razor-sharp plane and work diagonally across the panel. As figured woods have a tendency to tear out, take a very light cut. If you still have trouble with tearout, you can plane directly across the panel's width, although this will require more sanding later.

Use a freshly sharpened cabinet scraper to finish smoothing the tabletop (Fig. 4).

**5** Cut the tenon cheeks with a shopmade tenoning jig. Use a parallel jaw clamp to hold the apron to the jig.

**6** Saw the tenon shoulders with a miter gauge and extension fence. Note the parallel jaw clamp that acts as a stop.

**7** Cut the small shoulders with the apron on edge. Cut the waste piece off the tenon with a dovetail saw or band saw.

**8** Mark the curve on the long aprons, and saw just outside the line using a band saw or sabre saw.

**9** Remove the saw marks and smooth the apron's curve with a sharp spokeshave, or use a sanding drum on a drill press.

**10** Cut the groove in the aprons with dado blades in the table saw. The small lip on each button fits the groove.

## Making the Aprons

Rip and crosscut the stock for the table aprons to finished size. While the tenons can be cut in several ways, including using dado blades and by hand with a backsaw, you might want to use a shopmade tenoning jig on the table saw. Numerous commercial jigs are available, but most operate on the same principle of passing the workpiece vertically over the saw blade to cut the tenon cheeks.

The jig has a block of wood with a long, narrow piece of scrap screwed to it. The block rides against the table saw fence and the long, narrow piece acts as a backrest for the piece being sawn. The backrest is screwed to the block at 90°. The dimensions of the pieces used to make the jig aren't important as long as they provide the support for the workpiece. This means that the block should be long enough to accommodate the apron and backrest, and wide enough to provide an adequate bearing surface for a clamp to secure the workpiece.

It is important that the two pieces that form the jig have square edges. Any deviation from square in the jig will result in a tenon that does not fit the mortise properly.

Make a test cut on scrap before sawing the tenons. To do this, clamp a piece of scrap against the jig so its end rests on the saw table and its back edge butts to the backrest. Adjust the saw blade height carefully and run the test piece over the blade. If the saw cuts are correctly located, parallel and the right depth, you can cut the tenons (Fig. 5). If the test cuts are out of parallel, it means the jig is out of square. Any other adjustments can be made by moving the saw fence or changing the blade height.

Before cutting the shoulder cuts on the aprons, screw a long piece of straight scrap to the miter gauge to form an extension fence. Fasten a clamp to the extension fence to act as a stop, and test the setup on a piece of scrap before making the shoulder cuts. Saw the tenon shoulder first (Fig. 6), then saw across the apron's edge (Fig. 7).

Sawing the narrow shoulder in this way leaves a small piece of waste attached to the tenon. Remove this by cutting with a dovetail saw, or cut off the waste on a band saw.

Make a template from cardboard or hardboard of the curved bottom profile on the long aprons. Trace the shape on the apron, and use the band saw or a sabre saw to cut the curved shape (Fig. 8). Keep the saw blade barely to the waste side of the line as you cut.

You can clean off the saw marks on this edge and refine the curve by clamping the apron upright on the bench and taking short strokes with a sharp spokeshave

**11** Cut the mortises with a plunge router and fence. Place a scrap piece next to the leg blank to support the router.

**12** Square the mortise ends with a chisel. If the mortise is bored on the drill press, its sides must be pared flat.

**13** Cut the leg blanks to shape on the band saw. The curved profile is cut on the inside surfaces of each leg.

(Fig. 9). If you are careful, you can accomplish the same thing using a sanding drum on a drill press. Use light pressure on the drill press to avoid burning the wood or leaving crescents. Take fine cuts if you are using the spokeshave to avoid gouging. With either method, work down to the line in several passes.

Using dado blades in a table saw, cut the groove on the top inside surface of the apron pieces (Fig. 10). This groove will house the lip on the wood buttons for fastening the top to the base. Even a narrow dado blade tends to push a workpiece off the saw table, especially if the dado blades are dull. To avoid this, feed the workpiece slowly, and use a pushstick at the end of the cut to keep your hand clear of the dado blades.

If you find that the workpiece is riding up, despite these steps, try cutting the groove in two shallow passes.

### Making the Legs
The table legs are unusual in that they are made from stock far thicker than you find at an average lumberyard. You may be able to buy or order curly maple for the rest of this project at a local lumberyard that sells hardwood, but chances are such a yard may have difficulty finding curly maple that is this thick.

Using the mail-order source, the stock will arrive with rough-sawn surfaces. You need to have the stock planed to thickness at a lumberyard or plane it yourself.

If you plane the stock by machine, put a set of sharp knives in your planer. If you use hand planes, get ready for some exercise and sharpen your tools well before and during the operation. Either way, take very shallow cuts. The less you tear out the maple while planing it to thickness, the less cleanup you will have later with scrapers and sandpaper.

If you have the stock planed at a lumberyard, expect to pay a premium for this work—the yard may have to install a fresh set of knives and take extra time with the stock.

Once the stock is the correct thickness, rip and joint the leg blanks to $2\frac{1}{4}$ in. wide and crosscut them to

length. Draw the position of the mortises on the leg blanks using a sharp pencil and square, or use a mortise gauge. Hold a leg between bench dogs, and use a plunge router and edge guide to cut the mortises (Fig. 11). You also can bore out the bulk of the mortise on a drill press. Then pare the sides flat with a chisel. Either method will require that you also pare the mortise ends square (Fig. 12).

Make a template of the curved section of the leg and trace the curve on each leg. Note that the legs curve only on the inside faces. Cut the legs to shape on a band saw, staying just to the waste side of the line (Fig. 13). Clean up the curved face with a plane or belt sander.

### Assembly
To begin assembly, rip a strip of $\frac{3}{4}$-in.-thick stock to 2 in. wide, and crosscut it at least 24 in. long for making the wood buttons that fasten the tabletop to the base.

Use dado blades in the table saw to cut a $\frac{1}{4}$-in.-wide × $\frac{1}{2}$-in.-deep rabbet along one edge of the strip. As was the case with cutting the groove in the aprons, the workpiece may have a tendency to move away from the blade. If necessary, cut the rabbet in two passes.

Crosscut each button to length using an extension fence on the miter gauge (Fig. 14). Mark the length of the buttons with a strip of tape on the table-saw table. Slide the workpiece up to the edge of the tape and move it over the saw blade.

Bore and counterbore pilot holes in the buttons for the screws that attach them to the top.

Test fit the legs to the aprons without glue. If a joint is too tight, pare the tenon to fit with a sharp chisel, or use a chisel and block plane. If a joint is too loose, glue a veneer shim to the tenon cheek.

Once all the joints fit correctly, begin the assembly of the table base by joining the short aprons to the legs. Apply glue to both mortises and tenons and use a bar clamp to pull the joints snug. Compare opposite diagonal measurements of the assembly to check that it is square, and adjust the clamps if necessary (Fig. 15).

**14** Crosscut the buttons on the table saw using the miter gauge. A piece of tape on the saw table acts as a guide.

**15** Glue and clamp the short aprons to the legs. Measure diagonals to check the assembly for square.

**16** Clamp a stopblock and backrest to the drill press. Bore, then counterbore, the pilot holes in the corner blocks.

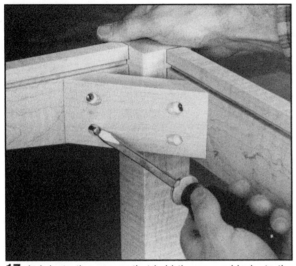

**17** Lubricate the screws that hold the corner blocks to the aprons with a little wax. Screw the blocks to the aprons.

**18** Invert the leg-apron assembly on the top with equal spacing all around. Screw the buttons into the top.

After the glue has cured, glue and clamp the two ends to the long aprons. Be sure to do this on a flat surface to avoid imparting any twist to the base.

Cut pieces of 5/4 stock for the corner blocks. Use either the table saw and miter gauge or a miterbox to cut the 45° angle on the block ends.

Bore and counterbore pilot holes in the blocks on the drill press (Fig. 16). It makes the process easier if you clamp a fence, 45° base and stopblock to the drill press table.

Next, screw the corner blocks to the aprons with 1¼-in.-long No.8 fh screws (Fig. 17). The screws will go in easier if you lubricate them with a little wax.

Carefully sand all the parts with 120-, 220- and 320-grit sandpaper. Then dust off everything thoroughly with a tack cloth.

The table shown has three coats of Waterlox Transparent finish. The finish is applied with a clean rag, allowing only a thin film to remain on the surface. After overnight drying, scuff the finish lightly with 320-grit paper, wipe it off with a tack cloth and apply the next coat. Repeat the process on the next coat. When the last coat has fully cured, rub it out with 4/0 steel wool and polish it with a soft, clean cloth.

To assemble the table, place the top upside down on a padded surface, then place the inverted base over it. Adjust the base for an equal overhang on all sides, then install the wood buttons and bore pilot holes in the top. Attach the base to the top by screwing through the buttons with 1¼-in.-long No.8 fh screws.

# Carpet buying guide

■ Because it provides a unifying focus that ties together walls, window treatments and furnishings, carpet may be the single most important element used in interior decoration. Carpet adds color and texture, provides soundproofing, insulates cold floors and offers under-foot comfort. Shopping for carpet, however, can be frustrating. You may be confused by the variety of choices available. To ensure that you make the right decision, be sure to choose your carpet dealer carefully and take the time to understand not only the basics of buying carpet, but also the ins and outs of carpet construction and proper care.

### Choosing a Carpet Dealer

Finding a reputable dealer shouldn't be difficult. Most department stores will have an established track record, so they'll be around to answer any future complaints you may have. An established neighborhood carpet store with a record of satisfied customers is also a good choice.

Approach discount carpet outlets with caution. If their deals sound too good to be true, they probably are neither good nor true. Never take the salesperson's word alone for carpet quality. Always ask to see the carpet sample specifications book and check the carpet manufacturer and the construction information. A dealer who has rolls of carpet in the showroom but can't provide sample books may be selling seconds—carpet that has a manufacturing defect. Some seconds may only show pattern errors that won't affect the wear characteristics of the carpet, but others are discounted

*Carpet Buying Guide* was written by Gary and Jim Branson. Illustrations by George Retseck.

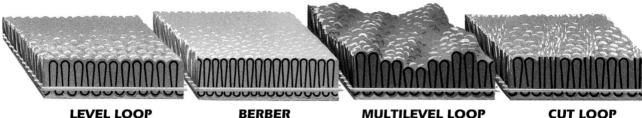

**LEVEL LOOP**          **BERBER**          **MULTILEVEL LOOP**          **CUT LOOP**

because of problems with adhesives or other materials. These problems may affect the life of the carpet.

Recently a new source of consumer carpet sales, the wholesale telephone carpet business, has shown rapid growth. Many shop-by-phone carpet dealers can provide a wholesale price quote for any carpet you want to buy, but you'll have to provide the legwork to provide the company with the name and description of the carpet in question. Some of these companies sell carpet only to a contractor or other large-volume accounts, while others solicit consumer business and sell in any quantity. A few shop-by-phone dealers will even send out sample books.

The advantage of buying carpet over the phone is that you may get wholesale prices. You will, however, have to pay shipping costs to your home.

When you've located a dealer and obtained the carpet sample books, check the carpet construction specifications for manufacturing information. Pay special attention to the brand name, warranty, style, density, weight and pile content. These are the variables that affect quality.

As with most purchases, buying carpet and selecting a dealer based on price alone may be only a short-term economy. The few extra dollars saved now are a small reward for carpet that doesn't live up to your expectations over the long term.

## Carpet Style

The most common carpet construction is called tufting. Tufting machines pierce the carpet-backing material with loops of yarn which form the carpet pile. If the loops of yarn are uniform in size and height, the carpet is a *level-loop* pile. *Berber* styles are level-loop carpets that have tight loops and maximum fiber density. Carpet with loops of uneven height is called *multilevel loop*. If some loops are cut and the carpet height is even, it's called *cut loop*. If some loops are intact and some are cut, but the pile height is uneven, the pile is called *random shear*.

If all carpet pile loops are cut and form a uniform $\frac{1}{2}$-in.-high pile, the carpet is called *Saxony*. A Saxony pile that's more than $\frac{1}{2}$ in. high and less dense may be called *velvet*, *plush* or *textured plush*. A carpet that has a mixture of straight tufts with twisted or curled tufts is called *frieze*. Friezes or twists, with their curled tufts, form a resilient textured pile that resists matting, doesn't

show footprints and is sometimes called trackless. Be sure these fibers are heat set to preserve the resiliency of the pile. The most durable carpets are the loop-pile carpet styles, so choose one of these for carpeting in high-traffic areas such as hallways and stairs.

## Density and Weight

Density and weight also help determine carpet durability. Density refers to the number of fibers found in 1 sq. in. of carpet and is called either stitches per inch (spi) or stitches per 3 in. (divide by 3 to get stitches per inch). The number of stitches shown should be a minimum of 9 to 10 spi for residential carpeting, 5 to 6 spi for berbers and 10 to 12 spi for level-loop or commercial carpets. After checking the specifications book, bend the carpet sample so it forms a 90° angle and check how much backing material you can see. The less visible the backing, the tighter the fibers and the more durable the carpet.

Check the carpet's pile yarn weight. Select a carpet that has no less than a 40-ounce pile weight (higher pile weight is better) for Saxonys, plushes or berbers. Buy commercial carpets that have a minimum 26-ounce pile weight. Note that pile weight refers to the weight of the carpet pile only. The total weight of the carpet, which includes the pile plus the backing, also will be listed.

## Pile Content

The carpet specifications also will list the type of fiber used in the carpet construction. This may be shown as pile content, pile yarn or simply as pile. The pile content is also an important guide to carpet durability and maintenance.

Carpet yarn or fiber may be nylon, olefin, polyester, polypropylene or natural fibers such as wool or cotton. Early polyester pile carpets were prone to matting and premature wear, but dealers now say that today's polyesters are more durable and crush resistant. Polyester fibers are sometimes used in a blend such as a polyester/nylon blend.

The most durable carpets, including commercial and long-wearing berber styles, are made with olefin fibers. Carpets made with pure olefin may feel rough to the touch, however. Berber carpets are also available in olefin/nylon blends or in 100% nylon construction. The olefin blends or pure nylon fibers feel softer than pure olefin. Nylon fibers are also durable, easy to clean and they resist matting, so nylon is always a good pile choice.

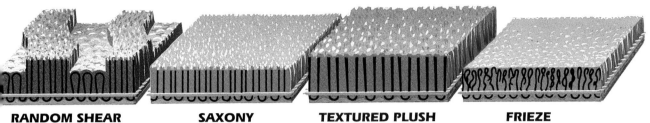

**RANDOM SHEAR**     **SAXONY**     **TEXTURED PLUSH**     **FRIEZE**

## Carpet Pad

A quality pad can extend the carpet's life, prevent the carpet from slipping and improve its feel underfoot—the pad choice can be as important as the carpet itself.

Pad materials range from felt and single-color plastic foam, to rebond and solid rubber pads. A pad that's too thick may interfere with good balance and may prove hazardous to the elderly or unsure of foot. A pad that's too thin may wear more quickly or deteriorate from impact, causing the carpet to wrinkle or even split at the seams. The best test for pad comfort is to lay the pad and carpet samples on the floor and walk on them.

For most applications, choose a 6- to 8-pound rebond foam pad. Rebond foam particles are bonded together with adhesives. Rebond pads will not lose their resiliency as will inferior pads.

To save money on your carpet pad, check the Yellow Pages under Carpet Installers, Equipment and Supplies. You can often buy the pad at half price from these wholesale-only dealers, but you may have to buy an entire roll (40 yards). Don't be put off by the fact that the dealer sells at wholesale—most will sell to the walk-in trade.

## Selecting the Carpet

If durability were the only criterion for carpet selection, you could simply pick the carpet with the best wear characteristics.

Other factors, including your budget and style, will help shape your final decision.

When making your carpet choice consider your lifestyle. Active families will need more durable carpets than retirees or working singles, and carpet traffic will vary from one area to another. While halls and stairs require high durability, bathroom carpet must be stain resistant and easy to clean. The luxury of a Saxony or the texture of a random plush may sway you more than the utility of a commercial or berber style.

Another crucial factor is carpet color. If possible, bring wallpaper and paint samples, or other examples of your home's color scheme to help you make a color choice. Bring home a carpet sample or large remnant of the carpet and place it in the room where you will use it. Color shifts will occur between sunlight and night lighting, so check the carpet's color under different conditions to be sure of an appropriate match.

---

### Carpet Care and Cleaning

Carpet costs represent a major portion of your decorating dollars, so it makes sense to follow good care and cleaning procedures. The following tips will help you extend the life of your carpet:

■ Use a quality pad to cushion the carpet.

■ Use commercial-type mats at entry doors.

■ Don't wear street shoes indoors.

■ Don't walk barefoot on carpet—natural skin oils soil carpet and retain dirt.

■ Clean up food or beverage spills immediately. Use a white cloth, dampened with water, to wipe up minor spills.

■ Invest in a quality, upright vacuum cleaner. Cheaper canister-type units often do not have sufficient power to remove deep-down dirt and grit.

■ Vacuum frequently—a carpet that bears heavy traffic should be vacuumed daily.

■ Have the carpet restretched if it shows any wrinkles or puckers.

■ Shade carpet from direct sunlight to reduce fading.

■ Move furniture frequently and put pads under legs to avoid dents.

■ If dents occur, remove them with a steam iron. Hold the iron about 2 in. above the carpet to steam the fibers. Then, brush and raise the fibers with your fingertips. Don't let the hot iron touch the carpet.

■ Have the carpets professionally cleaned to avoid a buildup of detergent residue. Professional equipment uses hotter water, stronger detergents and has better suction than typical home-use equipment.

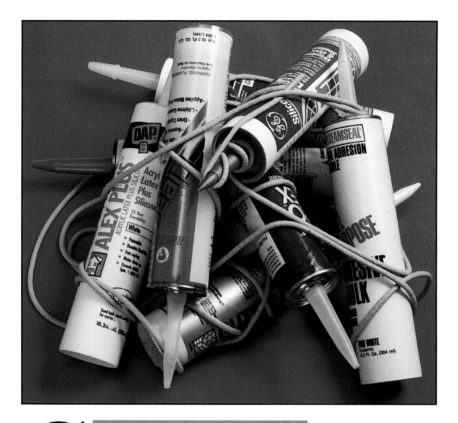

# C aulk
# buying guide

■ Choosing the right caulk for the job from a selection of tubes spread across a 10-ft. wall display in your home center can be intimidating.

### Many Shapes of Caulk

Caulk is a sealant and comes packaged in several forms. The most common type is a semi-liquid substance packaged in a $10\frac{1}{2}$-fluid-ounce tube. One tube of caulk should fill a gap roughly 48-ft. long, $\frac{1}{8}$-in. wide and $\frac{1}{4}$-in. deep. This type of caulk is applied with a caulking gun that uses a trigger mechanism to push the caulk out of the tube. Caulk also comes in larger tubes for professional use, and in smaller squeeze tubes for quick jobs.

Besides the tube-packaged types, caulk comes in a solid-putty form called *rope caulk* that's used temporarily to plug gaps or fill large voids. Another type comes in narrow strips ready to be pressed into place along bathtub tile joints or around a sink. Foam caulk comes packaged in an aerosol-type dispenser and is best for filling large voids, such as holes in walls where pipes pass through or the spaces between windows and wall framing.

### Type of Caulk

Despite what the caulk is called, what it is made from is the most important consideration in determining its use. What you want the caulk to adhere to and where you want to use it should determine the characteristics of the caulk you buy. For example, to caulk joints around doors and windows requires a sealant that's both flexible and long lasting, has good adherence to siding (wood, aluminum and vinyl), will resist extreme weather conditions and, if it's not painted over, will withstand UV radiation from direct sunlight. To seal flashing around a chimney, the caulk must adhere to masonry, roofing shingles and metal flashing, and stand up to the elements unpainted. The warm, wet conditions of a bathroom require a caulk that resists mildew and withstands moisture.

*Caulk Buying Guide* and *Caulking Tips* were written by Gene and Katie Hamilton. Illustrations by George Retseck. Photo by Stan Silver.

The package label should provide you with the information you need to determine if a particular caulk is suitable for your project. If it's not going to be painted, check to see if the caulk comes in a selection of colors so you can match it with adjacent colors of siding and trim paint. If you can't find a match, some caulks are also available in a clear formula.

The label also should state whether the caulk it paintable or stainable, what kinds of paints and stains it's compatible with and whether it requires priming before painting. The drying or curing time before painting also should be specified.

If you're working in cooler weather, check the recommended application temperature range. Some sealants can be applied at any temperature, while others require a minimum of 40°F or higher.

In some cases, reading the label won't give you a clear idea of exactly how well the caulk will perform. To help you choose the best caulk for the job, they have been grouped here in eight categories, based on formula type, and listed with some of their basic characteristics.

## Tripolymer, Copolymer and Compound Latex Caulks

If cost isn't a consideration, then the new tripolymer or copolymer caulks (about $4 to $6) are the best choices for versatility and durability. Proflex by Geocel and Lexel by Sasho are multitask sealants designed to adhere to dissimilar surfaces, such as metals, glass and untreated and treated wood. With excellent adhesion properties and more elasticity than other caulks, these newly developed sealants can replace some specialty caulks such as butyl-rubber and asphalt caulk. These new formulas, however, are also flammable and should be applied with caution and proper ventilation.

The high-end latex caulks, such as 230 by DAP, are also multipurpose caulks. The most popular formulas are latex-based variations, or combinations with silicones and acrylics. They are easy to use, clean up with water and are almost as durable as the polymer formulas.

## Silicone Caulks

Just as expensive are the 100% silicone caulks (about $4 to $6). These are the best choice when sealing damp, high moisture areas. They shrink very little, remain flexible, are water resistant and have good bonding power for joining dissimilar surfaces. They also can be applied in cold conditions. This is the best caulk to use around bathtubs, showers and sinks. Some silicones don't hold paint well, however, and they don't bond well to rot-resistant woods such as cedar, redwood and pressure-treated wood. As such, they're not as versatile as the compound-latex and polymer formulas.

## Acrylic Latex and Compound-Vinyl Caulks

In the midprice range are the acrylic latex formula caulks (about $2 to $3). These are the best all-around buy for many uses inside and outside, and they feature simple, water cleanup. As silicones are added to the formula, the caulk becomes more durable.

Included in this general category are adhesive caulks such as Polyseamseal by Darworth and Phenoseal Vinyl Adhesive Caulk. Besides sealing cracks, these caulks act as light-duty construction adhesives that join dissimilar materials. Replacing a loose ceramic tile, setting ceramic soap dishes and installing a vinyl baseboard molding are just a few of the jobs adhesive caulks can handle.

## Oil-base and Plain Latex Caulks

These inexpensive caulks (about $1 to $2) have been around for years and are suitable for indoor use only. Although oil-base caulks are inexpensive, they're not always the best buy because they have a limited life and require mineral spirits for cleanup. Plain latex caulks, on the other hand, are easy to apply and clean up with water. They're suitable for interior uses such as caulking woodwork when painting, but they are not a good choice for areas exposed to the weather.

## Butyl-Rubber Caulks

Butyl-rubber caulk is in the medium price range (about $2 to $4) and is traditionally used to caulk masonry-to-wood or metal joints. It's also good for caulking glass-to-metal joints and sealing aluminum and galvanized gutters. Butyl-rubber caulks require mineral spirits for cleanup, and are more difficult to work with than the newer formulas. Tripolymer and copolymer caulks can be used for similar applications.

## Polyurethane and Polysulfide

Both polyurethane and polysulfide formulas are expensive, high-performance caulks (about $4.50 to $14) used primarily in marine applications. They have excellent adhesion properties and are waterproof. They are toxic until cured, however, and precautions must be taken to provide proper ventilation and skin protection during application. Strong solvents are also required for cleanup.

While the expensive polysulfide formulas are generally reserved for marine use, Franklin International makes a popularly-priced polyurethane formula that is suitable for use around the home, and Titebond Wood & Window Caulk is a good choice for redwood and cedar siding. Polyurethane caulks have excellent adhesive properties.

## Foam Caulk

The best way to fill large cracks in difficult-to-reach areas is with foam caulk. It is sensitive to UV radiation, however, so it must be painted if it will be exposed to sunlight. The foam sticks to just about anything and is messy to work with, though. It also can cause skin or eye irritation, so wear eye protection and use the pair of plastic gloves provided with the product.

## Rope Caulk

Rope Caulk is an inexpensive, nonhardening, solid caulk used temporarily to fill cracks. It's best suited for plugging gaps between window sashes and doorjambs during the winter. Because it's designed not to adhere, it can be removed easily when the warm weather arrives. Rope caulk will last for a season outside, so it can be used to plug cracks between storm windows and other small gaps on the exterior of your house.

### Caulking Tips

Once you've bought the right caulk for the job, getting it out of the tube is a fairly straightforward process. To start, cut the tube's nozzle at a 45° angle (Fig. 1). The size of the gap you're filling determines how far up the nozzle to make the cut—the higher the cut, the wider the bead of caulk. Note that joints more that 3/8 in. wide and deep should be filled with a foam-rope backer or oakum to provide a base for the caulk. After cutting the nozzle, press a long nail through the opening to break the seal inside the tube.

Many caulking guns have a plunger rod with notches that the trigger engages to push out the caulk. To install the tube, first turn the rod so the notches face up and then pull the rod all the way out. After the tube is in place, rotate the rod so the notches face down, and squeeze the trigger until the caulk moves into the nozzle. Lay down a bead of caulk by holding the gun at a 45° angle, pressing the trigger and moving the gun at a steady rate (Fig. 2). When the bead is finished, turn the plunger rod so the notches face up to reduce the tendency for the pressurized caulk to continue flowing out of the nozzle. To ensure that the caulk adheres to the surface, always remove all old, loose caulk, paint and dirt from the area before applying new caulk (Fig. 3).

Deep, wide gaps are best filled with foam caulk. Wear goggles and gloves for this job, and use the long applicator tube to reach into confined spaces (Fig. 4). This type of caulk is especially useful for sealing the gaps between window casings and adjacent framing. Sealing cracks in interior woodwork is generally done after priming. Use a water-cleanup caulk and smooth the application by running a wet fingertip along the bead (Fig. 5). After the caulk is dry, you can apply the finish coat of paint. For seasonal protection around window sashes, storm windows and exterior gaps, inexpensive rope caulk is pressed into the gaps. This nonhardening caulk won't stick and should be removed when warm weather arrives (Fig. 6).

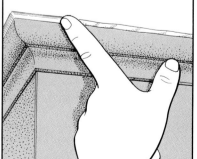  

**1** Use a sharp knife to cut tube nozzle at a 45° angle. Cut higher up the nozzle for a wider bead. Press a long nail through the nozzle to break the seal in the cartridge.

**2** Hold tube at 45° angle to run bead along joint. Use gentle trigger pressure and progress slowly. Then, turn rod so notches face up to reduce excess caulk flow.

**3** Before caulking, always scrape away all loose caulk, paint and dirt so new compound will adhere to the surface. Some caulks require priming before application.

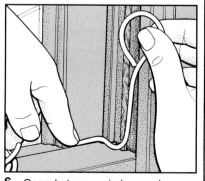 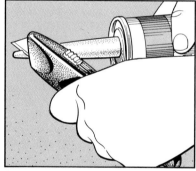 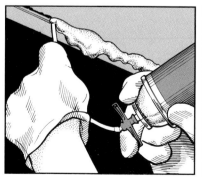

**4** Foam caulk is best for sealing large gaps, such as between a window and wall framing. Wear goggles and gloves for safety.

**5** Caulk joints between wood trim and walls before finish painting. Use a wet finger to smooth and press caulk into joint.

**6** Gaps between window sashes are filled with rope caulk in fall. After winter, nonsticking rope caulk is removed easily.

# Insulation buying guide

■ Insulation is one of those hidden home improvements that usually doesn't receive much attention. Few people even think about insulation unless they have to—when they're building a house, putting on an addition or if the cost of energy is going through the roof. But no matter what the circumstances, the amount and placement of insulation in your home helps determine your heating and cooling costs, as well as your comfort in the house.

## How Much Do You Need?

If we learned anything from the energy crisis of the late '70s and early '80s, it was the importance of making buildings energy efficient. Building codes now require insulation in new homes, and local utilities, government agencies and insulation manufacturers have spent the past decade spreading the word about the benefits of insulation in older homes. People who listened saved money on energy bills and, at one time, even earned a credit on their federal income tax.

But things are different now. Most people inclined to upgrade the energy efficiency of their homes have already done so. The question now is: Will adding more insulation make economic sense?

*Insulation Buying Guide* was written by Fran Donegan with illustrations by George Retseck. You can contact the Conservation and Renewable Energy Inquiry and Referral Service (CAREIRS) at (800) 523-2929. The insulation recommendations by Zip Code is Fact Sheet DOE/CE-0180. The Radiant Barrier Fact Sheet is No. DOE/CD-0335P. For more information on Air Krete installers, contact Palmer Industries, 10611 Old Annapolis Rd., Frederick, Maryland 21701.

## PLACES TO INSULATE

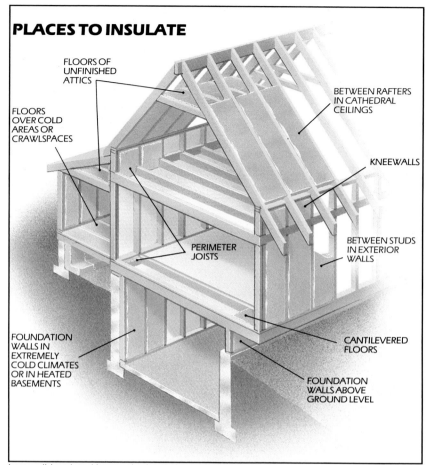

FLOORS OF
UNFINISHED
ATTICS

FLOORS
OVER COLD
AREAS OR
CRAWLSPACES

BETWEEN RAFTERS
IN CATHEDRAL
CEILINGS

KNEEWALLS

PERIMETER
JOISTS

BETWEEN STUDS
IN EXTERIOR
WALLS

FOUNDATION
WALLS IN
EXTREMELY
COLD CLIMATES
OR IN HEATED
BASEMENTS

CANTILEVERED
FLOORS

FOUNDATION
WALLS ABOVE
GROUND LEVEL

In a well-insulated home, the insulation acts as a blanket that covers surfaces adjoining cold areas. Special places to check are perimeter joists, crawlspaces and basements.

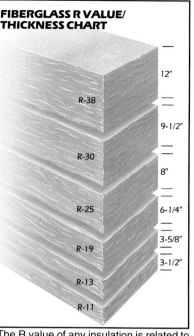

### FIBERGLASS R VALUE/THICKNESS CHART

R-38 — 12"
— 9-1/2"
R-30 — 8"
R-25 — 6-1/4"
— 3-5/8"
R-19 — 3-1/2"
R-13
R-11

The R value of any insulation is related to its thickness. This chart show current R values for standard fiberglass batts.

The answer is maybe—certainly if you add insulation where none existed before, and probably if you increase existing levels to current Department of Energy guidelines. The answer is no, however, if the cost of the upgrade exceeds projected savings.

To measure the energy efficiency of your house, take an insulation inventory to see where the insulation is and how much is in place. Your insulation should blanket all interior surfaces—walls, ceilings and floors—that are adjacent to a cold area (see drawing on this page).

Where you find insulation, try to determine its R value—the rating it's given that indicates its resistance to heat conduction. Some insulation lists this information on a paper or foil facing. If your insulation is unfaced fiberglass or loose-fill material, measure the thickness of the insulation and compare your findings with the Insulation Comparison chart on page 75 to make an estimate. Then, compare your estimated R value with what's recommended by the Department of Energy (see Recommended Insulation Based on Geographical Location chart, page 73).

For more specific information on R values for your area, the DOE has broken down its insulation recommendations by zip code. For a listing, contact the

Conservation and Renewable Energy Inquiry and Referral Service and ask for the Insulation Fact Sheet. CAREIRS is government funded and the fact sheet is free.

While it's a safe bet that installing insulation where there was none will save you money, the wisdom of adding *more* is trickier to figure out.

The way to decide is to calculate the payback period of the new material. If it takes a reasonable amount of time to save enough in energy bills to recoup the investment in insulation, it makes sense to add more.

One way to figure this out is to ask your local utility company. Most utility companies will provide an energy audit of your home and estimate the savings you'll realize in one year based on an insulation upgrade. Then take the cost of the new insulation, with the installation costs, and divide it by the savings per year to get the number of years it will take to pay back the investment.

Another way is to figure the present-value savings for additional insulation. The information in the Additional Attic Insulation Payback chart on page 74 was compiled by Oak Ridge National Laboratories and helps determine the economic sense of adding attic insulation for a number of geographic locations based

# RECOMMENDED INSULATION BASED ON GEOGRAPHICAL LOCATION

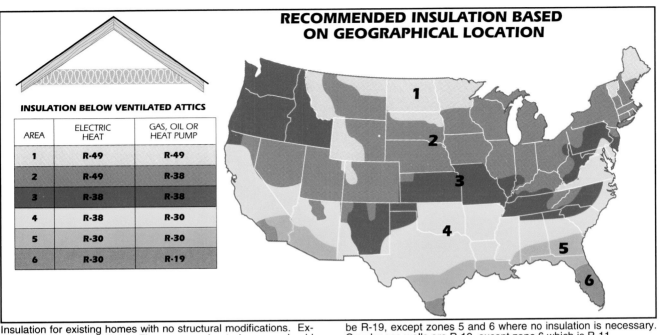

**INSULATION BELOW VENTILATED ATTICS**

| AREA | ELECTRIC HEAT | GAS, OIL OR HEAT PUMP |
|------|---------------|-----------------------|
| 1 | R-49 | R-49 |
| 2 | R-49 | R-38 |
| 3 | R-38 | R-38 |
| 4 | R-38 | R-30 |
| 5 | R-30 | R-30 |
| 6 | R-30 | R-19 |

Insulation for existing homes with no structural modifications. Exterior walls should be R-11. Floors over unheated spaces should be R-19, except zones 5 and 6 where no insulation is necessary. Crawlspace walls are R-19, except zone 6 which is R-11.

on current costs. Find a location near you, pick the appropriate column and then multiply the value given by the square footage of attic area to be insulated. If the number is higher than the estimated cost of adding the insulation, it makes economic sense to do so. The table deals with a payback over a 25-year period and makes a lot of assumptions about the price of energy, efficiency of heating and cooling equipment, and the like. For a more accurate reading check CAREIRS for the Radiant Barrier Fact Sheet.

Besides providing information on radiant barriers, this publication contains a worksheet for determining your precise Present Value of Energy Savings. Radiant barriers are reflective sheets often classified with insulation products. Their chief use is in lowering cooling costs by reducing the effect of radiant heat from the sun on you home's interior temperature.

## The Attic

The place to start checking your home is at the top because if your house has insulation in only one location, it's safe to assume that it's the attic. Attics are easy to insulate and the materials commonly used there are inexpensive and readily available.

Mineral fibers—fiberglass and rock wool in batts, blankets and loose-fill material—are the insulations most often used in attics. To increase present levels, add new batts or blankets at right angles to the material that is already there. This technique fills any gaps in the original installation and should cover the attic floor joists. Insulating the joists stops thermal bridging—heat loss by conduction across the solid wood joists. Adding new loose-fill material on top of the existing insulation accomplishes the same goal.

The job is straightforward, but there are two details to attend to when insulating attics: Keep insulation away from recessed light fixtures and provide adequate ventilation.

Electrical and building codes require a 3-in. air space between recessed light fixtures and insulation, unless the fixture is rated IC (insulated ceiling) and designed to be covered with insulation. Though mineral fibers won't burn, they can cause an unrated fixture to over-heat and start a fire in the ceiling. Sheetmetal shields that surround the fixture are available to create the safety zone. Do not pile insulation above the fixture.

Day-to-day life in an average house produces a lot of moisture in the form of vapor. Cooking, washing the dishes, taking a shower and even breathing all raise the humidity of the indoor air. When moist air condenses on cold surfaces, such as the framing in an unheated attic, the water can cause structural damage. There are two strategies for controlling moisture: blocking it with a vapor barrier so it can't reach cooler areas where it will condense, and venting it to the outside through gable, soffit and ridge vents before it can condense. Plan on installing 1 sq. ft. of vent area for every 150 sq. ft. of attic floor space. When you calculate the vent space, be sure to take the solid areas of louvers and screens into account and measure only the open area.

## Walls

To insulate the wall cavities in an existing house, without removing the interior walls, it's necessary to drill holes through either the interior or exterior and blow in loose-fill fiberglass or cellulose. The goal here is to fill every bay between the studs completely—a job that can be difficult because of fire stops and other blocking.

| ADDITIONAL ATTIC INSULATION PAYBACK | | | | |
| BASED ON A 25-YEAR PERIOD | | | | |
| EXISTING INSULATION | R-11 | R-11 | R-19 | R-19 |
| ADDITIONAL INSULATION | R-8 | R-19 | R-11 | R-19 |
| Albany, NY | 0.76 | 1.10 | 0.35 | 0.48 |
| Albuquerque, NM | 0.53 | 0.80 | 0.28 | 0.37 |
| Atlanta, GA | 0.50 | 0.71 | 0.21 | 0.29 |
| Bismarck, ND | 0.90 | 1.35 | 0.45 | 0.61 |
| Chicago, IL | 0.69 | 1.02 | 0.33 | 0.45 |
| Denver, CO | 0.64 | 0.96 | 0.32 | 0.44 |
| El Toro, CA | 0.33 | 0.48 | 0.15 | 0.20 |
| Houston, TX | 0.31 | 0.49 | 0.18 | 0.24 |
| Knoxville, TN | 0.53 | 0.78 | 0.24 | 0.34 |
| Las Vegas, NV | 0.47 | 0.70 | 0.23 | 0.32 |
| Los Angeles, CA | 0.22 | 0.33 | 0.11 | 0.15 |
| Memphis, TN | 0.52 | 0.74 | 0.22 | 0.31 |
| Miami, FL | 0.22 | 0.34 | 0.11 | 0.15 |
| Minneapolis, MN | 0.80 | 1.21 | 0.42 | 0.57 |
| Orlando, FL | 0.25 | 0.37 | 0.12 | 0.17 |
| Phoenix, AZ | 0.53 | 0.77 | 0.24 | 0.33 |
| Portland, ME | 0.73 | 1.09 | 0.37 | 0.50 |
| Portland, OR | 0.50 | 0.77 | 0.27 | 0.36 |
| Raleigh, NC | 0.50 | 0.72 | 0.22 | 0.31 |
| Riverside, CA | 0.49 | 0.70 | 0.21 | 0.29 |
| Sacramento, CA | 0.44 | 0.65 | 0.22 | 0.29 |
| Salt Lake City, UT | 0.65 | 0.97 | 0.32 | 0.44 |
| St. Louis, MO | 0.63 | 0.92 | 0.29 | 0.40 |
| Seattle, WA | 0.52 | 0.80 | 0.28 | 0.37 |
| Topeka, KS | 0.61 | 0.92 | 0.31 | 0.42 |
| Waco, TX | 0.41 | 0.62 | 0.21 | 0.28 |
| Washington, D.C. | 0.60 | 0.88 | 0.28 | 0.38 |

To calculate the potential payback of additional insulation based on present values, multiply the figure that corresponds to your insulation upgrade and a location near your home by the square-foot area of your attic floor. If the result is more than the cost of the upgrade, the insulation should pay for itself within 25 years.

This installation is best left to a contractor who has the proper pneumatic equipment.

When it's time to add new siding, many people take the opportunity to install rigid-board insulation before the siding goes on. This not only increases the R value of the wall, but it also insulates the studs, something fiberglass placed between the studs can't do. As when buying any insulation product, check the R value. Siding contractors have been known to pass off fiberboard-backed siding as insulated siding. Remember, when adding rigid-board insulation, it may be necessary to build up the trim around windows and doors.

The walls of a new addition offer the chance to achieve high R values in several ways. For example, framing with $2 \times 6$s rather than $2 \times 4$s allows for an extra R-6 when using fiberglass. You also can combine fiberglass with rigid-board insulation to get even higher R values. Rigid insulations used on interiors must be covered with fire-rated drywall.

### Basements and Crawlspaces
The walls of heated basements should be insulated. One method for doing this is to build a frame wall and install mineral fiber between the studs. Since the wall will not be load bearing, it can be pulled out a few inches from the foundation and the extra space filled with insulation. Another technique calls for attaching rigid-board insulation to the concrete walls with construction adhesive.

In new construction, extruded polystyrene can be attached to the exterior of foundation walls before the foundation is backfilled. Use extruded polystyrene because it stands up to the pressure of the backfill while expanded polystyrene will crumble.

In basements, the joist header, band or perimeter joist is often left uninsulated, providing an escape route for heat from the rooms above. Pack the sections between joists with fiberglass insulation to cut energy loss here.

The walls of crawlspaces should be insulated with either mineral fiber or rigid boards. Even after the walls are insulated, wrap pipes and heating and cooling ducts in crawlspaces with mineral or foam insulation.

The spaces between floor joists that are above unheated basements or crawlspaces should be packed with mineral fiber or insulated with a combination of mineral fiber and rigid board. Cover dirt floors in crawlspaces with 6-mil polyethylene vapor barrier to prevent ground moisture from entering the house. Keep the barrier in place with bricks or stones.

## Other Places for Vapor Barriers

Except for covering the bare earth in crawlspaces, standard advice has always been to install a vapor barrier on the warm side of a wall or ceiling.

A vapor barrier is any material, such as polyethylene film or aluminum foil, that significantly resists the flow of vapor. Fiberglass insulation is available with a kraft paper or foil backing that's intended as a vapor barrier. If you're going to use plastic film, or you're adding batts to existing insulation, unfaced fiberglass is all that's necessary.

By installing the vapor barrier on the warm side, it keeps moisture vapor from passing through the insulation and condensing on the cold surfaces beyond. This is why plastic film or the paper backing on fiberglass batts is installed facing the inside of a room. If paper-backed batts are installed in a floor over an unheated basement or crawlspace, the backing faces up.

Warm humid climates, however, often have outside relative humidities that are as high or even higher than the humidity levels inside houses. In these locales, the vapor drive, which is always from an area of high pressure to one of low pressure, is often from outside the house to the inside, rather than from the inside to the outside as it is during the winter months in cold climates.

To compensate, many insulators put a vapor barrier on both sides of the insulation, others omit the barrier altogether. The latest recommendation is to always put a vapor barrier on the warm side if the average January temperature is less than 35°F. If the average January temperature is higher than 35°F, no vapor barrier is necessary. To be on the safe side, though, it's best to check with your local building officials.

## A New Entry

Most of the insulation products on the market have been around for some time, but one of the newer products is called Air Krete. This is a cementitious foam that was developed to replace ureaformaldehyde foam in 1982. Then, ureaformaldehyde was being withdrawn from the market because it shrank after curing, leaving gaps for energy to escape. What was even more objectionable was that the material gave off fumes, called outgassing, which were harmful to some people.

According to Palmer Industries, the company that trains the Air Krete installers, this product corrects both problems. It is completely stable and there is no outgassing. It's a 2-part system that a trained installer pumps into the hollow cores of concrete block or into wall cavities. It has a 3.9 R value for each inch of thickness, it's fireproof and shrink resistant and it's completely nontoxic.

On the down side, there simply aren't many trained installers. The material is also more expensive than other insulations.

## INSULATION COMPARISON

| TYPE | R VALUE PER INCH | COST PER R VALUE PER SQ. FT. (CENTS) | COMMENTS |
|---|---|---|---|
| Fiberglass Batts, Loose Fill | 2.9 to 3.2 | 1.0 to 1.9 | Easy to work with, but can irritate skin, eyes and lungs—take proper precautions. Nonflammable, but paper facings can burn. |
| Loose Fill Mineral Wool | 3.3 | 1.9 | Uses and precautions similar to fiberglass. |
| Cellulose | 3.2 | 1.4 | Inexpensive, although professional installation can add significantly to cost. Must be treated with fire-retarding chemicals. |
| Extruded Polystyrene (rigid board) | 5 | 7.7 | Often used on exterior foundation walls and under slabs. Degrades in sunlight. Cover with fire-rated drywall when used inside. CFCs used in manufacturing. |
| Expanded Polystyrene (rigid board) | 4 | 4.6 | Not as strong as extruded type. Cover with fire-rated drywall indoors. |
| Polyisocyanurate (rigid board) | 7 | 7.7 | Commonly used as sheathing. R value may drop over time. CFCs used in manufacturing. |
| Air Krete | 3.9 | 8 | Foam applied by trained installer. Prices may depend on availability of trained personnel. |

Costs are estimates and may vary depending on geographical location and availability. CFCs are chlorofluorocarbons, which have been shown to have a negative environmental impact.

# Easy backyard deck

One area where builders often economize lies just beyond the back door. Open that door and it's usually one or two steps down to a modest concrete slab. These patios are often thrown down for around $100 and spend the ensuing years creeping steadily away from the foundation.

The advantages of this 10 × 12-ft. deck are that the deck is at floor level, it will never rot and it has frost footings—so it will stay put. Though it's small, it's large enough to accommodate a gas grill, a few chairs and a small table for the morning newspaper and first cup of coffee.

## Location

With a relatively small concrete slab, you can simply dig the post footings outside the slab perimeter. Here, a footing placed outside the slab would have extended the deck past the house by several inches. With this in mind, it was decided to cut the slab at each footing location, so the original 10 × 12-ft. footprint could be maintained.

## Material Selection

Although galvanized casing nails are acceptable, rust-proof coated screws were used in all instances where fasteners would be visible. These nails are shorter and heavier than common nails.

The lumber you choose will need to be rot-resistant. The most common choices are cedar, redwood and pressure-treated pine (CCA). Each has its advantages and its shortcomings. Redwood and cedar make the most attractive decks when new, but are a little pricey. To keep costs as low as possible, pressure-treated stock was chosen. Used also were 2 × 10s, 2 × 8s, and 4 × 4s for the structural components and 2 × 6s for the decking.

## Frost-proof Footings

As mentioned earlier, it was decided to cut the slab at each footing location. While sawing concrete may seem daunting, it's really fairly easy. All it will take is a circular saw and one or two masonry blades (around $7 each). While you can rent a demolition saw, you also can use an old circular saw. The goal is to score the concrete roughly one-third of the way through (Fig. 1). Then, break the slab inside the score lines with a 3-pound hammer.

**1** Begin by laying out the deck location. If concrete must be cut, use masonry blade in an old circular saw to score surface.

**2** Use a post-hole digger to dig pier footing holes below the frost line. Square off the bottoms of the holes.

With the concrete removed from the footing locations, use a post-hole digger to dig holes past the frost level in your area (Fig. 2). Fill the bottom 8 in. of 36-in. holes with gravel. Then, set the $4 \times 4$ posts on the gravel base and pack the soil firmly around each post.

As for the number of footings, place one at each outside corner and center one along the front of the deck. Also install one post on each side, halfway between the corner posts and the house. As such, the longest rim joist span was less than 6 ft.

## Easy Framing Method

Framing methods vary. Here it was desired to build a deck to hide the end cuts of the decking lumber. To achieve this no-reveal look, build the perimeter frame with $2 \times 10$ lumber. Then line them with $2 \times 8$ ledgers, securing them to the inside of the rim joists with $2\frac{1}{2}$-in. screws.

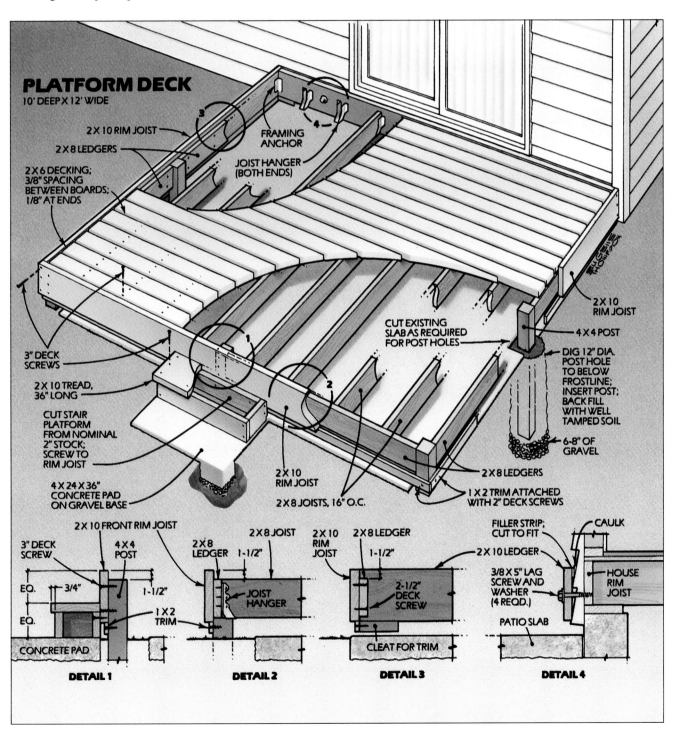

PLATFORM DECK
10' DEEP X 12' WIDE

2 X 10 RIM JOIST
2 X 8 LEDGERS
2 X 6 DECKING;
3/8" SPACING
BETWEEN BOARDS;
1/8" AT ENDS
3" DECK SCREWS
2 X 10 TREAD, 36" LONG
CUT STAIR PLATFORM FROM NOMINAL 2" STOCK; SCREW TO RIM JOIST
4 X 24 X 36" CONCRETE PAD ON GRAVEL BASE

FRAMING ANCHOR
JOIST HANGER (BOTH ENDS)

CUT EXISTING SLAB AS REQUIRED FOR POST HOLES

2 X 10 RIM JOIST
4 X 4 POST
DIG 12" DIA. POST HOLE TO BELOW FROSTLINE; INSERT POST; BACK FILL WITH WELL TAMPED SOIL
6-8" OF GRAVEL
2 X 8 LEDGERS
1 X 2 TRIM ATTACHED WITH 2" DECK SCREWS

2 X 10 RIM JOIST
2 X 8 JOISTS, 16" O.C.

**DETAIL 1**
3" DECK SCREW
4 X 4 POST
EQ. — 3/4"
1-1/2"
EQ.
1 X 2 TRIM
CONCRETE PAD
2 X 10 FRONT RIM JOIST

**DETAIL 2**
2 X 8 LEDGER
2 X 8 JOIST
1-1/2"
JOIST HANGER

**DETAIL 3**
2 X 10 RIM JOIST
2 X 8 LEDGER
1-1/2"
2-1/2" DECK SCREW
CLEAT FOR TRIM

**DETAIL 4**
FILLER STRIP; CUT TO FIT
CAULK
2 X 10 LEDGER
3/8 X 5" LAG SCREW AND WASHER (4 REQD.)
HOUSE RIM JOIST
PATIO SLAB

**3** If the house siding leaves a large gap between siding and ledger, tack a strip of treated lumber to the ledger.

**4** Attach the ledger to the house siding with a couple of screws, then bore four lagbolt clearance holes in the ledger.

**5** Slide a lagbolt and washer into each ledger hole and tap with a hammer. Then drive into the rim joist with a wrench.

**6** After screwing the side rim joists to the house ledger from the outside, nail a corner bracket to both on the inside.

**7** After setting the 4 × 4 posts, plum them in place. Then screw the rim joists to them with three or four long screws.

**8** With the rim joists squared and fastened to the posts, mount the 2 × 8 ledger plates to the inside with screws.

**9** Lay out the outside rim joist for the deck joists and install a joist hanger at each mark. Slide joists into place.

**10** Use spacer sticks to maintain ⅜-in. gap between deck boards and a ⅛-in. space alongside the rim joists.

**11** To keep screw rows straight, draw a line across the boards above each joist. A drywall square was used to do this.

## Step by Step

After digging the post footings and adding the gravel, put off installing 4 × 4 posts until the box is built and squared up. To build the box, start by trimming a 2 × 10 joist (because of its position against the siding, now called a ledger) 3 in. short of the overall deck width. If your home has lap siding, and if the gap left between the top of the deck ledger and the siding is more than ¼ in., you'll want to cut a strip of lumber to fill this gap. The best approach is to tack this strip to the rim before mounting it on the siding as shown in Fig. 3. Keeping it level, screw or nail this ledger to the house (Fig. 4). Then, bore holes through the ledger at four

points along its length and use 5-in. lagbolts to bind it to the rim joist of the house (Fig. 5).

With the 2 × 10 ledger mounted on the house, cut the side joists to length and prop them up temporarily. Then, screw them to the ends of the ledger on the house. For added strength, nail a corner bracket to the inside of this joint (Fig. 6). Finally, cut the front rim joist and screw it to the fronts of the side joists, using 3-in. screws.

With the basic box completed and propped up temporarily, measure from corner to corner to square it. If necessary, tack braces diagonally across the corners to keep it square while you install the posts. At this point, you'll also want to level the deck in all directions.

To install the posts, simply set them in the post holes and mark and cut them to the correct length. Be sure to hold the tops of the posts $1\frac{1}{2}$ in. below the rim to accommodate the decking. Finally, plumb each post in its hole and secure the rim to the posts with 3-in. deck screws (Fig. 7). Screw the corner posts from both directions, With all posts secured, backfill around them.

Your next step will be to screw the $2 \times 8$ ledger plates to the three $2 \times 10$ rim joists (Fig. 8). Remember to hold these exactly $1\frac{1}{2}$ in. down from the top of the rim joists. (The $2 \times 10$ ledger on the house will not need an additional $2 \times 8$ ledger, because the joint hangers can be tacked directly to it.)

With the ledgers in place, lay out the $2 \times 8$ joists on 16-in. centers along the front rim and on the house-side ledger. Then cut the joists to length and set them in the hangers (Fig. 9). Finally, nail the joist through all openings in the hangers, using special hanger nails.

## Decking

Choose the straightest $2 \times 6$ you can find for the first deck plank. Then, screw it to the joists and ledgers using 3-in. screws. Start the decking at the front of the deck and proceed toward the house.

While the first plank can be placed against the rim, all subsequent planks should be spaced roughly $\frac{3}{8}$ in. apart. To maintain this spacing, make a spacer stick and use it at each screw location (Fig. 10). When dealing with warped lumber, screw the nearest point and pry the rest of the plank over one joist at a time, securing it as you go. Use two screws per plank, per joist.

For the best nailing, it's a good idea to draw a straight line across the boards above each joist (Fig. 11). For ease of installation, you can use a screw gun instead of a standard drill to drive in all the deck screws (Fig 12).

## Building a Step

For the step, all you need to do is build an open box (Fig. 13) and screw a plank on top of it. If you need two steps, build two boxes. You can set the box on buried concrete blocks, or you can pour a small concrete pad. Just make sure your step support is level.

Generally, a step's rise should not exceed $7\frac{1}{2}$ in. and its tread should be at least 10 in. deep and 36 in. wide. Minor compromises are acceptable. Here, to split the difference between pad and deck, which was 14 in., the box was built $5\frac{1}{2}$ in. high. After screwing the box to the deck (Fig. 14), a $2 \times 10$ plank was screwed over it, making an even, 7-in. rise (Fig. 15).

## Finishing Touches

Before applying stain or waterproofing, take the time to caulk the top of the ledger board (Fig. 16) and to sand away any imperfections on the surface of the deck. These include rough spots, grade stamps and pencil marks. Then, apply an even coat of oil-base stain and keep off the deck for several days (Fig. 17).

**12** Drive the deck screws with a standard drill or a screw gun. Set screws just below the surface.

**13** Preassemble a box step using the drawing as a guide. Set it on a poured concrete pad or a few concrete blocks.

**14** Make sure the top of the box is parallel to the top of the deck. Then attach it to the deck with screws.

**15** Complete the step by installing a tread. Use at least three screws on the sides and several along the front and

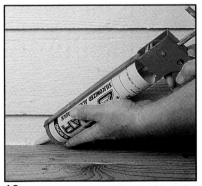

**16** To protect the siding behind the ledger from water exposure, seal the top joint with a bead of silicone caulk.

**17** After sanding away any rough spots and removing the dust, cover the deck with wood sealer or an oil-base stain.

# Painting aluminum siding

■ Aluminum and steel sidings, which took the nation by storm in the '50s and '60s, are showing their age. Of course, the allure of these products was the maintenance relief they offered—namely an end to regular and costly painting. To a great extent, aluminum and steel sidings have fulfilled that promise. But with much of it in place for nearly a generation now, a good many homeowners have opted to dress it up, ironically, with paint.

In many cases, tastes have simply changed. Yesterday's visionary colors have become today's eyesores. Moreover, the factory applied paint coatings keep chalking over, leaving a dusty, lackluster appearance. This chalking (easily seen by rubbing your fingertips over the siding as shown in Fig. 1), while unattractive, is no accident. Paint coatings made for metallic surfaces are designed to chalk. Chalking allows the paint to slough off tree sap, bird droppings and other natural stains.

If the chalking is your only complaint, then a good scrubbing may be all your siding needs. If you've wondered if your steel or aluminum siding would hold a coat of paint without initiating the very cycle of repainting that you spent good money to avoid in the first place, the answer is a qualified yes.

While your paint job will not likely hold up as well as a factory coating, metallic surfaces generally hold paint better than wood or composite-fiber surfaces. The reason is that metal does not absorb and release moisture with changes in the temperature and humidity. This breathing process is what causes paint to blister and lose its grip on wood and hardboard sidings.

Text and photos for *Painting Aluminum Siding* by Merle Henkenius.

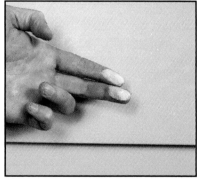

**1** Wipe your fingers across the siding to check for chalking. If heavy dust comes off on your fingertips, consider painting.

**2** Rinse the siding with water first, then scrub the surface with a mild household detergent and stiff cleaning pad.

## Paint Choices

Choosing the right paint is critical. You'll want to do this only once, so a garden-variety latex is out of the question. Instead, choose a high-quality, and slightly higher priced, 100% acrylic pant. The 100% acrylics bond well to metal siding and dry to a hard, smooth finish. Just as importantly, acrylics have what the paint industry calls good leveling characteristics. Simply put, when brushed on, the paint levels out any of the brush marks before skinning over. As such, the paint doesn't look as though it was swabbed on with a broom.

## Surface Preparation

As you've guessed by now, the most critical step in surface preparation is the removal of chalk buildup. While the pros often use power washers and detergent, a bucket of warm soapy water and a scouring pad will work just as well (Fig. 2). Use a mild household detergent that can be easily rinsed away. Simply scrub a manageable area and rinse it thoroughly before moving on.

You'll also want to seal any seams between exposed wood and siding (Fig. 3). Just use a top-quality silicone exterior caulk that can expand and contract with the seasons. Pay particular attention to plumbing and electrical opening (Fig. 4), as well as dryer vents and phone and cable-TV entrances (Fig. 5).

If one or two laps of siding are badly damaged, your options will vary. Check with a siding wholesaler or installer about replacement. A perfect match, however, may not be possible. Many older manufacturers have long since gone out of business and new siding locking systems may not be compatible.

## Applying the Paint

Painting aluminum requires no special skills, but close attention to detail improves the final appearance. As always, start painting from the top and work down. Paint the field first, then the trim. Make sure you load the brush with plenty of paint and smooth out your strokes carefully.

When it comes to painting the inner surfaces of J-molding and the siding that abuts it, the brushwork can be tricky. It's easy to load too much paint into these narrow strips, and because your brush must lay against the siding, it's easy to drag fresh paint off the siding near the J-molding. If this is a problem, paint the inside channel of all J-molding first. Then paint the rest of the siding after this paint dries.

 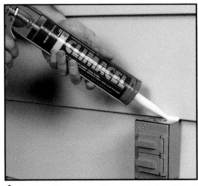 

**3** Use silicone caulk to seal all joints where the wood and siding meet. Pay special attention to windows and doors.

**4** Apply silicone caulk around all outdoor electrical fixtures to prevent any water from entering these boxes.

**5** Fill any holes, like these that were left when a phone line was moved. Keep caulk flush with the surrounding surface.

# Foolproof vinyl flooring

■ The thought of installing sheet-vinyl flooring can be intimidating, especially when you consider that one or two mistakes can ruin a whole sheet. The problem is compounded because few rooms are truly square, and most have obstacles and offsets to accommodate.

When a room is complicated, a pro will make a paper pattern of the room and transfer that pattern onto the vinyl. The paper becomes a one-of-a-kind template and every offset and obstacle is factored in before cutting.

There's no reason why you can't do the same thing. In fact, the Armstrong flooring people have come up with an installation kit that allows you to do just that. The kit includes the pattern paper, instruction booklet and transfer tools.    While there are enough sheets of 3 × 6-ft. paper to accommodate a 600-sq.-ft. room, and you could easily add your own paper to fit a larger room, this flooring project was a good deal smaller.

*Foolproof Vinyl Flooring* was written and photographed by Merle Henkenius. For more information on the installation kit shown, contact Armstrong Customer Response Center, P.O. Box 3001, Lancaster, PA 17604.

**1**  Begin floor preparation by removing the baseboard shoe molding with a flat pry bar. Pull nails from the back of board.

**2**  New vinyl flooring should be installed under, not around, a toilet. Remove the toilet and reset it later.

## Advance Considerations

The first thing to decide is whether you'll take up the existing flooring. If your floor has suffered water damage and dry rot, or could simply use a layer of underlayment to make it more uniform, then by all means make those corrections before installing the new vinyl. (Do keep in mind, however, that laying underlayment on a floor can be quite a bit of work. Not only will you have to scribe all the sheets to fit, you also may need to cut off the bottom of any doors to allow clearance above the now-thicker floor. The cracks between the underlayment panels must be filled and the depressions caused by the numerous nails required to install the panels also must be filled.) If not, there's no reason why you can't lay your new vinyl directly on top of the old. In fact, there are several good reasons why you might.

At the top of the list is because, as described above, installing underlayment is a lot of work. Next in line is the disquieting notion that many resilient flooring and flooring adhesives installed prior to the early 1980s contained asbestos.

This asbestos is perfectly safe when left in place but tearing it up will send some of it airborne, unless precise EPA abatement procedures are followed. A vinyl-over-vinyl installation is a good choice. Of course, you'll need to do some pretty exacting surface prep to make the job last.

## Materials

There are two types of vinyl for this kind of installation. One requires gluing the entire floor, the other just the perimeter. When choosing your flooring, make sure that both you and your supplier know which type you've chosen and that your methods are adjusted accordingly.

Secondly, if your existing flooring has an embossed surface pattern, you'll need to fill these depressions with embossing leveler. Without it, the old floor's pattern will telegraph through your new flooring.

Because resilient flooring is designed to repel just about everything, you'll also need to degrade and prep the surface with an etching solution and primer. Beyond these steps, it's pretty much a measure, cut and glue sequence.

Besides the Armstrong pattern kit, only common household tools were used, and all support products were from a typical flooring supply store.

## Step by Step

Start by removing all of the base shoe (quarter-round). Just pry it loose with a small pry bar (Fig. 1). If it comes off intact, you can reuse it. If not, installing a new base shoe often goes a long way toward improving the final appearance of your installation.

If your room is a bathroom, you'll also need to take up the toilet. Just shut off the water and bail out the tank and bowl. Then, loosen the closet bolts at the base of the toilet and the compression fitting on the water supply tube. Lift it from its flange and carry it to another room (Fig. 2). Remember to lift with your legs, not with your back. Be sure to set the toilet on newspapers to keep the bowl wax from making a mess. If you damage the wax seal, replace it with a new one before reinstalling the toilet. To keep sewer gases from invading the room, plug the drain flange with a rag.

Finally, if your old flooring was caulked along a tub or cabinet, carefully slice away the caulk with a razor blade or blade scraper.

This done, it's time to cut the surface glaze on the old flooring. The etching fluid used here came in concentrated form and needed to be diluted with water. Even so, this is a very caustic solution. Wear rubber gloves when mixing and when applying it with a brush or sponge. Carefully paint the solution on with a brush around the perimeter. Then, roll the rest of the floor

**3** For best results, apply an etching solution—using a disposable roller—to deglaze the surface of the old floor.

**4** Once the etching is dry, apply two coats of primer. The second coat should be at a right angle to the first.

**5** Lay down the paper sheets around the perimeter of the room. Then fill in the middle and tape all the sheets together.

with a paint roller and inexpensive disposable roller cover (Fig. 3).

After the etching liquid has dried, coat the old vinyl with a quality floor primer, again using a paint roller and brush. It's a good idea to use two coats of primer, allowing time for drying between coats. Roll the first coat in one direction and the final coat in the opposite direction (Fig. 4).

### Making a Paper Template

Before applying the embossing leveler, put down the template paper and mark all cuts. The object is to cover the entire floor, keeping the paper $\frac{1}{4}$ to $\frac{1}{2}$ in. away from the baseboard and fixtures. Overlap the individual sheets and tape them together with masking tape (Fig. 5). To hold the paper in place, randomly cut 1-in. triangular slots from the paper and tape across the openings (Fig. 6). With the entire floor covered, use the kit's edging disc and ballpoint pen to trace the perimeter (Fig. 7). The disc will roll along the edge, leaving a trace line on the paper that is $\frac{3}{4}$ in. from the baseboard.

If your sheet goods must abut an irregular edge, such as a brick or stone wall, use the kit's transfer tool to transfer the exact profile of the wall. Place the pen into the center hole of the tool and draw the tool's pointed edge along the wall. When tracing around doorjambs and trim, use the transfer tool for the straight lines and draw in any sculpted features by hand. If you are unsure of this method, practice with scrap paper until you've rendered the trim's profile exactly. Then tape that paper to the larger paper.

When fitting around plumbing or heating pipes that enter through the floor, cut the appropriate holes in the paper and slice directly from that hole to the nearest

wall, usually a few inches away. These cuts also will be transferred to the vinyl.

With the template made and marked, loosely roll it up, leaving the tape in place over the triangular slots. Carry the template to the waiting sheet vinyl and press it in place over the vinyl. If your vinyl has a linear pattern, be sure to align the trace lines with this pattern.

With the inside edge of the transfer tool on the trace line of the paper, use the ballpoint pen to transfer the line to the vinyl on the opposite side of the tool (Fig. 8).

### Cutting to Fit

This kit's transfer tool also doubles as a vinyl cutter. Just insert the hook-shaped blade into one end of the tool. Pierce the vinyl on the transfer line at a convenient corner, then, very carefully, draw the blade along the transfer line (Fig. 9). Cut the entire perimeter of the vinyl in this manner. Finish by trimming out the pipe openings.

### Applying Leveler

The embossing leveler you use should have the consistency of tile grout. Just mix the powdered leveler with a compatible bonding agent until it has the correct consistency. Using a straightedged trowel, spread it over the old floor (Fig. 10). The object is to leave compound in the recessed areas only. Use the edge of the trowel to scrape away all excess. Because embossing leveler dries quickly, you may wish to mix and apply small amounts at a time.

This done, carry the sheet vinyl into the room and dry-fit it. Carefully roll back one-half of the sheet and spread adhesive on the floor, using the kit's plastic applicator (Fig. 11). With the adhesive spread evenly, roll the vinyl back in place, pressing it down along the edges. Then, glue the remaining half in like fashion.

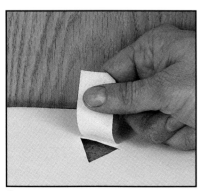

**6** To hold the paper in place, cut 1-in. triangular slots every couple of feet and apply tape across the slots.

**7** To scribe the exact perimeter of the floor, insert the ballpoint pen into the roller disc and trace around the room.

**8** Once the outline is complete, roll up the paper and lay it over the vinyl. Draw a cutline directly onto the vinyl.

All new vinyl must be rolled with a weighted roller to seat it properly in the adhesive. You might rent a 100-pound flooring roller, but a home remedy can work just as well. Just borrow the rolling pin from your kitchen and roll the floor with it (Fig. 12). Because weight is important, exert as much downward pressure as you can on the rolling pin. Roll the entire floor in this way.

If there are any areas abutting fixtures or cabinets, which will not be covered by base shoe, caulk those right after rolling the floor. The pros often use silicone caulk, but silicone requires a practiced hand. Instead, choose a latex tub-and-tile caulk, which is available in a variety of colors.

Trim the applicator tip to its smallest opening and dampen the seam to be caulked. Then apply a clean, continuous bead, doing your best to maintain even pressure (Fig. 13). If you don't like the first attempt, wipe away the caulk with a wet rag and start over.

If you've installed a seam between plumbing pipes and walls, there are two ways to create an invisible seal between pieces. You might try a commercial seam seal, which is fed into the joint with an applicator, or you can use the less expensive tub-and-tile caulk. Press the two halves together and apply the caulk over the seam. Then, with a damp cloth, wipe cleanly across the joint. The caulk remaining in the seam will shrink to a water-tight, nearly invisible line.

## Joining Other Flooring Materials

Flooring supply stores should offer splicing options for laying vinyl next to other flooring materials. While these options may include marble thresholds, most are pretty basic.

When adjoining carpeting use a metal tack strip. Simply nail the strip over the vinyl and lock the carpet onto the strip's spikes (Fig. 14). Then bend the edge over the carpet with a rubber mallet.

When meeting hardwood floors, a variety of hardwood reducing strips are available. Used here was a grooved, $\frac{3}{8}$-in. oak reducer to fit the tongued parquet squares (Fig. 15).

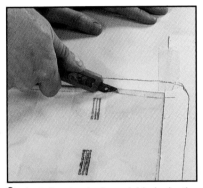

**9** Install a hook-shaped blade in the transfer tool and then cut the vinyl by drawing the blade along the cutline.

**10** To smooth out embossed flooring, apply leveler to the surface. Once recesses are filled, scrape away the excess.

**11** Apply vinyl adhesive to the floor with the kit's notched applicator. Cover only half the room at a time.

**12** Lower vinyl sheet onto adhesive, then roll surface smooth using a flooring roller or kitchen roller pin.

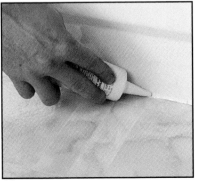

**13** Seal around the entire perimeter of the room—and around any plumbing fixtures—with latex tub-and-tile caulk.

**14** When laying vinyl next to carpet, use a metal tack strip. Nail the strip onto the vinyl and bend it over the carpet.

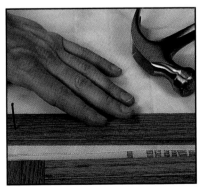

**15** When laying vinyl next to hardwood flooring, buy a hardwood reducing strip and glue or nail it in place.

# Sidewalk repairs

Sidewalks take a beating, from the very beginning. While a house is under construction, a new sidewalk often floats high on a bed of fill-sand, which eventually erodes from the sides and is swallowed up by utility trenches. Then, before the expectant family moves in, their new sidewalk will bear the weight of countless delivery trucks and the grating assault of landscape tractors, usually before the concrete is fully cured. As the years go by, all this is exacerbated by the ire of preschoolers with hammers and adults with ice hoes. Meanwhile, the soil beneath the hapless sidewalk heaves and settles. It's no wonder so many sidewalks look the way they do.

Of course, a damaged sidewalk can be more than an eyesore. It can be a barrier to the physically impaired and a hazard to everyone, especially when adjoining sections settle unevenly. Questions of legal liability also arise. More often, though, a damaged sidewalk simply invites more damage. As such, a little care can prolong the life of a walk considerably.

Text and photos for *Sidewalk Repair* by Merle Henkenius. The product used for narrow patches was Sure-Fix Pour-n-Patch, which is manufactured by the W.R. Bonsal Co., in Charlotte, North Carolina. The acrylic bonding agent used was Sure-Fix Super Concrete Patcher, also from Bonsal.

## Dealing with Cracks

Sidewalk cracks range from minor fissures to gaping faults. Left unattended, most cracks will continue to spread. The severity and location of a crack will dictate how you deal with it. The goal is to seal out water because wet soil beneath a sidewalk only exacerbates the problems of frost heave and settling.

Narrow cracks, in the less than $\frac{1}{2}$-in. range, should be caulked shut with liquid-polymer crack sealer.

Most concrete crack fillers will not cure properly when applied more than $\frac{1}{2}$ in. deep. If the crack you hope to repair is deeper, you can either pack the joint with some form of backing, such as foam-plastic backing rod, or pour the filler in two or more applications, each $\frac{3}{8}$ in. deep.

In any case, clean the joint with a stiff-bristle brush and water, if necessary, then let it dry and pour the joint full of crack filler (Fig. 1). Cover the joint for a day or so to keep foot traffic from damaging filler.

## Repairing Surface Problems

Several conditions will cause the portland-rich surface of a sidewalk to pop loose. The problem may be caused by a poor concrete mix, an aggregate that was not sufficiently clean or the failure to protect the surface from certain extremes in weather.

Of course, cold weather can damage a fresh concrete surface, because the surface is the most susceptible to frost. More often, however, the problem is caused by heat. When concrete is poured on hot days, the surface dehydrates faster than the cement below it, causing the slab to weaken and separate just below the surface. Fresh concrete should always be covered on hot days.

## Material Options

Standard masonry mortar has little bonding strength when applied in such thin layers. If you intend to use standard mortar, mix a prescribed amount of acrylic bonding agency into it for greater adhesion.

The patching material used here is a dry mortar mix with a granular vinyl resin as a bonding agent. Add water, and the bonding agent is activated.

Surface pops appearing at the edges of the walk are quite common. To maintain a uniform appearance, form the edge of the walk as if for new concrete. Chisel a shallow trough, or keyway, into the concrete to give the patch a compound surface to cling to (Fig. 2). To keep the patch from sticking to the young lumber, line

**1** Brush away debris from any cracks, then pour in liquid-polymer crack filler to a level just below the surface.

**2** On edge cracks or breaks, undercut the edge of the concrete with a cold chisel to increase the bonding surface.

**3** Install a foam board against the side of the slab. Then cover the board with masking tape to keep patch from sticking.

**4** Thoroughly remove any debris from the damaged area. Make sure to dampen the surface with water prior to patching.

**5** Apply the patching material to the crack using a small trowel. Feather the patch to match the surrounding surface.

**6** To install a new sidewalk section, first break up and remove the old concrete, then build rough 1 × 4 forms.

the edge of the form with masking tape (Fig. 3). Then, keep the area clean and wet it thoroughly (Fig. 4).

To mix the mortar patch, pour a small amount into a container and add cold water. Stir the mix to a working consistency; then allow it to rest for 10 minutes. Without adding more water, stir it into a working consistency again. Then press the patch material firmly into the recesses of the surface pop and keyway groove (Fig. 5). Once the surface is smooth, form the edge with an edging tool and finish by smoothing the surface with a small trowel, feathering the edges where the patch meets the surrounding concrete. Wait a day or two for the patch to dry; then remove the form.

## Replacing a Section

When a sidewalk is too badly cracked or when a settled section of sidewalk creates a trip hazard, no amount of patching will help. In these cases, it's best to replace the entire section.

While replacing concrete can be hard work there's nothing particularly complicated about it. Start by breaking up the old section with a sledgehammer. When you've reduced the old concrete to manageable pieces, haul them off. Don't even be tempted to use some of the broken pieces as filler.

With the removal complete, form both sides with 1 × 4 or 2 × 4 lumber and wooden stakes (Fig. 6). Let the adjacent sidewalk sections determine grade, and drive in at least three stakes on each side, nailing the stakes into the form lumber. Then, level the bed by excavating high spots and adding fill-sand to the low spots. Avoid using soil as fill, as you'll only encourage your new section to settle as its predecessor did.

With the form ready, you'll need a float, a finishing trowel, an edging tool and a straight piece of lumber to use as a screed board.

As for the concrete, the best you can buy will be that mixed in a batch plant and trucked to the site. Specify a 6-bag, or 3000-psi, mix. When pouring only a single section, order 1/4 yard from a cash- and-carry plant and tow it home in one of the small trailers these firms provide. The less you buy, of course, the more you can expect to pay per yard.

If you decide to mix your own concrete on site, go for a rich mix. One shovel of portland cement to five shovels of aggregate material—or if sold separately in your area, one part portland to two parts sand and three parts gravel. One final caution: Don't add water to your concrete to make it easier to work. Wet concrete is weak concrete.

## Pouring and Finishing

Pour your mix into the form and smooth it out with the screed board (Fig. 7). On the first pass, simply drag off the excess. Then, make a second and third pass, sawing from side to side as you move forward.

Now for the hard part: Just wait. Don't work the concrete until the pour has had time to stiffen substantially. Then, dress the surface with a wooden or magnesium float, pressing firmly through each arc (Fig. 8). A float is not a finishing trowel, so don't try for a finished look. The float's only jobs are to bring water and cement to the surface and to level any high spots or voids. If water puddles behind the float, however, you haven't waited long enough.

With the floating complete, use an edging tool to round the edges on all four sides (Fig. 9). If the edger leaves a distinct ridge, stop and let the concrete set up a bit more, then try again.

Before smoothing the surface with a finishing trowel, press your fingertips into the concrete. As long as they sink in easily, the mix is too wet. When your fingers leave only a slight impression, it's ready to finish.

Hold the trowel nearly flat and sweep in wide, overlapping arcs. If the trowel leaves chatter marks, flatten it even more. Two trowlings, 15 to 30 minutes apart, may be needed for a perfectly smooth finish. After another brief wait, drag a soft-bristle broom across the section to make a slip-resistant surface. Then, cover it with plastic and wait two days before disturbing it or the forms.

**7** Pour the concrete between the forms and level the surface by moving a screed board back and forth across the forms.

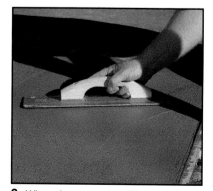

**8** When the concrete stiffens, work the surface with a float. Smooth the top until puddles just start to form, then stop.

**9** Use an edging tool to round off all edges. Then, gently retrowel the surface and brush lightly with a broom.

# Fixing broken windows

Have you ever looked at the glazing putty around your windows? If so, chances are you noticed some cracked, broken or entirely missing strips of putty. All single-pane windows need reglazing periodically. Replacing cracked putty when it appears will save energy and prevent rot from invading your windows.

Of course, your maintenance job will be hastened if you happen to have a broken window. But take heart, reglazing is not difficult or expensive. All it takes is a few dollars worth of glazing compound and the most common of household tools.

Text and photographs for *Fixing Broken Windows* by Merle Henkenius.

**1** Remove the storm window, if necessary, then use a putty knife to pry the old putty from around the broken glass.

**2** Once the putty is out, find the glazer's points and remove them with needle-nose pliers or a screwdriver.

## Glazing Compounds

Today's glazing compounds are wonderfully smooth and easy to apply when fresh. With time on the shelf, however, the oils in them can settle, leaving a drier, less workable putty at the top of the container. To correct this problem, have your salesperson put the can on a vibrating paint mixer for a few minutes before you leave the store. The putty can be reconstituted in this way.

While the old pros used to add a splash of linseed oil to putty to achieve the same effect, most manufacturers now recommend against the use of thinning agents.

## Preparation

Start your glazing project by removing any screen, storm or combination window that might be in place. Then look to the most deteriorated strip of putty and start chipping it away with a rigid, chisel-edge putty knife (Fig. 1). Putty that is cracked and has begun to lift off will usually break away easily. If the putty you encounter is rock-hard and solidly in place, as it sometimes is on very old windows, you may need to use heat to soften it. (In these cases, you'll only be removing putty to access a cracked or broken pane.)

While some sources suggest taking a propane torch to hardened putty, a good deal of caution is in order. Old window sashes can be as dry as tinder, and a smoldering ember can work its revenge hours later. If you must use heat, opt for an electric heat gun and concentrate the heat on the glass side of the glazing. Use no more heat than is necessary.

After prying all the old putty from the window, look for the half-dozen glazer's points that lock the pane against the sash frame (Fig. 2). These points will either be diamond-shaped metal points, usually shot into the wood with a spring-loaded gun, or formed metal clips that were pressed into the wood with a flat-blade screwdriver or putty knife. In either case, these points must be removed to free the glass. Needle-nose pliers or a screwdriver will easily unseat them.

With the putty and glazer's points removed, go indoors and press evenly against the bottom of the glass pane. When the glass pushes just past the bottom rail of the sash, go back outside, grasp the pane (with gloves) and pull down steadily. Because the glass is usually seated firmly in a slot in the top rail of the sash, you may need to twist and tweak it a bit until it breaks free.

Of course, if the window pane is badly broken, you'll want to remove the loose pieces of glass first, starting with the smallest and proceeding to the largest pieces (Fig. 3). Again, wear gloves and use caution. This is no time to hurry.

**3** When the putty and points are gone, gently remove the broken glass. Be sure to wear heavy gloves to prevent cuts.

**4** Use a wire brush or sharp chisel to clean off the sash. Wipe away loose particles before installing a new pane.

**5** If your sash has a groove to hold the edge of the glass, be sure it's cleaned out thoroughly before proceeding.

**6** Slide the new pane in place from below. Guide it into its upper slot and gently press the bottom against the sash.

**7** Install the glazer's points and start fitting around the pane with compound. Soften the putty before using it.

**8** Smooth the putty by drawing a clean knife firmly along the joint. Carefully trim away any excess when finished.

When the glass pulls free, brush the L-shaped recess with a wire brush and whisk away the debris (Fig. 4). Then use a utility knife to pry the remaining putty from the top slot of the sash (Fig. 5). If your window is quite old and the wood supporting the glass is soft and ragged, paint the putty recess with a top-quality primer. If you find the wood to be in good shape, priming won't be necessary.

### Installing New Glass

With the broken pane removed and the joint cleaned, ease the new glass pane into the top slot of the sash and press the bottom of the pane against the bottom sash member (Fig. 6). If the pane won't slide into the recess at the bottom, slip a putty knife into the recess and gently pry the glass up until it clears the recess edge. Remove the knife and press the glass firmly into the recess. Then, secure the pane with glazer's points. Two points per side and bottom will do. Press the points into the frame with a screwdriver or a putty knife.

### Applying Glazing Compound

If the putty you buy is soft and creamy, simply dip into the container with the knife and press a measure of putty firmly into the recess (Fig. 7). If the putty seems stiff, or clings to the knife as you pull it away, try kneading it first. Simply dig out a glob of putty and roll it into a $\frac{1}{2}$-in. rope between your hands. The resulting friction, and the heat from your hands, will soften the putty and make it more manageable.

Install a bead of putty all around the window, including the small gap in the top slot. Then, with a clean putty knife, smooth the putty at a uniform angle (Fig. 8). The finished depth should not be higher than the recess, as viewed from inside the house.

Usually, you'll want to paint the glazing when it's had a few hours to skin over (Fig. 9). There's no need to be too careful about getting paint on the glass. When the paint dries in a few hours, just scrape it off with a single-edge razor blade (Fig. 10). Not only is overpainting the glass easier, but it also helps seal the joint and picks up the oily film left on the glass by the putty. If you don't overpaint, you'll need to wait a few days and remove the film with mineral spirits.

### Double-Glazed Windows

What if yours are double- or triple-glazed insulated windows? You won't need to reglaze this type of window, as the sash members are assembled around the sandwiched glass at the factory. The glazing, such as it is, simply doesn't break down the way it does on single-pane windows.

If one of these windows breaks, or its seal is broken, you have to call on a professional. Even then, a pro is not likely to rebuild the frame surrounding the glass. In many cases, an entirely new sash, with glass installed, is ordered from the factory. Sash replacement is quickly becoming the only option.

You may be able to get this repair done for less money by removing the sash yourself and taking to a glazer's shop. This eliminates the service call which, in turn, should lower the price. Removing the sash on a double-hung window can be as simple as removing the stop piece that holds the sash in place. Just use a pry bar to pull off the strip and to remove the nails from its backside so it can be used again.

Casement and awning windows are held in place with different types of hardware. Just find the screws that hold the hardware, remove them and the sash should come free.

Despite the type of window you're working on, you'll need to make some provision for closing in your house while the sash is being repaired. Probably your best option is to tack up a piece of polyethylene plastic over the window. Something at least 6 mils thick is best.

**9** After the putty sets, apply fresh paint to the putty and the sash. Slightly overpainting the glass is recommended.

**10** Once the paint has partially dried, use a single-edge razor blade to scrape away excess paint and other blemishes.

# Warm water outdoor faucet

■ Have you ever wondered, maybe while washing the car, filling the kid's pool or handling any of a dozen other outdoor water chores, why someone hasn't designed a hot-and-cold water outdoor faucet? Because day-dreaming costs so little, wouldn't it be nice if that faucet allowed you to dial in just the right mixture of hot and cold water for each job? Of course, your dream faucet also would be designed to resist a freeze and prevent a contaminating backflow.

By now you've guessed that such faucets already exist. In fact, they've been used at the commercial level for years, but for some reason they've seldom made the trip to the residential side of the street.

It could be because they're a bit pricey, but more likely it's because few of us know that they exist. We don't ask, and the plumber doesn't think to suggest.

## Installation

Begin installation by choosing a joist space convenient to both outdoor watering tasks and indoor plumbing lines. As the body of the valve must fit through a sizable opening in the rim joist, you'll need to cut (not drill), the siding and joist. Use a tape measure and level to mark the siding for the cut. Taking the measurement from the back of the faucet's faceplate, mark for an opening $2\frac{3}{4}$ in. high and $9\frac{1}{2}$ in. wide. This opening, and ultimately the faucet faceplate, must be kept level.

With the cutout marked on the siding, bore the four corners with a $\frac{3}{4}$-in. bit (Fig. 1). Then, use a reciprocating saw to cut between the holes (Fig. 2). With the opening made, lay a bead of caulk around its edge (Fig. 3). Then press the faucet into the opening (Fig. 4). To hold the faucet in position until the piping is connected, support the valve body above the sill plate with a block of wood. As with all frost-proof, self-draining faucets, you'll want the drain chambers (pipes) behind the faceplate to pitch down slightly. A slope of $\frac{1}{8}$ to $\frac{1}{4}$ in. will be plenty.

> Text and photographs for *Warm Water Outdoor Faucet* by Merle Henkenius. The unit shown is a Woodford model No. HC65 hot-and-cold mixer. It's available from Woodford Mfg. Co., Colorado Springs, Colorado.

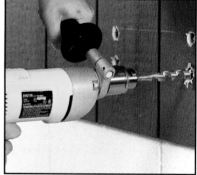

**1** Once the cutout is marked, bore saw-blade entry holes at the four corners. Use a $\frac{3}{4}$-in. bit for good clearance.

**2** Use a reciprocating saw, or a sabre saw, to cut between the holes. Working slowly will yield the straightest cut.

Before fitting any piping to the faucet, you'll need to install the check valves in the hot and cold mixing-valve ports. But because the nylon and neoprene parts within the check valves can be damaged by heat, it's a good idea to make up and solder the 90° turns and let them cool before threading them into the check valves.

You'll need two ¾-in. copper male adapters, two short stubs of pipe and two 90° street ells. Street fittings have one male end and one female end, and in this case, their use allowed critically short turns into the vertically aligned valve ports. Because both sides of a fitting should be soldered at the same time to avoid leaks, install 4-in. pipe stubs in the female ends of the street ells. The supply piping could then be soldered to these stubs, using sweat couplings with 45° fittings.

With the 90° turns made, soldered and cooled, thread the adapters into the check valves (Fig. 5). Be sure to use Teflon tape on the threads to prevent leaks. Then, thread the check valves into the valve ports, again using Teflon tape (Fig. 6). You'll find this prefitting preferable to spending undue time inside the cramped confines of a joint space.

## Tapping Into the Plumbing System

Because the faceplate of this faucet has no mounting screwholes, it was clearly designed to be mortared into a masonry wall. On a framed home, the faucet must be held in place by the tightness of the joist cut, the caulk seal and the tension and support of the plumbing pipes. With this in mind, go outside and press the faucet firmly against the siding once more before cutting into the plumbing system.

With the water shut off at the meter and the piping system drained, cut into your home's hot and cold water supply lines. Most of these lines are made of copper, as they are in most homes built after 1950. To make the connection between the water supply lines and the new faucet, simply splice copper tees into the trunk lines and continue piping toward the faucet. With connections made, solder all fittings with lead-free solder and support the piping at least every 6 ft. with pipe hangers (Figs. 7 and 8).

## Soldering Tips

Like many chores, sweat soldering plumbing fittings looks more complicated than it is. The basic requirements are simple: Cut the tubing cleanly and squarely, and clean all mating surfaces so they are free of dirt and other contaminants. To get a good clean cut, use a high-quality tubing cutter to perform all the cuts. To make sure everything is clean, rigorously rub all mating surfaces with steel wool, and then coat them with flux before joining them. Also keep in mind that lead-free solder requires more heat to melt than other solders. Just hold your propane torch on each joint longer before applying the solder.

**3** Once the opening is cut, check the faucet for fit. When satisfied, apply a bead of caulk to the rim of the opening.

**4** Carefully press the faucet into the opening until it seats completely in the caulk. Then brace it in place.

**5** Solder copper street ells to stubs and male adapters. Let assemblies cool, then thread them into the check valves.

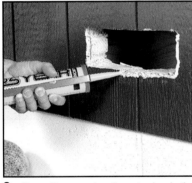
**6** Once the soldered turns are joined to the check valves, thread these assemblies into the faucet's valve body.

**7** Join the supply tubing to the valve with lead-free solder. Protect any nearby framing members with sheetmetal.

**8** Cut into the hot and cold supply lines, and solder tees in place. Then connect the faucet tubing to the tees.

# Basic basement waterproofing

*Basic Basement Waterproofing* was written and photographed by Merle Henkenius. The bonding agent used was Elmer's Concrete Bonder from Borden Inc., Columbus, Ohio. The silicone mortar caulk was from Macklanburg-Duncan, Oklahoma City, Oklahoma. Finally, the masonry waterproofing produced was UGL's Drylock, made by United Gilsonite Laboratories in Scranton, Pennsylvania.

As we all know, a wet basement can be a very costly thing. It not only robs the homeowner of valuable living space, the dampness also plays host to a variety of molds, which are common allergens. Wet soil against a basement wall can eventually destroy that wall.

What many homeowners don't realize is that wet basements can often be corrected easily and inexpensively. The obvious exception is when the culprit is ground water. Then, the only sure solution is to install drainage tile around the outside of the wall and sump pumps inside. Still, the vast majority of wet basements can be attributed to simple neglect.

**1** Check the perimeter of your foundation for depressions in the fill-soil, like this 12-in. recess at a window well.

**2** Add soil to any depressions around your foundation. Then tamp the soil firmly into place and plant grass seed.

## Finding the Water Source

While this selection is about repairing leaky walls, it's important to keep in mind that basement walls don't cause leaks. Water causes leaks, and the presence of water is usually the result of poor drainage and poorly maintained gutters. Without first correcting these problems, basic wall repair is a losing battle.

Here's why: The backfilled soil around a basement will always be more porous and more absorbent than the soil outside the excavation line. Moreover, fill-soil will always settle, and keep settling for years. If this band of fill is not brought back to grade periodically, or if rainwater is not diverted at least 3 ft. beyond the foundation, the relatively loose soil next to the foundation will absorb a disproportionate volume of water. Some of this water will be forced, laterally, through the basement walls.

In Northern states, this scenario carries an additional penalty. Wet soil expands more than dry soil when it freezes. When wet backfill is sandwiched between virgin soil and a basement wall, the wall will always be the first to yield. With enough of these freeze/thaw cycles, the wall can collapse inward.

You should bring all backfill around your foundation back to grade (Fig. 1). If window wells have settled, raise them (Fig. 2). An ideal grade will slope steadily away from the foundation for at least 3 ft., at a rate of at least 1 in. per foot.

If you have an area defined by landscape timbers, make sure this area slopes outward as well. Downspouts should extend 3 ft. beyond the house, and where landscaped areas abut the foundation, downspouts should extend past them. Gutters also should be cleaned frequently.

## Material Choices

There are two basic kinds of basement waterproofing materials. The first are masonry patch items. They range from mortar caulk to premixed mortar to hydraulic putty. Because this basement was not leaking at the time of repair, simple standard masonry mix was chosen and a latex bonding agent added to improve adher-

ence. Had there been a continuously seeping hole in the wall, then hydraulic putty would have been chosen. Hydraulic putty bonds extremely well and cures quickly, even when wet and under pressure.

The second category includes a variety of rubberized coatings, which usually contain portland cement. As these products are expensive (more than $20 per gallon), cover only 75 to 125 sq. ft. per gallon, and produce noxious fumes when they cure, they should only be used when drainage improvements and wall repair come up short. (Manufacturers say that nontoxic, latex coatings will be on the market soon.) In the right situations, however, they will work.

## Wall Preparation

Before coating a masonry wall with waterproofing compound or paint, you'll need to patch all holes and eliminate all forms of surface degradation. Surface problems can take the form of blistered paint, molds embedded in existing paint, waterborn iron stains and efflorescence.

To remove blistered paint, use a wire brush (Fig. 3). Sand any remaining hard edges with coarse sandpaper before repainting. Rust and hard-water stains may also be removed in this fashion. Efflorescence, on the other hand, appears as a white, chalky substance on masonry surfaces. The substance is actually crystallized mineral salts that have leached from the concrete or mortar. To remove efflorescence, scrub the area with an abrasive pad and muriatic acid. Then rinse with water.

As for mildew and mold growths, you'll need to kill them before sealing. The simplest approach is to scrub all visible mildew spots with a solution of household bleach and water (Fig. 4).

## Patching

Water migrates through walls where holes and cracks appear. Most midwall cracks are stress cracks, caused by the freeze/thaw cycle. These cracks are usually horizontal, but may step diagonally along mortar joints. Water also may seep through the structural seam between the walls and the floor.

**3** Remove any blistered paint from the interior of your foundation wall with a wire brush and coarse sandpaper.

**4** Scrub mildew with an abrasive pad and a mix of household bleach and water. Use muriatic acid on efflorescence.

**5** Caulk small, leaky cracks with a silicone-mortar caulk. Smooth with a putty knife dipped in mineral spirits.

If these cracks are small, in the ⅛-in. range, then a good, silicone-mortar caulk forced deep into the crack will work. Cut the applicator at a 45° angle and apply enough pressure to force the caulk into the joint (Fig. 5). Then, smooth the bead with a putty knife dipped in mineral spirits.

If the cracks are larger, or if there's loose mortar, then the best approach is to enlarge the joint with a chisel and tuck-point new mortar into the gap. To remove loose mortar, or to enlarge a crack so that it will accept enough new mortar, use a mason's chisel (Fig. 6). Start at the largest point in the opening and remove all cracked and crumbling mortar. Then, brush the masonry dust from the crack and wet the joint with a mix of water and latex bonding agent.

Next, blend the premixed mortar with water and bonding agent until the mortar will stand up when you slice through it with a trowel (Fig. 7). Then, stack a little mortar on the back of a small trowel, place the

trowel against the crack and push the mortar into the joint with a pointing trowel (Fig. 8). Pack the entire joint, then scrape away the excess and smooth the joint with a joint-striking tool (Fig. 9). Use the same methods to fill any gaps or cracks around utility pipe holes (Fig. 10).

## Waterproofing Coatings

Before deciding to paint a wall with waterproofing, wait a few weeks. If it rains and your basement stays dry, chances are you won't need it. If you don't see any obvious leaks, but the masonry surface is damp, then a sealant is a good idea.

The masonry waterproofing product used here is a high-solvent specialty coating that requires plenty of ventilation. Be sure to open windows and use fans to circulate the air in your basement. You'll also want to shut off the furnace and any other pilot lights and open flames.

**6** Remove loose or cracked mortar between blocks with a tapered mason's chisel, and clean the joint thoroughly.

**7** Fill any gaps in the foundation's mortar joints with a mixture of premixed mortar, water and a latex bonding agent.

**8** Pack fortified mortar into the wall joints using small mason's trowels. Make sure the entire space is filled.

**9** Finish the new mortar with a joint-striking tool. Once the mortar has set, brush off the joint to remove any burrs.

**10** Use the same mortar mix to fill gaps around utility pipe entrances. Pack and smooth the mortar with a brick trowel.

*Installing Fiber-Reinforced Wallboard* was written by Gene and Katie Hamilton. Illustrations by George Retseck. Wallboard shown is called FiberBond and it's manufactured by Louisiana Pacific.

# Installing fiber-reinforced wallboard

■ For more than 10 years, a wallboard material made of fiber-reinforced gypsum plaster has been used in European construction and remodeling. The material, which is made of gypsum and recycled paper, has made its way across the Atlantic and a similar product is now being distributed in the United States.

Walls finished with the material have a look and feel that is closer to traditional plaster than drywall. The wallboard is a denser, nonlaminated material without paper facing or backing.

It is available in $4 \times 8$-, $4 \times 10$- and $4 \times 12$-ft. sheets, from $\frac{3}{8}$ to $\frac{5}{8}$ in. thick. Because of its denseness, a $4 \times 8$ sheet of $\frac{1}{2}$-in. board weighs about 25% more than a comparable sheet of drywall. The manufacturer claims that the product is stronger and more fire resistant than drywall and that its high density helps to deaden sound. It also claims that the material is more moisture resistant. Unlike ordinary drywall, the new paneling is beveled on all four edges and tape isn't required on flat seams—only on inside corners.

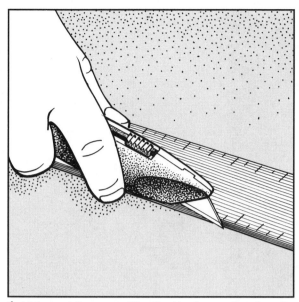

**1** Make straight cuts on FiberBond by first scoring along the cutline with a utility knife. Then bend to snap the piece in two.

## Trying it Out

Working with a drywall contractor, 60 sheets of ½-in.-thick, 4 × 8 fiber-reinforced paneling were installed in a 100-year-old house. Because of its strength and density, the material is a lot tougher than drywall. Because the panels are heavy, they're harder to move around and position. The material is also harder to cut.

On the plus side, the new paneling's strength and density make it a much more forgiving material to install on old walls. Hanging the board with glue and nails is easier than hanging drywall because it's almost impossible to crush the surface with an overzealous hammer blow. Drywall screws are harder to start, but you can't drive the head right through the board as with

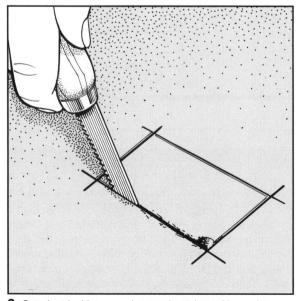

**2** Cut electrical box openings and notches with a sabre saw or drywall saw. Bore a hole at one corner to start the cut.

drywall. Once in place, the screw draws the board up tight against the wall framing. The board also can be installed with an air-powered stapler which is the fastest method for hanging the material.

Fiber-reinforced paneling isn't as flexible as drywall, and since it has tapered edges on all four sides, the corners are vulnerable to breaking off and chipping. In fact, it's not difficult to accidentally break in half a sheet of the wallboard if you're not careful in handling.

In principle, installing fiber-reinforced paneling is the same as installing standard drywall. It unique characteristics, however, demand a few changes in technique.

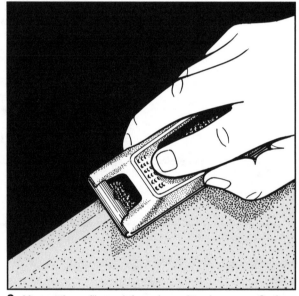

**3** After cutting a fiber-reinforced panel to size, use a Surform tool or coarse rasp to chamfer the square edge.

## Cutting

The material is much harder to cut than drywall, but the same basic tools are used to get the job done. To cut straight edges, use a utility knife and a straightedge to score the panel (Fig. 1). Then snap the board in two by bending it back on the side opposite the score.

Notching or cutting inside corners can be handled by several means, including using a sabre saw or a drywall saw. Use a drywall saw to cut holes for outlets and switches (Fig. 2). Because the material is so tough, however, it's best to begin these cutouts with a hole bored at the inside corner.

Keep in mind that, unlike drywall, you can't hack away small areas with a utility knife to get a stubborn piece to fit. The best method is to measure carefully and accurately before you cut. Because this is a solid material, you can, however, use a rasp or Surform tool to fine-tune a cut.

The tapered edges make installing full sheets easy, but as soon as a full sheet is cut, there's a nontapered edge to contend with. To help ensure a smooth seam at this square edge, it's best to chamfer the edge before hanging. Use a Surform tool, or coarse rasp to cut a ½-in.-wide, 45° bevel along the edge (Fig. 3).

## Hanging

Fiber-reinforced wallboard is hung like ordinary drywall, except a ⅛-in.-wide gap must be left between the edges of adjacent sheets. Nails are easily driven through the material. You will use wallboard adhesive the same way you do with drywall, applying it with a caulking gun (Fig. 4).

For most applications, a wallboard installation with horizontal seams creates the best results. First hang an upper panel against the ceiling, then install the lower sheet. Make the lower sheet about ½ in. to 1 in.

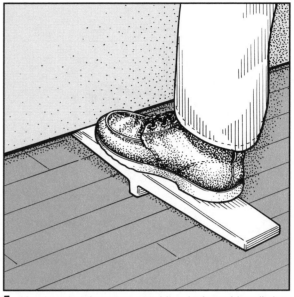

**5** After hanging the upper panel in a horizontal installation, use a drywall jack to lift the lower panel into position.

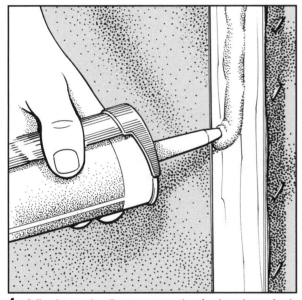

**4** Adhesive and nails are one option for hanging. Apply ordinary drywall adhesive to studs in a generous bead.

narrower than the actual distance from the edge of the upper sheet to the floor so that the panel goes in place easily. To lift up the lower sheet to the upper sheet, use a drywall jack. Simply push the front of the jack under the panel and step on it to raise and hold the board in place for fastening (Fig. 5). Once the board is in position, drive drywall nails, setting the heads slightly below the surface (Fig. 6). If you have to cut this lower panel, install the cut edge toward the floor.

Drywall screws are a little more difficult to get started but, otherwise, they work the same as they would with standard drywall. To get the screws seated below the board's surface, set the depth adjustment of your drywall gun deeper than you would for ordinary drywall. You'll also have to push harder to keep the driver bit firmly seated in the screwhead. Fastening with screws is an especially good choice when installing fiber-reinforced panels over old plaster.

In addition to standard drywall screws, nails and adhesives, staples can be used because they don't pull through. A heavy-duty air-powered stapler is required to shoot the staples through the board and into the wall studs (Fig. 7).

When installing ordinary drywall overhead, a set of T-braces is all but essential, and the extra weight of the fiber-reinforced paneling makes having the T-braces an absolute must. Make the length of the braces the same or slightly longer than the distance from the floor to the ceiling. Then, have a helper wedge the T-brace between the panel and the floor as the panel is lifted to the ceiling. Once the brace is secure, install the fasteners (Fig. 8).

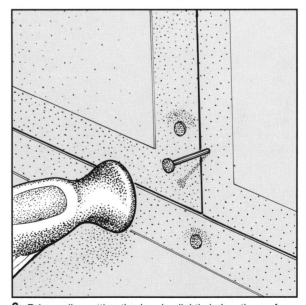

**6** Drive nails, setting the heads slightly below the surface. Fiber-reinforced panels accept nails close to the edge.

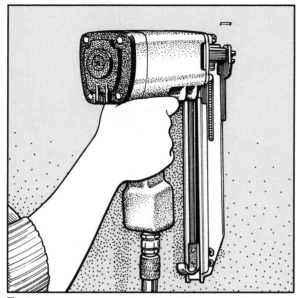

**7** For the fastest installation, use a heavy-duty air-powered stapler to hang fiber-reinforced wallboard.

**8** Use T-braces to support wallboard during overhead installation. Drywall screws draw panel tight to ceiling.

## Finishing

Finishing fiber-reinforced wallboard is probably the most unique part of the whole process. In contrast to traditional drywall, the flat joints do not have to be reinforced with paper or fiber-mesh drywall tape.

Begin finishing the flat joints by applying a basecoat of FiberBond Dri Mix joint compound that fills the hollow area created by the tapered edges. Avoid covering the area outside the tapers, and trim the application flush with a drywall knife.

Allow the Dri Mix base compound to dry thoroughly because it shrinks slightly, like most other compounds. After it's dry, apply a second topcoat of standard, ready-mixed drywall joint compound and spread it to a feathered edge several inches beyond the edges of the base coat application (Fig. 9). When the topcoat is dry, it's ready to be sanded.

The inside corners are finished as they would be with standard drywall. First, apply the Dri Mix compound

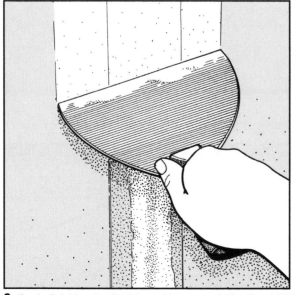

**9** Begin finishing the flat joints with a coat of FiberBond Dri Mix—no tape is required. Remove excess with a drywall knife.

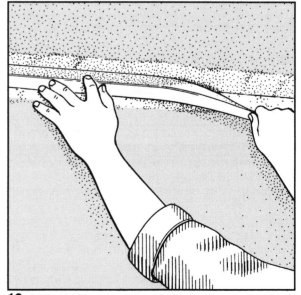

**10** At the inside corners, apply base compound and add drywall tape. Then smooth the compound with drywall knife.

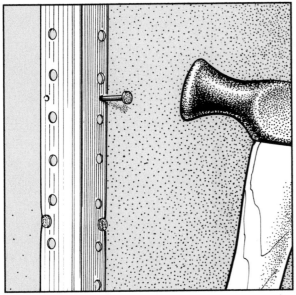

**11** Attach metal corner bead to outside corners in preparation for compound. Use nails, screws or staples for the job.

**12** After corner bead is installed, apply ordinary joint compound, let dry and then apply a second coat.

to the joint, and then lay the tape in the compound (Fig. 10). Smooth and press the tape in place with a 4-in. knife. Once the joint is dry, apply a topcoat of joint compound and spread it several inches wider than the joint.

Outside corners are also treated in the same manner as standard drywall finishing. Nail, screw or staple metal corner bead to the outside corners (Fig. 11), and then cover the bead with a 6-in. band of joint compound (Fig. 12). You don't need the Dri Mix basecoat for outside corners. One coat of joint compound will almost do the job, but a second coat makes it perfect.

Cover nails, screws or staples with a first spot coat of Dri Mix compound. Then, after any necessary sanding, follow with joint compound applied at right angles to the first coat (Fig. 13).

When it comes to sanding the joints, you'll really appreciate the benefits of this solid wallboard. Because there's no paper top layer, there's no chance of scuffing the surface next to the compound. In fact, this wallboard is finish sanded at the factory and additional sanding has no effect, except to further smooth the surface (Fig. 14).

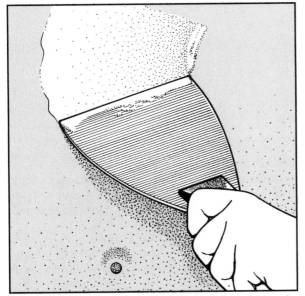

**13** Use Dri Mix base compound for the first coat over the fasteners. Then, apply a second coat of joint compound.

**14** Smooth the compound with fine sandpaper and use a sanding stick to easily handle hard-to-reach areas.

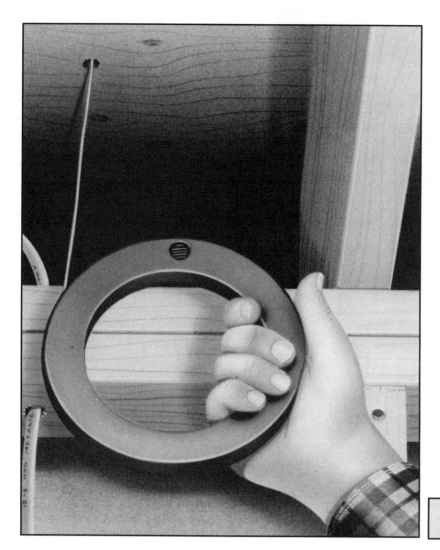

*Retrofit Wiring* was written by Merle Henkenius. Illustrations by George Retseck.

# Retrofit wiring

■ Have you ever wondered how you might add a switch, light or receptacle to your home with all those finished walls, ceilings and floors concealing the wiring? With a little careful measuring and a complement of luck, you can easily run cable through the ceiling and wall cavities and with little or no drywall repair.

Fishing cable, as it's known, is not new. Electricians have been upgrading electrical systems in this manner for years, and you can do it too. Although the job is time consuming, it's not that difficult.

### Circuit Size

To find the code-legal capacity for an existing circuit, count how many receptacles are on each circuit. To do this, shut off one circuit breaker a time (at the service panel) and count the de-energized outlets.

Just move around the house with a voltage tester, desk lamp or power tool, and plug it into every receptacle. Assign each de-energized receptacle on a circuit a value of 1.5 amps.

At that rate, a 15-amp circuit will, according to the National Electrical Code, accommodate 10 receptacles, and a 20-amp circuit, 13 receptacles. The amperage ratings are found on the breaker switches. You can add additional outlets and fixtures to any circuit that does not have its full allotment of outlets or fixtures (the addition must not exceed the capacity of the circuit). Also, if you find a free space in your service panel, you can add a new circuit.

A few cautionary words are in order. Circuits dedicated to appliances, such as a clothes washer, are best left alone. Don't tap into an appliance circuit to add a ceiling fixture. Instead, tap into an existing lighting circuit. Similarly, don't tap into the circuit that runs power to outlets above the kitchen counter.

Remember to match existing wire sizes. A 15-amp circuit will generally contain 14-gauge wires, while a 20-amp circuit will require 12-gauge wires. If the existing circuit is grounded, then the cable you install should contain a grounding conductor as well. If the electrical system in your house is old, or you are unsure of how to ground the new wiring or circuit, consult an electrician.

Of course, always flip the circuit breaker or pull the fuse on any circuit you are working on.

## The Right Equipment

In many cases, all you need to fish electrical wire are a cut-in box, sheathed cable, a screwdriver, utility knife and drywall saw. In some cases, a length of sash chain is handy.

For a short run, a piece of coat hanger will serve as a fish tape. For longer reaches, a factory-made fish tape will save you hours of frustration. This costs about $20.

Fish tape is a thin, coiled steel ribbon that has a hook on one end. It's rigid enough to push through a wall cavity, yet flexible enough to make tight radius bends.

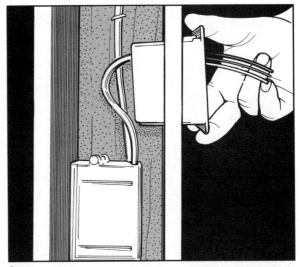

**3** To gain access to the wall cavity from the attic, bore through the 2 × 4 (or nailer) that forms the top of the wall.

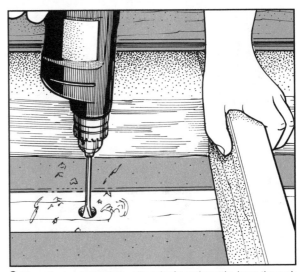

**2** Mount the cut-in box a few inches away from the box that's nailed to the stud. The cut-in box mounts to the drywall.

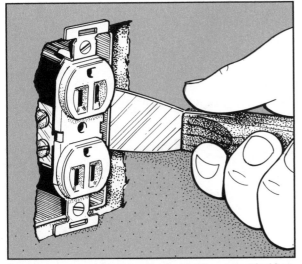

**1** To determine which side of a stud holds an electrical box, slide a putty knife between the drywall and the box.

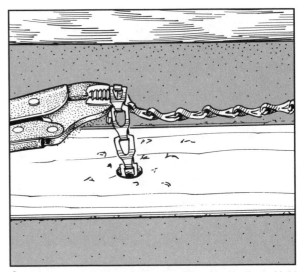

**4** Drop a sash chain through the hole bored in the 2 × 4. Hold the sash chain in place with locking pliers.

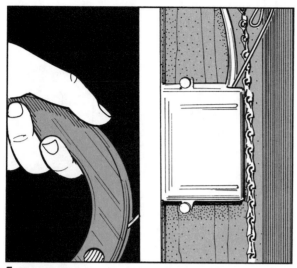

**5** Poke the fish tape through the electrical box and snag the sash chain. Bring the sash chain into the box.

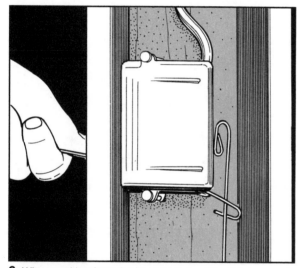

**6** When working from the basement, feed the fish tape up to the electrical box. Snag the tape with a piece of wire.

## A Back-to-Back Route of Access

Some circuits are easy to expand. If you want to add an outlet on a living room wall, check the wall's back first. Often, you can pull power from a receptacle on the wall's opposite side.

To do this, start by measuring carefully from a common feature on the wall, such as a door. The existing receptacle box will be mounted on a stud. The new box, known as a cut-in box, will not be mounted on a stud.

To determine where to put the cut-in box, poke a putty knife between the outside of the receptacle box and the edge of the drywall (Fig. 1). Do this on both sides of the box. The putty knife will go in up to the stud on one side, but on the other side it will not hit the stud. This is the side on which you should install the cut-in box.

On the opposite side of the wall, mark and cut the opening for the cut-in box a few inches from the existing box. Run wire from the existing box to the opening. Push the wires through the cut-in box and install the box in its opening (Fig. 2). Now, install the new receptacle in the cut-in box.

## Moving Laterally Along a Wall

When extending cable along a wall, in most cases, you will have to run cable from the basement or the attic. Which way you run the cable depends on which is unfinished. If both are unfinished, it's generally easier to work from the basement.

If you work in the attic, you'll need to move the insulation aside to find the top of the walls through which you will bore holes to run cable. The wall will run parallel to the ceiling joists or perpendicular to them. If it runs parallel to the joists, look for a drywall nailer (two $2 \times 4$s or one $2 \times 8$) that appears to lay on top of the drywall (which is the back of the ceiling

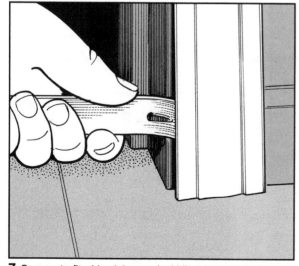

**7** Some retrofit wiring jobs require hiding the cable behind the trim. Begin by prying off the door casing.

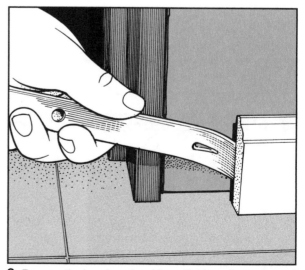

**8** Remove the baseboard molding. Begin prying at the end nearest the door, and work toward the molding's other end.

below). A wall perpendicular to the joists is evidenced by the horizontal 2 × 4 that forms the top of the wall.

After measuring carefully from a reference point, bore one hole to tap into the circuit and another to run the cable (Fig. 3). Next, lower an 8-ft.-long sash chain into the stud space from above. Secure the chain with a pair of locking pliers (Fig. 4).

Poke the fish tape through the box opening (the one you are pulling power from) and snag the dangling sash chain (Fig. 5). Pull the chain into the box, and attach the new cable to it. Pull the chain and cable into the attic. From the attic, feed the cable into the next hole and push it down to the new opening.

Do not lay cable on top of the ceiling joists. If the cable runs across a joist, bore a hole through the joist and run the cable through the hole. If the cable runs parallel to a joist, staple the cable to the joist's side. Space staples 4 ft. apart.

When working from the basement, instead of using a chain to gain access to the existing box, push the fish tape into the stud space from the basement and snag it through the box with a coat hanger (Fig. 6). Then use the fish tape to pull the cable through the box and into the basement.

### Fishing Cable Through a Completely Finished Home

It's difficult to fish cable in homes built on concrete slabs and those where both the basement and second floor are finished. If your electrical work is on the first floor, you won't be able to work from the attic or basement.

Let's say, for example, you want to replace a pull-chain ceiling light with a newer fixture, and you want to control the new fixture from a wall switch near the door.

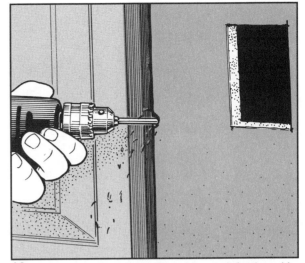

**10** Bore into the stud space to provide a path for the cable. Cable will run from the switch and along the door jamb.

**11** Run the cable into the cut-in box. Fold down the wing fasteners on the box's back and install the box.

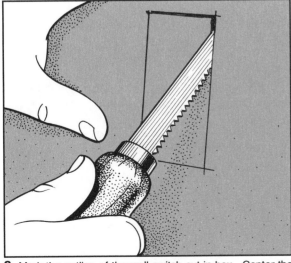

**9** Mark the outline of the wall-switch cut-in box. Center the box 46 in. from the floor and cut the opening.

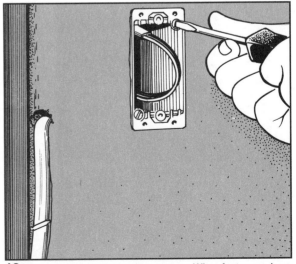

**12** Tighten the cut-in box's screws. Wing fasteners bear down against the drywall, holding the box in place.

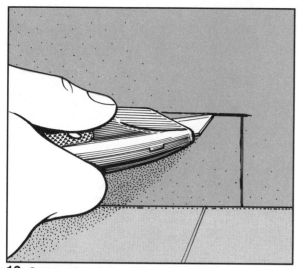

**13** Cut a section of drywall from where the trim was removed. The opening should be about 2½ in. high.

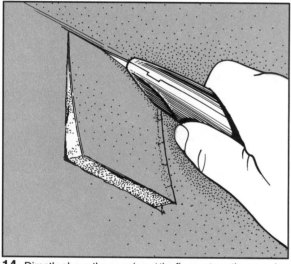

**14** Directly above the opening at the floor cut another opening where the wall and the ceiling meet.

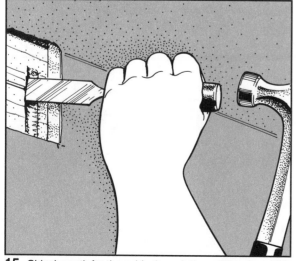

**15** Chisel a path for the cable through the wall framing. This is done most quickly by making a V-shaped cut.

**16** Poke the fish tape down through the wall. Bend the cable around the fish tape and tape the two together.

This procedure requires that you fish the wire along the joists, and not across them. You must first determine the direction of the joists relative to the wall on which you will mount the switch.

Joists generally run in the same direction that the roof slopes. If the wall switch will be mounted perpendicular to the joists, then you can fish the cable straight from the wall to the ceiling fixture.

If the wall switch is to be mounted on is parallel to the joists, you will have to fish the cable to one wall and around the corner to the wall that is parallel to the joists.

Begin the installation by carefully prying off the door trim and baseboard using a flat pry bar (Figs. 7 and 8). Mark for the cut-in box and cut its opening (Fig. 9). Center the box 46 in. from the floor.

Next, bore at an angle from the door jamb into the stud space (Fig. 10). Feed the switch cable into the stud space and the cut-in box opening. Leave yourself enough excess cable to install the receptacle. Then, press the cable near the box into the space between the drywall and the door jamb. Hold the cable in place with a staple and install the box (Figs. 11 and 12). Run the cable to the floor, stapling it as you go.

Next, cut a hole in the wall at floor level and across from the fixture (Fig. 13). The hole must be at least 2½ in. high, but not so high that it will show above the reinstalled baseboard. Next, directly above this hole, cut another hole at the corner where the wall and ceiling meet (Fig. 14). This opening must be about 3 in. wide × 4 in. high.

With the drywall cut away, use a chisel to cut a V-shaped channel in the wall framing for the new cable (Fig. 15).

Push the fish tape down from the corner hole to the hole at floor level. Tape the cable to the fish tape and pull the cable up to the ceiling (Figs. 16 and 17).

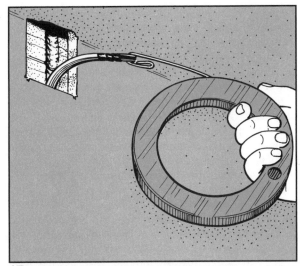

**17** Pull the cable through the wall with the fish tape. Pull up some excess cable and leave it dangling.

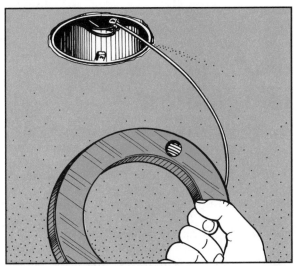

**18** Feed the fish tape through the ceiling fixture and push it through the ceiling cavity to the cable.

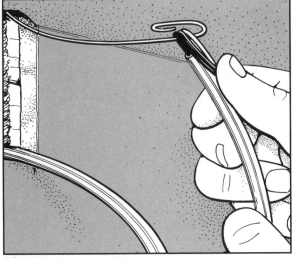

**19** Hook the cable around the fish tape. Pull the cable through the ceiling cavity and out through the fixture.

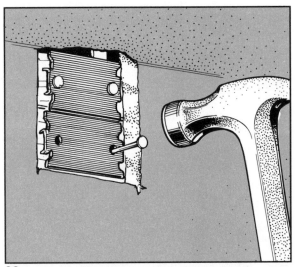

**20** Before patching the hole, nail metal protection plates over where the cable crosses the wall framing.

Push the fish tape through one of the cable openings in the existing ceiling box (Fig. 18). Feed the fish tape through the joist space to the corner hole and pull it through. Connect the cable to the tape and pull both back to the ceiling box (Fig. 19). Install the new fixture and wire the switch loop.

To complete the job, nail metal protection plates over the cable to keep drywall nails from piercing it and tuck the cable neatly under the drywall (Figs. 20 and 21). As for replacing the trimwork, remember where the cable runs and nail accordingly. Of course, if you live in a code-enforced area, be sure to call for an inspection before you conceal your work.

**21** Tuck the cable neatly into the space below the drywall. Be careful later not to nail through the cable.

# Dishwasher installation

■ Of all the rooms in your home, your kitchen is probably the most space hungry, while at the same time being the most difficult to modify. Adding another major component to an already overcrowded kitchen may, therefore, seem like an impossibility.

If you've wondered how you could squeeze a dishwasher into your kitchen, however, you might consider sacrificing a base cabinet to create the needed space. While this isn't always an acceptable tradeoff, in many cases it's the only affordable alternative.

Cabinet-for-dishwasher swaps won't work in every home, however. Cabinets that were built in place or were not built to standard dimensions simply pose too many problems. Another roadblock can be a countertop that was nailed or screwed down from the top before the plastic laminate was installed. In this case, removing a base cabinet for a dishwasher means you'll have to look at a new countertop as well.

Luckily, the best cabinets for this switch are also the most commonly installed. These are factory-built, modular units that are screwed together through their stiles, which makes them easy to remove. They also come with corner brackets mounted on the inside walls of each unit near the top. The countertop is screwed to the brackets from underneath so it can be easily removed.

If your kitchen has these types of mix-and-match cabinets, and you find a 24-in. base unit near the sink, you can install a standard dishwasher. (There are also models available that fit into an 18-in.- wide base cabinet space.)

*Dishwasher Installation* was written by Merle Henkenius. Illustrations by George Retseck.

## Basic Requirements

Besides the dishwasher, you'll need a 6-ft. drain hose and two standard hose clamps. If your sink has a garbage disposer, you'll need a dishwasher connector kit to connect the dishwasher drain hose to the disposer. Without a disposer, a dishwasher waste tee that is spliced in the sink drainpipe is required. In either case, the hose you buy must be heat and detergent resistant. You can find ready-made dishwasher drain hoses, but a ⅝-in. automotive heater hose is a common alternative.

To bring water from the sink's hot-water pipe to the dishwasher, you'll need about 5 ft. of ⅜-in. O.D. soft copper tubing and a dishwasher ell—a right-angle fitting with a ⅝-in. male pipe thread on one side and a ¾-in. compression fitting on the other—to attach the tubing to the dishwasher. You'll also need a dual compression stop to replace the single compression stop that's on the hot-water pipe connected to the faucet. Both hot and cold stops are usually found at the base cabinet floor, and they're connected to the pipes with compression fittings.

Your electrical code will require a dedicated circuit for your new dishwasher, so don't be tempted to pull power from a nearby receptacle. In some jurisdictions, a dishwasher may share a circuit with a garbage disposer, but each appliance will need its own disconnect switch inside the sink base cabinet. Codes vary, so be sure to check.

To run power from a dedicated circuit, you'll need a free slot on your service panel, a 15-amp circuit breaker and at least 6 ft. of flexible metal conduit to house the wires in the sink and dishwater area. To carry the power, you'll need enough 14/2 w/g (14-gauge, 2-wire cable with ground) to bring power from the panel to the sink cabinet, plus insulated black, red and green wire to go from the sink cabinet to the dishwasher. You also can run insulated black, white and green wire in standard conduit from the service panel to the sink. You'll also need box connectors, a grounding clip, a single-pole switch and a surface-mount switch box with cover plate.

Finally, double check that the modular cabinet space will be adequate for a standard dishwasher. The cabinet space dimensions must be 24 in. wide, 24 in. deep and 34½ in. high, measuring from the floor to the bottom of the countertop edge band.

## Removing the Base Unit

You'll probably find the base cabinet screwed to the kitchen wall, the countertop and to the stiles of adjoining base units. It also will be locked in place by the trim that spans the toe kick along the bottom of all the base units. This may be glued-in-place vinyl, vinyl-wrapped particleboard, wood or hardboard. Glued-in-place vinyl is on the units shown (Fig. 1). After the toe-kick trim is freed, remove the screws from the counter, back cabinet wall and stiles (Fig. 2). Then, simply grasp the front of the cabinet and ease it out a little at a time (Fig. 3).

**1** Begin freeing the cabinet by removing the toe-kick trim. This will be cut to fit around the dishwasher and reinstalled later.

**2** Remove screws in stiles that secure the cabinet to adjoining units. Then, remove countertop and back screws.

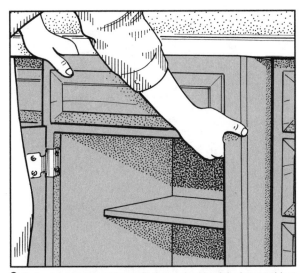

**3** Pull out cabinet from the wall. A standard modular base cabinet should leave a space 24 in. wide and deep by 34½ in. high.

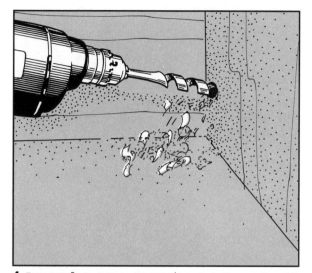

**4** Bore two ⅝-in. holes and one 1⅛-in. hole through the side of the sink unit wall for water supply, conduit and drain hose.

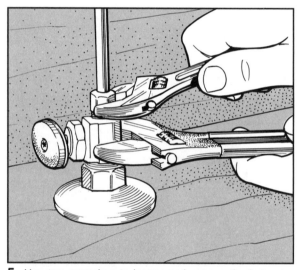

**5** Use two wrenches to loosen and remove the hot-water compression stop (valve) within the sink base cabinet.

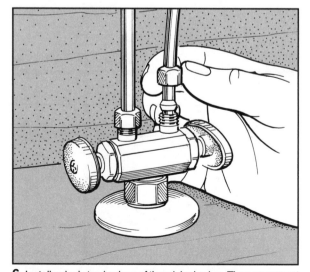

**6** Install a dual stop in place of the original valve. Then, reconnect the faucet pipe and attach the dishwasher supply tubing.

## Plumbing Provisions

Before installing the dishwasher, it's best to run the plumbing and electrical conduit into the opening. The dishwasher can then be pushed in place and the final connections can be made at the bottom front of the unit with the dishwasher's front access panel removed.

Begin by boring three holes in the sidewall of the sink base cabinet adjacent to the dishwasher space and near the cabinet floor. Be sure to arrange these holes vertically within 1 in. of the back wall to avoid interference with the dishwasher frame. Make one hole 1⅛ in. diameter and the other two ⅝ in. (Fig. 4).

Feed the drain hose through the larger hole and pass the copper tubing through one of the smaller holes. The remaining hole is for the conduit. To connect the copper tubing that supplies hot water to the dishwasher, first shut off the main valve to turn off the water supply to the house and drain some water from the pipes. Then, disconnect the hot-water supply pipe to the sink at the top of its compression stop and remove the stop. The compression nuts and ferrules from this valve will remain on their respective pipes (Fig. 5).

In place of the single compression stop, install a dual compression stop and connect the faucet's hot-water supply pipe to one side with the existing ferrule and nut. Fasten the dishwasher supply line to the remaining port using the nut and ferrule supplied with the new valve (Fig. 6).

One critical drainage requirement must be met before connecting the drain hose to the sink drain. To protect against a contaminating backflow, the hose must be looped and secured high inside the sink cabinet. Simply loop the hose at the top of the cabinet and fasten it with a hose strap or a conduit bracket (Fig. 7). Some codes also may require a vacuum breaker in the drain line. Install the vacuum breaker in the extra fourth sink hole next to the faucet, or through the countertop. Be sure to check your local code to see if a vacuum breaker is required.

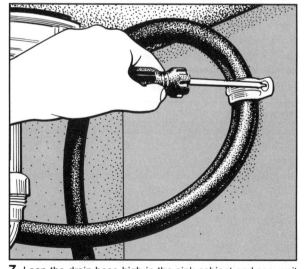

**7** Loop the drain hose high in the sink cabinet and secure it to the side with a conduit bracket or hose strap.

If your sink has a garbage disposer, use a screwdriver to knock the plug from the disposer's dishwasher inlet fitting and then connect the drain hose with a dish-washer connector kit. In the installation shown, a dish-washer waste tee was spliced into the sink drainpipe. A part of the drain tailpiece that extends down from the sink was cut away and the tee installed in its place. As plastic waste kits use nylon compression washers, the nuts need only be hand tight. With the tee installed, slide the hose over its fitting and secure it with a hose clamp (Fig. 8).

## Electrical Provisions

Begin by shutting off the main disconnect switch on your breaker panel. Then install a 15-amp circuit breaker in an open slot of your service panel (Fig. 9). If you are not completely confident of your electrical skills, hire an electrician to install the breaker and make all panel connections. Then, run 14/2 w/g cable from the service panel to the sink cabinet. Just before the cabinet, run the wires through the conduit. You can either strip the plastic sheathing back to the cabinet and feed the wires through the conduit—allowing some overlap between the conduit and plastic sheathing—or feed the sheathed cable through the conduit.

Once inside, install a metal switch box on the wall of the sink base cabinet (Fig. 10). Use box connectors to join the incoming and outgoing conduit to it, and pass the outgoing conduit through the remaining hole into the dishwasher space. Then, feed one black, one white and one green wire through the outgoing conduit. In-stall a single-pole switch in the box, ground the box with a pigtail and grounding clip, then finish with a cover plate (Fig. 11).

**9** Install a new 15-amp circuit breaker in panel for a dedicated dishwasher circuit. Work with the power off.

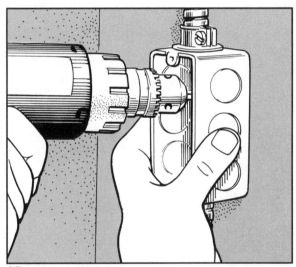

**10** Join incoming and outgoing conduit to switch box with connectors, and screw box to sink cabinet floor.

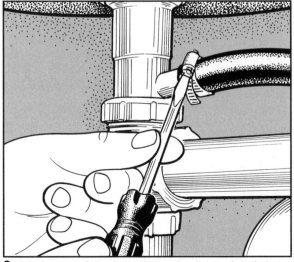

**8** Join the end of the drain hose to the dishwasher drain tee installed in the sink drain. Secure with a hose clamp.

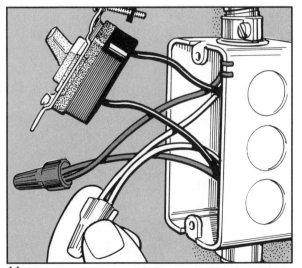

**11** Wire switch by joining white to white, both blacks to switch, and ground to box via pigtail and grounding clip.

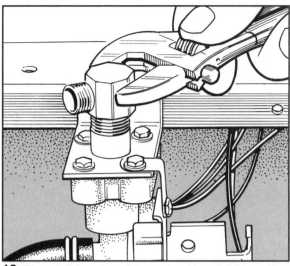

**12** Thread dishwasher ell into solenoid, and tighten with a wrench. Use pipe compound or Teflon tape on threads.

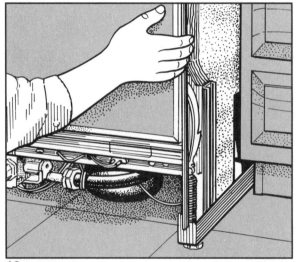

**13** After screwing in adjustable legs all the way, carefully slide the dishwasher into its cabinet space, taking care not to damage the floor.

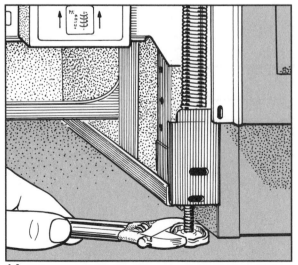

**14** Raise and plumb the dishwasher by extending the legs until the counter brackets meet the edge of the countertop.

## Installing the Dishwasher

With the plumbing and wiring completed within the sink base, tip the dishwasher on its back and thread the four extension legs in completely so the dishwasher will slide under the counter easily. Next, coat the threads on the dishwasher ell with pipe joint compound or Teflon tape and thread it into the dishwasher's solenoid fitting (Fig. 12). Then, tip the dishwasher up and, without scarring the floor, slide it into the cabinet space (Fig. 13). Placing an old towel or floor mat under the dishwasher legs can make sliding the unit easier and prevent damaging the floor.

Press the dishwasher against the back wall so that its frame is flush with the cabinet stiles, and adjust all legs upward until the front of the unit is plumb and the counter brackets at the top front of the dishwasher meet the bottom of the countertop edge band (Fig. 14).

Carefully bend the copper water-supply tubing to meet the dishwasher ell and slide the compression nut and ferrule over the tubing end. Then, thread the nut onto the ell and tighten (Fig. 15). To connect the drain hose, simply slide it over the hose fitting on the discharge pump and tighten a hose clamp over it (Fig. 16).

To complete the wiring, remove the unit's electrical box cover and fasten a box connector to the dishwasher's frame. Then, using twist connectors, join the black circuit wire to the black dishwasher lead, the white wire to the white lead and the green ground wire to the grounding screw on the frame (Fig. 17). Finish by covering the wires with the unit's electrical box cover (Fig. 18).

## Finishing Touches

Turn on the water and screw the dishwasher's counter brackets to the bottom of the counter's edge band (Fig. 19). Then, turn on the circuit and run the unit through one complete cycle to check for leaks and balance. If a compression nut leaks, tighten it one more turn. If the dishwasher vibrates excessively, look for a leveling leg that's not carrying its share of the load. If you find water backing up into your sink, you'll have to clear the drain line with a snake or hire a specialist to do it. Once cleared of soap and grease, the force and heat of the discharged water will keep it clean. To finish installation, first replace the dishwasher access panel (Fig. 20). Then, measure the toe-kick area on both sides of the dishwasher, cut the pieces to fit from the original toe-kick trim and install the trim.

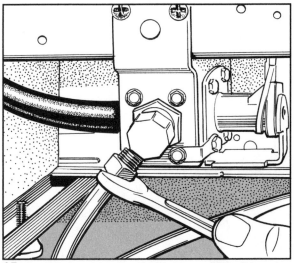

**15** Carefully bend the supply tubing to meet the dishwasher ell, and join the tubing with a compression nut and ferrule.

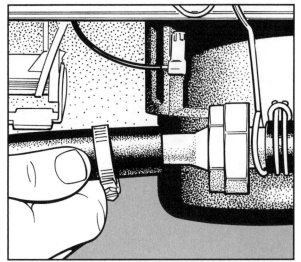

**16** Slip a hose clamp over the drain hose and slide the hose over the pump's discharge fitting. Then tighten the hose clamp.

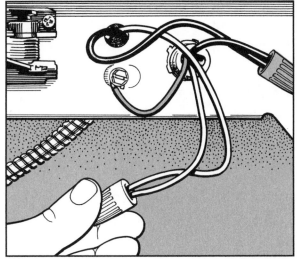

**17** After connecting conduit to frame, join black and white wires to like-colored leads. Join green wire to grounding screw.

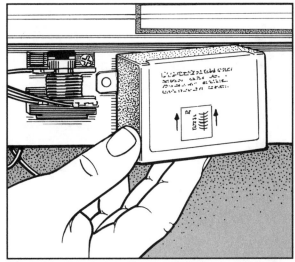

**18** Finish wiring by installing the dishwasher's electrical box cover over wires. Then turn on circuit power and water.

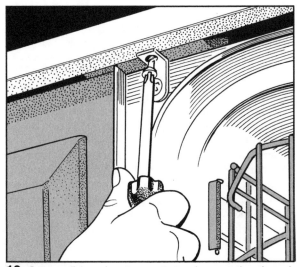

**19** Secure dishwasher to countertop by screwing through dishwasher's counter brackets into underside of counter edge.

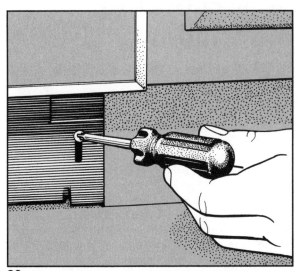

**20** After checking for leaks and proper balance, replace dishwasher access panel and reinstall toe-kick trim.

# Renovating old windows

Old, worn-out double-hung windows are the largest source of drafts and energy loss in many older houses. Replacing even a modest double-hung window may cost as much as $250, but it can be renovated for a fraction of the cost using a jamb liner kit, which typically costs about $50.

Years of opening and closing, the settling of the house and the effects of the weather take their toll on a window. Wood sashes are durable, but the jambs they ride in wear out. The sash becomes loose in the jamb, and large gaps develop at the center meeting rail, allowing air to leak between the jamb and the sash and between the inner and outer sash.

Although the damage done to the window may have been years in the making, the renovation takes only a couple of hours per window.

Jamb liner kits made of vinyl or a combination of aluminum and stainless steel provide fully weather-stripped channels for old sashes to ride in. These replacement jambs, teamed with a high-quality exterior storm window, give the window a heat-loss efficiency equal to many double-glazed replacement windows.

*Renovating Old Windows* was written by Gene and Katie Hamilton with illustrations by George Retseck.

The new replacement jambs have weatherstripped tracks that fit old window sashes snugly. Friction holds the windows open, eliminating the need for sash weights. This makes it possible for you to insulate the sash-weight compartments, and stop another source of air infiltration.

### Measuring

The jamb liner must be at least as long as the existing window jamb is high. The manufacturer of your jamb liner may have specific instructions about measuring for the liner. For instance, one manufacturer asks that you measure the glass area of your window and then consult a chart to determine the correct size of the liner to purchase.

If you have a nonstandard site-built window or one with different-size sashes, measure the distance inside the window channel between the bottom of the sash (not the window sill) and the top of the sash. Purchase a jamb liner kit that is at least as long, or longer, than this measurement.

### Preparing the Jamb

Remove the inside stop, inside sash and parting stop in that order. You will reinstall the inside stop, so remove it carefully.

Use a stiff putty knife or small pry bar to remove the inner stop (Fig. 1). Push the blade between the stop and jamb, and gently pry up. If the stop is covered with many coats of paint, try to drive the putty knife between the stop and window jamb from the window track side of the stop. Be careful—if the sash-weight cords are broken or the window is very worn, the sash can fall out of the jamb when you remove one of the stops.

The outer sash is held in place by the parting stop in the center of the window jamb. This piece of molding is usually set into a groove cut in the sash. If the outside window sash is not painted shut, you may be able to remove it by prying it out of the groove (Fig. 2). Don't worry about breaking this molding—it gets discarded.

**2** The parting stop holds the outside sash in place. Remove it by prying it out of the slot in the jamb or chisel it flush.

**3** If the sash cords are still in place, cut them off with a utility knife and let the sash weight pull them through.

**1** Remove the inside sash by prying off the inside window stop. To prevent breaking the stop, pry where it is nailed.

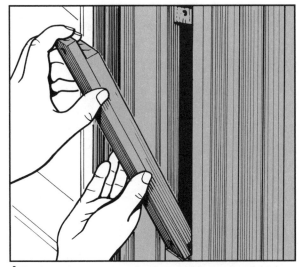

**4** Back out the screw or nail at the top of the sash-weight door, then remove the door. Take out the sash weights.

**5** Remove the screws that hold the sash-weight pulleys, and pry the pulleys from the jamb using a screwdriver.

**6** Stuff fiberglass insulation into the jamb weight cavity. Tear the insulation into little pieces, and use a pushstick.

**7** Scrape and sand off paint globs, and remove embedded hardware that might interfere with the jamb liner.

You also can chisel the parting stop flush with the jambs. You don't have to remove it from the slot, just carve off the protrusion so the outside sash can be removed. Remove one stop, and pull that side of the sash toward you to remove it. If the window won't budge, it's probably because it's painted in place. In that case, you must break the bond between the paint and window from the outside.

When both sashes are out, cut the sash cords with a utility knife (Fig. 3). Then, lift out the access doors to the weight compartment located in the lower section of each side of the jamb (Fig. 4). Some are held in place with a screw, others with nails.

Next, remove the screws holding the pulleys in place. Some pulleys are nailed down, in which case you will have to pry the pulley loose. Pry each pulley out of its mortise with a screwdriver (Fig. 5).

Remove the old weights and fill this cavity with insulation. The easiest way is to pull apart a piece of fiberglass insulation and push small pieces of it into the cavity with a small stick (Fig. 6). Pack the insulation in tight. Your goal is to stop air infiltration through the opening. When the weight pockets are full, reinstall the access doors.

The face of the jamb must be flat. Scrape away old paint and weatherstripping, and remove any embedded hardware that interferes with the new liners (Fig. 7).

The liners are cut to fit the jamb. Their bottoms are cut at an angle to match the slope of the sill. The angle at the bottom makes the jamb liners fit either the right or left side, so be careful to cut off the square end of the jamb liner. Also, double-check that you are cutting the correct piece if the sides of your jamb are different lengths.

If the windows are very old, the angle of the sill may not match the precut angle on the bottom of the jamb liners. Here, copy the sill angle of your window and transfer it to the bottom of the jamb liner with a sliding bevel gauge. Cut the bottom of the liner to match the sill angle using a hacksaw (Figs. 8, 9 and 10).

**8** On old windows, you may have to cut the jamb liner to fit the sill angle. Copy the sill angle with a sliding bevel gauge.

The top parting stop must be notched at the jamb by about ½ in. to clear the parting stop on the new jamb liner. Measure the exact height of the center parting stop and weatherstripping on the new liner. Then, measure from the jamb toward the center of the window and mark the stop. Cut through the stop with a handsaw (Fig. 11), and knock out the small piece with a hammer and chisel.

Put the two sides of the liner in place and check the fit. They should not be too tight. This is especially important for the vinyl jamb liner because it may bow away from the jamb and make the window difficult to operate. Don't secure the jamb liners yet. The sash must be inserted before the liners are permanently installed.

### Preparing the Sash

Remove the window weight cords from the sash if they have not fallen off. Some are nailed in place, others are held in place by a tight-fitting knot pushed into a slot.

Scrape off old paint from the sides of the sash, especially in the area that will be in the jamb liner track. Since the sash is out of the window and easy to work on, it's a good time to replace any broken glass, repair the putty and paint the sash if necessary.

Place the sash in the jamb liners and check the fit. If there is paint buildup on the sash, it probably will fit very tight. Sand the sides of the sash so they make a snug fit in the jamb liner, but they should not fit too tight.

Check the fit of the inside and outside sashes at their meeting rails. The sashes often wear at the point where each meeting rail rubs on the parting stop. The weatherstripping on the jamb liner may seal this gap. If a large gap exists because the jamb liner has a smaller parting stop than the one you removed, you will need to correct this (Fig. 12). To fill the gap, glue a small block of wood to the sash in the area and shape it to fit the new parting stop (Fig. 13).

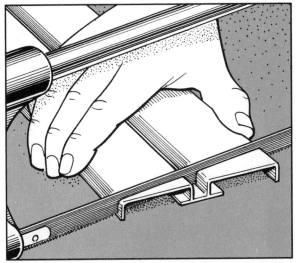

**10** Cut the jamb liner to length with a hacksaw. Other fine-tooth saws, such as a backsaw or dovetail saw, also work.

**11** Cut the parting stop at the top of the jamb to accommodate the new parting stop in the jamb liners.

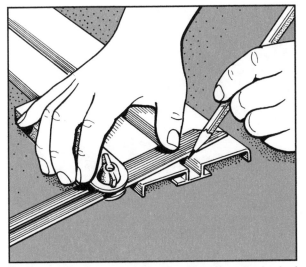

**9** Use the bevel gauge to copy the sill angle on the back of the jamb liner. Be sure the angle slopes the right way.

**12** Old windows wear out where they rub against the parting stop. If there is a large gap at the arrow, repair the sash.

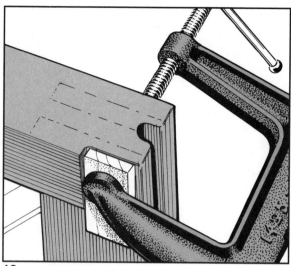

**13** Glue a small piece of wood on the sash where it rubs against the parting stop. Shape the block to fit the stop.

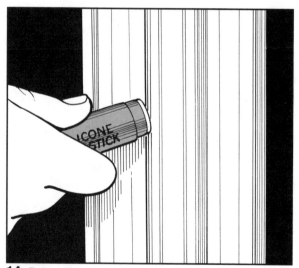

**14** Rub a stick of silicone lubricant (supplied with the jamb kit) on the jamb liners so the sash slides easily.

**15** Place the inside and outside sash in the jamb liners. Set the assembly on the window sill and push it in place.

Prime and paint all exposed wood before you install the sash.

### Installing the Jamb Liners

To install the new liners, first lubricate the edges of the jamb weatherstripping with the silicone lubricant provided in the kit (Fig. 14). Next, place the windows in the jamb liners and check that the angled bottom of each liner faces down. Slide the windows together to the center of the jamb liner, then place the bottom of the liner into the old jamb (Fig. 15).

Raise the jamb liners and windows so the pointed end of the liners are as far forward as possible in the old jamb and rest against the outer stop. When the liners are fully upright, temporarily secure the top of the jamb liners with a nail or screw—but don't drive the fastener all the way home.

Slide the windows up and down, and check their fit in the jamb. They may be difficult to move at first, but the jambs will loosen after some use. If everything checks out, fasten the jamb liners to the old jambs with a nail or screw driven through the top of the jamb. The inside stop holds the jamb in place, so these fasteners are needed only until you install this stop.

### Weatherstripping the Sash

V-strip, self-adhering vinyl weatherstripping is the easiest to apply and does a good job of sealing the window. The spring brass version of this weatherstripping is more durable but harder to install. In either case, apply the weatherstripping to the upper edge of the outside sash with the point of the V facing in (Fig. 16).

Next, apply a strip to the back edge of the meeting rail of the outside sash (Fig. 17). Keep the point of the V-strip facing up. Then, apply weatherstripping to the bottom of the inner sash with the point of the V facing in.

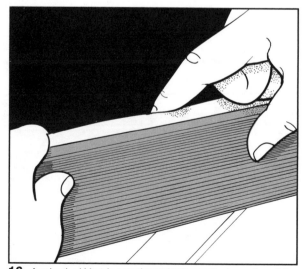

**16** Apply vinyl V-strip weatherstripping to the top edge of the outside sash. The point of the V faces inside.

**17** Pull down the outer sash, and apply V-strip to the outer sash meeting rail. The weatherstripping must point up.

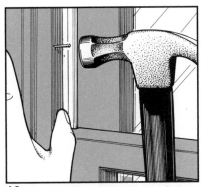

**18** Renail the inner stops snug—but not tight—against the inside window. Set the nailheads and putty the holes.

**19** A jamb liner with a spring-loaded channel on the left side of the window allows the window to be removed.

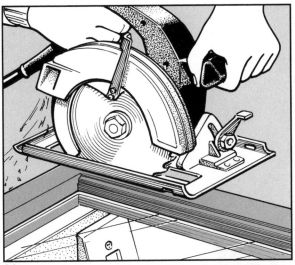

**20** Use a circular saw to rip about ¾ in. off the left side of the sash to accommodate the spring-loaded jamb liner.

**21** Push the sash against the left jamb liner to compress the springs, then push the window into the track on the right.

## Trimming Out the Window

Before you install the inner stop, run a light bead of latex silicone caulk along the joint between the jamb liner and the old jamb. Also caulk the joints between the liner and jamb at the top and bottom. Caulk any gap between the parting stop on the liner and the top parting stop. Wipe up any excess caulk with a damp rag before it has a chance to set up.

Renail the inner stop. Use longer finish nails or reposition the nails so they will hold the stop firmly (Fig. 18). Check that the windows still move smoothly after renailing the stop. Set the nails, putty over the nail holes and paint the stop.

## Installing Jambs for Take-out Sash

Installing spring-loaded jamb liners allows the sashes to be removed for cleaning and repair. This job is only a little different than installing standard replacement jambs. These jamb liners are made from aluminum with a stainless-steel wear strip. They are not available in vinyl.

The spring-loaded channel is screwed or nailed to the left side of the existing jamb (Fig. 19). A jamb liner is snapped into place on top of this, and a standard jamb liner is installed on the right jamb.

Next, to accommodate the increased thickness of the spring-loaded channel, cut off about ¾ in. from the left side of the sash (Fig. 20).

Push the sash against the left jamb liner to compress the springs, then push the window into the track on the opposite side of the jamb (Fig. 21). Spring tension keeps the sash in place.

*Basic Deck Care* was written by Neal Barrett.  Illustrations by George Retseck.

Decks and other exterior structures need regular maintenance to keep looking new. Periodic applications of deck sealer will help keep weathering to a minimum.

# Basic deck care

■ If you're like many homeowners, the backyard deck is the focal point for warm-weather activities.  Whether used as a gathering place for dining and socializing, or as a quiet spot to read the newspaper or catch a nap, the deck extends your living space to the outdoors and enhances your leisure hours.

   As with most parts of your home, however, a certain amount of routine maintenance is required to keep your deck structurally sound, safe and looking its best.  If your deck is several years old, it's time to evaluate its condition, fix trouble spots that need immediate attention and use a little preventive maintenance.

   The design and construction of a deck can vary considerably from a simple square or rectangle resting right on the ground to an elaborate, multilevel polygon supported on posts or piers.  While it would be impossible to cover every particular condition that might need attention, the following tips and techniques will apply to most situations.

   Chances are your deck is built of either cedar, redwood or pressure-treated yellow pine.  These are the most commonly used materials because they are resistant to rot and insect damage.  When exposed to the elements, however, any wood will show signs of weathering.  Even if the deck was originally treated with a stain or preservative, this treatment eventually needs to be renewed.

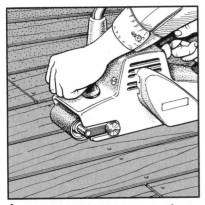

**1** Use a belt sander to remove roughness and splintering from a weathered deck. Smooth rails with a sanding block.

**2** Apply a deck brightener with a stiff brush to remove stains and weathering. Follow manufacturer's instructions.

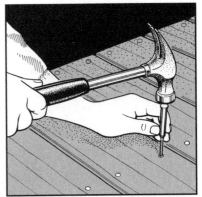

**3** If decking nails have popped above the surface due to wood shrinkage, use a nail-set or punch to drive them back in place.

**4** To repair slightly cupped boards, first pull nails with a pry bar. Use a thin piece of plywood to protect deck from marring.

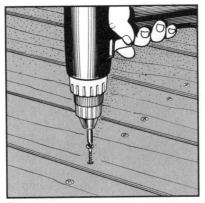

**5** Install galvanized decking screws to draw cupped board flat. Use a power screwdriver to simplify the job.

**6** Flatten severely cupped boards by sawing a series of parallel kerfs on the underside. Then, screw the board in place.

**7** If a deck board shows signs of cracking, remove it by first using a sabre saw to cut across the board near the crack.

**8** Then, use a pry bar to remove both pieces. Cut each at the joist positions and reinstall. Then install a filler piece.

**9** Crawl under the deck to inspect joist fastenings. Install toenails to strengthen joint and add hangers if necessary.

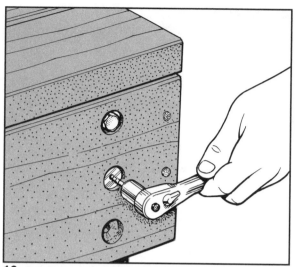

**10** Reinforce rim joist-to-post joint with lagbolts. Counterbore lagbolt holes for washers and bolt heads.

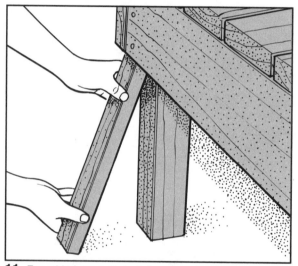

**11** For added strength, install a support under the rim joists at the posts. Secure support with galvanized nails or screws.

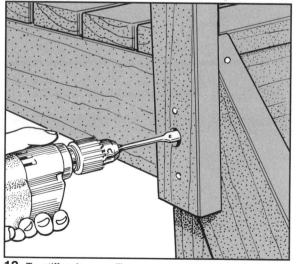

**12** To stiffen loose railing supports, bore and counterbore lagbolt holes and install lagbolts and washers.

## Surface Treatments

First, inspect the surfaces of the deck and railing for excessive splintering. If splintering is a problem, sanding the surface is the simplest solution. Use a belt sander to smooth the boards on the deck surfaces. Sand only in the direction of the grain and keep the sander moving evenly to avoid gouging (Fig. 1). On the railings, hand sand with a sanding block or use an orbital pad sander to remove roughness and hazardous slivers.

You'll find many stains and sealers designed specifically for your deck. Several manufacturers offer products called deck brighteners (actually bleaches), which remove stains and weathering from the wood surfaces. Apply these products according to the manufacturer's directions, usually with a stiff-bristle brush, and rinse off the deck thoroughly before applying any top coat (Fig. 2). Be sure to wear gloves and eye protection.

Sealers protect your deck from moisture and are available in clear or tinted, which acts as a stain. Sealers need to be renewed periodically to offer continuous protection. Stains are offered in a range of opacities for either completely hiding the grain or allowing it to show. When it comes to choosing a stain and sealer for your deck, check that both products are compatible and suitable for the type of wood used in your deck.

After a new deck has been exposed to the elements for a year or so, shrinkage of the lumber can cause nails to pop up above the deck surface. If the boards are still flat, reset the nails slightly below the deck surface using a nailset or punch that matches the size of the nailheads (Fig. 3). If the deck boards have cupped due to drying, there are several ways to approach the problem. If the cupping is not too severe, first remove the nails with a pry bar (Fig. 4). Then, install galvanized decking screws to pull the board flat (Fig. 5). If the board is too severely cupped to do this, use a pry bar to remove the board. Then use a circular saw to make a series of relief cuts along the back, convex surface of the board, equal in depth to about one-third of the board's thickness (Fig. 6). Replace the board and fasten it with galvanized decking screws. If this technique fails to bring the board flat, install a new board in its place.

Occasionally a deck board will develop a serious crack or break, either from an accident or as the result of an original structural flaw in the lumber. To fix this problem, first use a jigsaw to cut through the board near the crack (Fig. 7). Then pry up the pieces on either side of the cut (Fig. 8). Drive the nails back through the boards and remove them with a pry bar. Then, mark the boards and cut them to break in the middle of the joists to either side of the damaged area. Replace the board sections, cut a new piece to fit in the gap and nail or screw it in place. Remember to always use galvanized nails or screws when working on a deck.

## Structural Fixes

Next, check your deck for structural problems. Crawl under the deck and examine the joints between the floor joists and the deck rim joists. Although joist hangers usually are used, they may not be. If there are joist hangers, check to be sure they are properly nailed. If there are no joist hangers, drive two or three toenails into a loose joist to reinforce its attachment (Fig. 9). For extra security, install joist hangers on all the joists.

Keep in mind that while minor problems can easily be handled with simple tools and a free weekend, serious structural fixes such as post replacement may require a building permit and approval from your local building inspector. Check your building code to be sure.

If the rim joists on your deck are simply nailed to the posts, check to see that the joints are secure. While nailing may have been adequate when the deck was built, cupping of the joists or vibration of the deck may have loosened the nails. The remedy is to install lag-bolts through the rim joists into the supporting posts. Drill pilot holes and counterbore for the lagbolt head and washer. Use a socket wrench to install the bolts—usually two or three per joist end are adequate (Fig. 10). To further support the structure, install a 2 × 4 support underneath the rim joist and nail or screw it to the supporting post (Fig. 11).

Likewise, the supports for the deck railing can come loose if they're only nailed in place. To stabilize the rail supports, bore and counterbore holes for lagbolts (Fig. 12), and install the new fastenings.

The steps that lead from your deck to the ground also can become the site of needed maintenance. Through frost heaving or settling, the earth or pad that supports the bottom of the stairs can move. This loosens the attachment of the stair to the deck. The first course of action is to readjust the bottom support of the stair. If your steps sit directly on the earth, shim the stringers with flat rocks or shovel new earth in place. If your steps rest on a masonry pad, you have to lift and shim the pad. Then, reinforce the attachments at the top of the stairs by driving toenails through the stringer into the rim joist.

Through use, the nails that hold the stringers to the stair treads can become loose. Use a long clamp to draw the stringers tight to the tread and drive new nails to hold the assembly together (Fig. 13).

When a tread develops a crack, which might later prove to be a hazard, it's best to replace it before the problem gets worse. Cut the tread in half with a hand-saw and pry the two haves from their housings in the stringers (Fig. 14). Use a hammer to drive the nails back through the stringers and remove them with a pry bar. Cut a new tread and slide it into position, fastening it in place with new galvanized nails (Fig. 15).

**13** If step stringers have moved away from the treads, draw the joint tight with a long clamp. Then, secure with nails.

**14** To remove a cracked or weak step, first saw the step in two with a handsaw. Then, remove each half with a pry bar.

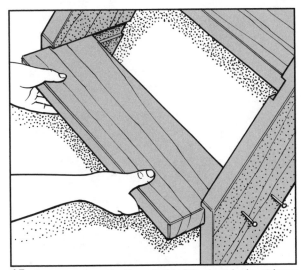

**15** Cut a new tread to fit, and slide it in place in the stringer slots. Then, secure with galvanized nails or screws.

# Post-hole footings

■ Whether you're reconstructing a deck, adding a porch, or building a gazebo, the job begins with footings that penetrate your climate's frost line. Often, a simple post-hole footing is ideal. This type of footing is quick, easy and relatively inexpensive. If you plan an enclosed addition, of course, you'll want a continuous footing that surrounds a crawlspace beneath the floor. Anything short of a major structural addition will rest firmly on simple posts and spot footings.

### Check Your Building Codes
Before you begin digging, visit your local building codes office to find out what the requirements are for your area. Local codes may vary, but generally, spot footings will need to be 8 in. in diameter and at least 36 in. deep. Don't be tempted to get by with shallower holes. If you don't dig below the frost line, you run the risk of seasonal shifting and structural damage.

Warmer climates will often allow shallower footings, and some codes may stipulate a square hole. Some areas require a galvanized bracket to secure the post to the footing, and others require an anchor bolt. Most codes will specify the spacing of the footings as well. Regardless of your area's requirements, it's always better to have accurate information on hand before you begin.

### Tools and Materials
Pouring a post-hole footing requires very little in the way of tools and materials. At the start, you'll need a post-hole digger—either the scissors type shown or an auger type. You'll also need a tape measure, level, shovel, galvanized post brackets and concrete.

Use a mortar box or wheelbarrow to mix the concrete. If you plan to pour a series of footings in a row, stretch a string between two stakes placed beyond the first and last post-hole locations. With this in place, the holes can be aligned and each bracket can be positioned accurately.

If you plan to pour only a few footings, it's easiest to buy bags of premixed concrete—you simply add the water. Each 60-pound bag will make 1 cu. ft. of concrete. An 8-in.-dia. × 36-in.-deep footing will take about two bags.

Text and photographs for *Post-Hole Footings* by Merle Henkenius.

A concrete footing set below the frost line provides a stable base for deck and porch construction. Premixed concrete is the easiest solution for small jobs.

**1** A scissors-type post-hole digger works well in digging deep narrow holes and squaring the hole bottoms.

**2** Use a tape measure to check that the hole extends below the frost line. Codes vary, but a 36-in.-deep hole is common.

**3** Mix premixed concrete in a wheelbarrow and shovel it into the hole. Two bags should handle one 36-in. hole.

## Digging and Pouring

After laying out and marking the footing locations, rough out each hole with the post-hole digger (Fig. 1). There's nothing complicated about digging a hole, but make sure it doesn't taper. Make the bottom of the hole the same diameter as the top and keep the sides consistent. When you've reached the required depth (Fig. 2), trim the bottom of the hole flat and clean out all loose dirt.

With the holes ready, mix the premixed concrete one or two bags at a time. As a drier mix is always stronger than a wet mix, add only enough water to make the concrete workable. Then, shovel it into each hole until it reaches the grade level (Fig. 3). Finally, float the tops of each footing so that the concrete is level and relatively smooth.

Keep in mind that this isn't a finished surface and you needn't spend a lot of time with a trowel. If you don't have a trowel, a small piece of lumber will do the job as well.

## Setting Brackets and Posts

Setting a bracket in wet concrete is easy enough, since you position it exactly where you need it. Again, a taut string helps in positioning a row of brackets. Lacking the string, you can simply measure from a common point such as a foundation wall. With the brackets settled into the concrete, use a level in both directions to level the units (Figs. 4 and 5).

After the concrete as set for several days, you can begin building on your footings. The mix will not reach full strength for several weeks, so avoid side stress on the brackets while building. When nailing lumber to a bracket, remember to use approved bracket nails (Fig. 6). These nails are short and thick and designed for optimum shear strength. While a standard galvanized nail may seem an acceptable substitute, many building code authorities won't agree.

**4** A post bracket has tabs that penetrate the concrete. Press brackets in place so the tabs are fully embedded in surface.

**5** Use a tape measure or taut string to determine the exact bracket position. Then, level the bracket in both directions.

**6** When fastening support posts to the footing bracket, use approved bracket nails for maximum joint strength.

# Bath and utility room addition

■ More than 60% of the 80 million single family homes in this country are over 20 years old. Most of these are tiny compared to the excessive, 5000-sq.-ft. monsters we so often see in architecture and design magazines today. But these basic, child- tested, bread-and-butter homes aren't obsolete, though often they are a little short on pleasant amenities, like sufficient closet space and some extra elbow room at the bathroom sink.

While some shortcomings can be expensive to change, others, like this simple bath and utility room addition, won't break the budget and will add bonus space right where it's needed.

Some preliminary plans considered for this project were pretty ambitious and expensive. One even sported an outdoor shower enclosure and a special 8 × 8-ft. alcove for an oversize, all-season whirlpool bath. After that first design splurge, however, a more sensible plan was decided on. Two factors had to be considered. First, there had to be more room so that two could use the vanity at the same time and second, a lot more storage space was needed in the utility room.

Along the way, it was also decided to improve the mechanical systems. The utility room held a Rube Goldberg maze of plumbing connections, an old inefficient furnace and a large interior flue that made any layout changes very difficult.

The final plan is what you see here. The back house wall was extended only 5 ft. 4 in. The bathroom was immediately more comfortable, and the previously dark and cramped utility room now has an airy feel with tons of closet space. A new patio door that opens onto a small covered entrance deck was installed. This lets the utility room do double duty as an all-purpose mud room.

There is also a more modern heating system, instead of an old white-elephant furnace, plus all-new plumbing and wiring. Because this furnace model has such a high efficiency rating, a PVC vent could be used to release combustion gases, not the typical masonry flue. So, away went the annoying interior flue and in its place is an alcove for the washer and dryer.

By cutting down the square-footage requirements, two other benefits resulted: First, there was more money to devote to better windows, doors, bath fixtures, appliances and heating equipment. Second, the small bulge on the house's footprint hardly raised an eyebrow at the local building department.

*Bath and Utility Room Addition* was written by Mike McClintock. Photos by J.R. Rost with technical art by George Retseck.

The previous bathroom only accommodated two people if one was in the shower. Now two can comfortably use the vanity.

Extra square footage in the utility room allowed for more efficient placement of the washer and dryer and a wall of storage cabinets.

## The Bath

While the hardcore mechanical guts of this job are in the utility room, the nicest touches are in the bathroom. Though it's difficult to keep even a modest bath remodeling like this from eating up the budget, after the demolition, digging and disruption—which are so much a part of the job—you should include a couple of extras just to take the edge off the hassles that are bound to occur.

One good approach is to splurge a little on color and pattern. The job shown used a mosaic of ceramic tile on the floor which followed the outline of the room's perimeter. This created some subtle visual interest in an otherwise small and subdued room. The color on the cabinetry complemented the floor but remained light so the room felt airy and expansive.

Because it was desired to flood the room with exterior light without sacrificing privacy or the only wall for an oversize vanity mirror, narrow windows were chosen. These frame the sides and top of the mirror which reflects light into the room. With the fixed unit above, this makes the room seem even larger. The fixed unit above lets in the most light. But the two casements on the sides do provide lots of light and great ventilation. There is still privacy, and room for two at the vanity.

This job also provided the opportunity to change plumbing fixtures, opting for ones that were a neutral color. In the future, the looks of the room can be changed by simply changing the decorating, not the fixtures. Top-of-the-line faucets and other hardware were purchased with the money saved by building a smaller room.

An exhaust fan on a timer switch was also installed. It is vented directly to the outside and does a great job of ridding the room of excess moisture.

One last grace note in the bath: The exact location of all towel bars was planned so framing could be added between the studs at these locations.

## The Utility Room

The old utility room was dark and dingy. There was just one small window over the washer and dryer. In the new utility room, wall space was again too precious to award to windows, but room was made for a patio door to give access to the backyard, a huge amount of screened ventilation in the summertime and a great source of natural light all day long. The door has two panels of equal size, one center-hinged to swing back on the other. A full screen door slides across the opening. Although a sliding door would have had many of the same advantages, this version was chosen because it's easier to operate, looks great and locks more securely than standard sliding glass doors.

The door opens onto a small covered back porch, which creates a nice transition between the house and the backyard. Not only does it break up what would otherwise be a flat facade, it also shields the door from the weather. So, during most rainstorms, the door can remain open to catch the cooling breezes.

To make room for the patio door, a new location for the washer and dryer had to be found. This was done by creating an alcove along the bathroom wall. This layout change was possible once the interior flue that the old fuel-guzzling furnace required was removed. When the new furnace was closed in, the resulting alcove allowed the new washer and dryer to recede from the center of the room for a builtin custom look. Another nice touch is the removable box shelf placed behind the washer dryer. This gives room to make all the mechanical connections and still avoid the cavern behind most washers and dryers that always seems to gobble up socks.

The wall cabinet above the washer and dryer offers room for general-purpose storage, and its lower rail extends far enough below the cabinet floor to hide a fluorescent fixture, right over the machines. The last touch in the appliance alcove is a narrow cabinet

This small addition—amounting to less than 100 sq. ft.—increased the comfort and efficiency of both rooms immensely. With increased maneuvering room at the bathroom vanity and the washer and dryer, everyday operations became easier. The increased storage space in both rooms reduced the clutter.

between the washer and dryer, just wide enough to store detergent and other laundry supplies.

Once the washer and dryer had a new location and the patio door was in place, the old entrance door could be eliminated, winding up with a full wall for storage cabinets behind louvered doors. These doors are harder to paint but make the wall look more interesting than a succession of flat doors. Each closet has an overhead light.

Some of the most interesting improvements are hidden behind the doors to the furnace space. In a very tight spot there are a new furnace, air cleaner, water softener and water heater.

The 94%-efficient furnace, called a combo heater, is a 2-unit fixture but still a space saver for remodelers. A heavily insulated hot-water tank feeds domestic hot-water lines and a heat exchanger coil above the furnace fan. This system is so efficient that a stainless-steel exhaust coil in the water tank gives up the last drop of gas heat and produces a tepid exhaust that's vented through PVC pipe. An electronic air filter was added—to cut down on dust accumulations in the house—just below the fan in the return air plenum.

One bonus of the whole project was the chance to right a wrong that had been there for years. The entrance to a small workroom—now converted to a home office—had always been through the old utility room. By extending the hall a few feet farther, as shown in the drawing, the room now opens directly into the hall, the way it always should have been.

# Electrical system maintenance

A properly installed electrical system is remarkably durable, especially given the number of devices and connections in the average home. Still, some maintenance is often required. Perhaps several receptacles will suddenly stop working, or a light switch will work erratically. Circuit breakers may begin to trip even though you're not using substantially more power. You also might notice a momentary flickering of a ceiling light every time someone shuts a door. These are all simple electrical problems with easy solutions.

Text and photos for *Electrical System Maintenance* by Merle Henkenius.

## Loose Connections

While troublesome switches and receptacles simply need to be replaced, most other routine electrical problems can be attributed to loose wiring connections. Though the hundreds of wiring connections in a home were originally made securely, they almost always loosen over time. The source of the problem is a combination of vibration and heat.

What would cause a house to vibrate? Just about everything that moves—including nearby cars, trains, airplanes and even our own feet. Such relentless vibration eventually causes twist connectors and screw terminals to loosen their grip on the wires they hold in place.

Once a connection loosens—even slightly—resistance to current flow increases. With resistance comes heat. Each time current passes through a loose connection, the wires and connector heat up, causing them to expand. When the current is stopped, they cool and contract. This repeated expansion and contraction further loosens connections, causing more heat, which eventually trips a circuit breaker or causes wires to back out of their connectors entirely.

**1** Begin by shutting off power at the service panel main switch. Then, remove the screws that secure the service panel cover.

**2** With the screws removed, lift off the service panel cover to reveal the circuit breakers, bus bars and circuit wiring.

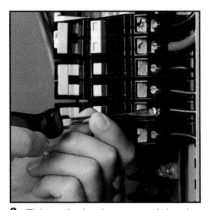

**3** Tighten the hot lugs on each breaker with a sturdy screwdriver. Tighten the lugs until snug, but avoid excessive torque.

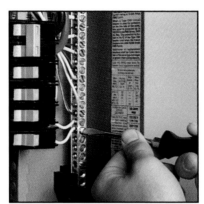

**4** Follow by tightening each lug holding a wire on the neutral bus and the grounding bus, if the service panel has one.

## Loose Service Panel Lugs

We all have a healthy respect for the power inside service panels, and rightly so. But with care, you can work within a panel safely. The task at hand is to tighten any loose screws that hold the circuit wires.

Start by shutting off all power to the circuit breakers and their circuits by switching off the main disconnect switch. Then, loosen the screws for the panel cover and pull off the cover (Figs. 1 and 2). This will reveal all the wire terminals, both on the breakers and the neutral bus bar. (Some panels will have a separate grounding bus as well.) Even with the power off, you'll need to exercise some care, as the service conductors leading to the main disconnect and neutral bus will remain hot— make sure that your screwdriver touches only the screw to be tightened.

Tighten each terminal screw that binds a wire or set of wires within the panel (Figs. 3 and 4). First do all the breaker terminals, then all the neutral bus terminals, then all grounding bus terminals if you have a dedicated grounding bus. As it's possible to overtighten these terminals, don't be tempted to torque the screwdriver with a wrench. Simply tighten each screw until it's snug, and leave it at that. With all lugs tightened, replace the panel cover and move onto the next trouble spot.

**5** To service a flickering light fixture, start by removing the fixture's globe or diffuser to access the fixture base screws.

**6** Loosen the screws that secure the fixture base to the ceiling box. Then, carefully pull the fixture down from the ceiling.

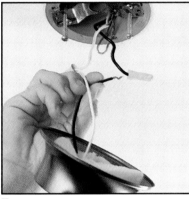

**7** Check each connection. If a wire is loose, the connection may separate completely when the wires are disturbed.

**8** Twist stranded fixture wire around the solid circuit wire and thread the twist connector back over them.

## Flickering Lights

When a ceiling light flickers with the slightest vibration, expect a loose wire connection to be the problem. The most likely spot to look is in the ceiling box. First, shut off the power to the circuit at the breaker, then simply undo the fixture globe or diffuser, drop the base down and pull the wires from the box (Figs. 5 and 6).

A bad connection may be obvious, as when a wire falls out of its twist connector with the slightest disturbance. If this is the case, undo the twist connector, twist the wires back together and tighten the connector back over them (Figs. 7 and 8). When joining a stranded fixture lead wire to a solid circuit wire, carefully wrap the stranded wire around the end of the solid wire before twisting the connector over them.

If none of the wires is obviously loose, remove each connector, twist the wires together and replace the connector. If you find that the stranded wire in one or more connectors is frayed, cut off the affected section and strip about ⅝ in. of insulation from the new end. Then, twist the wires together and install the connector.

If you don't solve the problem at the ceiling box, expect a loose connection in the switch box, usually on the neutral side of the circuit. If redoing the switch-box twist connectors doesn't help, it may be time for a new switch.

## Replacing Defective Switches

Switches do wear out, often displaying a variety of symptoms. In some cases, the switch simply will remain either on or off, no matter which way you flip the toggle. A more likely scenario has the switch behaving erratically before it fails completely. It may work only when used slowly, or when pressure is applied at an angle, or with any number of other special touches. Regardless of you how you get it to work, an inconsistent switch is on its last legs and needs to be replaced.

Replacing a switch is a simple operation, requiring little or no knowledge of electricity. With the circuit power off, remove the cover plate and yoke screws and pull the switch from the box (Figs. 9 and 10). No matter what wiring configuration is in place, you'll find that only the hot wires will be switched. The white neutral wires will be joined with a twist connector and do not need to be disturbed.

Cut the wires near the switch and strip about ½ in. of insulation from the ends of each (Figs. 11 and 12). Then insert one wire in each round hole at the back of the switch (Fig. 13). Finally, mount the switch in the box and replace the cover plate.

The only variance from this procedure will be if the defective switch is a 3-way or 4-way switch that allows the light to be controlled from more than one location.

Here, three or four wires will need to be transferred to the appropriate terminals on the new switch. Be sure to transfer only one wire at a time to prevent mixing them up.

### Replacing a Defective Receptacle

When a receptacle fails, it may affect only that outlet, or it may discontinue power to the several outlets following it on that circuit. The difference is in how the receptacle is wired. In years past, it was common to fasten incoming and outgoing wires directly to the receptacle, thereby making the entire circuit dependent on each receptacle. If one receptacle failed, the circuit to the others was broken.

Today, most codes require a continuous circuit, with pigtail connectors joining each individual receptacle to the circuit. In this way, the circuit will remain intact, even when one of the receptacles fails.

Replacing a receptacle is also a quick and easy task, but if several outlets are dead, you'll need first to determine which receptacle is the culprit. The simplest approach is to shut off the power to the circuit, remove the cover plates of the first and last boxes in the series of dead outlets and inspect the wiring. One box will contain incoming and outgoing wires (two whites, two

blacks and two grounds), the other will have only incoming wires (a single black, white and ground). The problem will lie in the box having both incoming and outgoing wires.

With the problem outlet identified, pull it from the box and cut the incoming and outgoing black, white and bare ground wires from the defective receptacle (Figs. 14 and 15). Then, strip $\frac{5}{8}$ in. of insulation from each wire and use a twist connector to join all like-colored wires with an insulated pigtail of the same color (Fig. 16).

Next, fasten the white pigtail to the silver terminal on the receptacle, the black wire to the copper terminal, and the ground wire to the green grounding screw (Fig. 17). Mount the receptacle in the box and replace the cover plate.

### Restoring an Interrupted System Ground

Most electrical codes require a home's electrical system to be grounded through the copper or galvanized-iron water supply pipes that lead from the water main to your faucets. This is done by clamping the ground wire from the panel to a pipe. A problem can arise, however, when a homeowner unknowingly disrupts this continuous ground by splicing a length of plastic pipe into the water system.

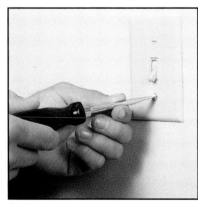

**9** To replace a switch, begin by removing the switch's cover plate. This will reveal the yoke screws that hold it to the box.

**10** Remove the switch's yoke screws and pull the switch out from its box to gain access to the fixture wires.

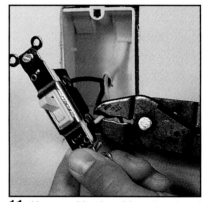

**11** Use a multitool or side cutters to cut the wires. To replace 3-way switches, transfer one wire at a time to the new switch.

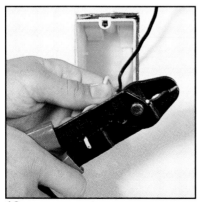

**12** Strip roughly ½ in. of insulation from the ends of each switch loop wire. A wire-stripping tool best handles the job.

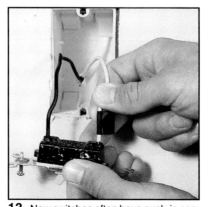

**13** New switches often have push-in connectors as well as screw terminals. Simply push each wire into its respective hole.

**14** Remove a defective receptacle just as you would a switch. Take off the cover plate and remove the switch yoke screws.

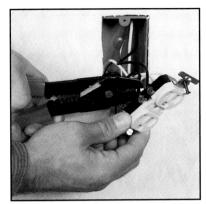

**15** Cut the incoming and outgoing black, white and bare ground wires from the defective receptacle.

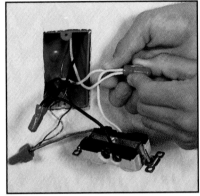

**16** Join like-colored wires to an insulated pigtail. Attach white pigtail to silver screw, black to brass, and ground to green screw.

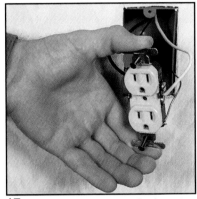

**17** End-of-the-run receptacles have two circuit wires attached (plus ground). Fasten wires directly in old or new installations.

Though not allowed by code in many areas, plastic water piping has enormous appeal to those uncomfortable with traditional piping materials and methods. If a part of your home's water supply piping has been replaced with plastic, you can still have the protection provided by a proper and legal ground.

To reestablish the ground, simply fasten approved grounding clamps to the metal piping on each side of the plastic splice (Fig. 18). Then span the gap with a short length of No.4 solid ground wire. Bind the wire tightly in the clamps and the job is complete (Fig. 19).

**18** To reestablish an interrupted ground, secure an approved clamp to the metallic pipe on each side of the plastic pipe.

**19** Connect the two grounding clamps with a length of No.4 ground wire. Tighten the fastening screws securely.

# Plumbing system maintenance

Unlike your car, VCR, home computer and countless other high-tech components of modern living, the plumbing system that services your home runs on technology that's much the same today as it was in your grandfather's day. The materials and fixtures may be new, but the idea is the same. Keeping the system in shape requires little more than a few basic skills with a wrench and screwdriver and the resources of your local hardware store.

Most residential plumbing systems hold up remarkably well, given the amount of work they do. Even so, some maintenance is occasionally required.

The good news is that maintenance is always cheaper than replacement and repair. This is especially true of plumbing, where faucet washers cost only a few pennies and toilet repairs a few dollars. A little attention now will save you plenty down the road.

Text and photos for *Plumbing System Maintenance* by Merle Henkenius. The toilet flapper valve replacement kit shown was made by Fluidmaster. The new toilet valve shown is the Fluidmaster 400 that costs about $8.

**1** To change the temperature setting on an electric heater, first remove the panel covers to access the thermostats.

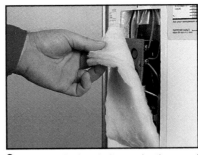

**2** Remove the insulation under the panel cover. Be sure to replace it so thermostat reads tank temperature accurately.

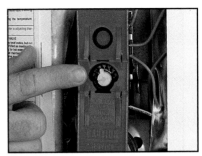

**3** The thermostats on an electric heater have temperature indicators and adjustment knobs with screwdriver slots.

**4** To remove a spent magnesium anode rod, first use a 1¹⁄₁₆-in. socket wrench to loosen the anode rod nut.

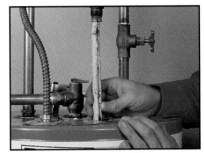

**5** Lift the old anode rod from the heater, then slide in the new rod. Apply a light coating of joint compound to the threads.

## Extending the Life of a Water Heater

With two exceptions, functioning water heaters are best left alone. The first exception will cost nothing and save you plenty. It's simply this: Turn the thermostat down to 130°F or less. A heater that runs hotter, say 150° to 160°F, puts unnecessary stress on the tank and costs more to operate.

Use a cooking thermometer to test the temperature at your faucets and adjust the heater thermostat accordingly. With a gas heater, simply turn the temperature control knob. With an electric heater, remove the electrical access panels to reach both thermostats (Fig. 1). Be absolutely certain that the fiberglass insulation is returned to its position over the thermostat before you replace the panel cover so ambient room temperature won't affect heater operation (Fig. 2). After resetting the thermostat (Fig. 3), wait several hours before testing the temperature again.

The second exception involves your heater's built-in rust protector. Every heater (except the very latest nonmetallic models) contains a sacrificial magnesium anode in the form of a rod suspended from the top of the tank. It operates on the principle that all metals corrode at different rates. Here, magnesium corrodes faster than iron. As the magnesium breaks down, it sheds electrons which migrate to the pinhole flaws in the tank's glass lining. In such an electron-rich environment, the iron tank will not corrode. When the anode is spent, in four to five years, the tank begins to rust.

This is why standard, single-anode heaters come with 5-year warranties and why 10-year-warranty heaters often have two anodes, or a larger, single anode. If you replace the anode rod (about $30) before the tank starts leaking, you could coax another five years out of the heater.

In many cases, the anode nut is visible at the top of the heater. In others, the top of the anode appears as a 2-in. silver-colored nipple at the hot-side piping connection. Here, you'll need to disconnect the hot-water outlet pipe to back the anode from the outlet opening.

Assuming that there is a visible, top-side nut, shut off the water and power and drain about 2 gallons of water from the heater. Then, use a socket wrench to back the rod out of the tank (Fig. 4). If the rod nut is stuck, heat the tank fitting slightly. When the rod spins freely, lift it out and slide the new one into place (Fig. 5). Use only a light coating of pipe-joint compound on its threads—the threads must make metal-to-metal contact with the tank for the anode rod to be effective.

**6** Shut off the water at the stop and loosen the supply tube's compression nut before lifting the toilet from the floor.

**7** Use a screwdriver to pry up the decorative caps that cover the closet bolts on each side of the toilet base.

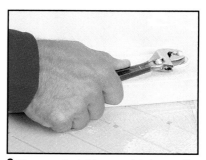

**8** Use an adjustable wrench to loosen the closet bolt nuts. Then, lay down newspaper to rest the toilet on after it's removed.

**9** Lift the toilet by grasping the bowl only. Holding the tank can damage the seal between the bowl and the tank.

**10** Use a putty knife to thoroughly scrape the old wax from the flange. Also check and remove wax from the toilet base.

**11** New closet bolts make reinstalling the toilet easier. Slide the bolts into the flange slots and press a new wax over the flange.

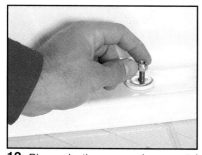

**12** Place plastic cap washers, metal washers, and chrome nuts on the bolts. Then tighten and saw off excess bolt thread.

**13** Reconnect the water supply tube by inserting it into the stop and tightening the compression nut.

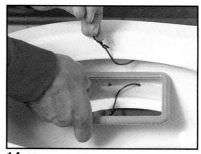

**14** Use a coat hanger and hand mirror to clear bowl rim holes. Then flush and check for a good water flow down the sides of bowl.

## Resetting a Toilet

When water appears on the floor around the base of a toilet, it means the wax bowl gasket has lost its seal. While the leak may seem sporadic and small, don't put off replacing the gasket. Water that seeps between the subfloor layers can cause rot and major damage.

The only parts you'll need will be a bowl wax and a set of closet bolts (about $4). Start by shutting off the water at the supply stop or at the water meter. Then, flush the toilet and sponge all water from the tank. Next, dip all remaining water from the bowl with a paper cup.

With the toilet empty, loosen the compression nut on the supply tube (Fig. 6). Then, pry up the plastic caps that cover the closet bolts at the base of the toilet (Fig. 7) and remove the nuts and washers from each bolt (Fig. 8). The toilet is now ready to lift from the floor.

Place newspaper on the floor next to the toilet. Then, grasping both sides of the bowl (not the tank), lift straight up and set the toilet on the newspaper (Fig. 9). Use a putty knife to scrape the old wax from the piping flange (Fig. 10). If you see only a little wax on the flange, tip the toilet on its side and scrape the remaining wax from the toilet outlet horn.

You'll also need to replace the old closet bolts, as getting the nuts started on them once they've been used can be a chore. With the old wax and bolts discarded, insert new closet bolts into the flange slots and press a new wax onto the flange (Fig. 11). For added leak protection, you can use a bowl wax with a built-in plastic sleeve. If the drainage line is larger than 3 in., however, stay with the standard wax, as the sleeve type can dislodge when set on 4-in. flanges.

With the wax and bolts in place, carefully lift the toilet to a position directly over the flange. Then, using the bolts as guides, set the toilet onto the new bowl wax. Make sure that the toilet tank is parallel to the wall, and press down firmly on the bowl to seat the wax. Place the washers and nuts on each closet bolt and tighten them, then reconnect the supply tube (Figs. 12 and 13).

Keep in mind, as you tighten the closet bolt nuts, that the toilet is made of vitrified clay. If you overdo it, you may break the bowl. Use a small wrench and tighten each side until it feels snug. Then, put your full weight on the bowl several times and take up the slack with a turn or so. If you are still unsure, use the toilet for a week and then tighten each nut again. Finally, cut off the tops of the bolts with a small hacksaw and snap the caps in place.

## Routine Toilet Repairs

Besides being a nuisance, a toilet that doesn't work properly wastes water. When water bleeds past fill valves and flush valves in a relentless trickle, it deposits calcified minerals on the bowl and in the rim holes. All this leads to a toilet that can't be kept clean.

If you've noticed that you have to clean your toilet more often lately, expect calcified minerals to be the problem. A calcite accumulation reveals some fairly obvious symptoms once you know where to look.

Check the water streaming from under the bowl rim with each flush. This water should scour the sides of the bowl in a rigorous, diagonal pattern. If, instead, it slips lazily down the sides, calcification has partially clogged many of the rim holes.

To remedy this problem, use a coat hanger to ream the hardened minerals from the openings. Simply poke the hanger into each hole repeatedly until the calcite breaks up and falls away (Fig. 14). This done, it's time to move onto the source of the problem and check the fill and flush valves.

## Replacing a Flush Valve Flapper

A defective flush valve seal is indicated when the toilet comes on by itself, runs for a few seconds, and then shuts off again. In most cases, the toilet will do this all day in half-hour increments. What is really happening is this: Water leaks slowly through the flush valve and into the bowl. As the water level in the tank recedes, the fill valve opens, adding water until the proper level is restored.

Usually, simply replacing the flapper or tank ball (about $3) will solve the problem. Just shut off the water, disconnect the old flapper or ball from the flush valve and snap a new one in its place (Fig. 15). Then, attach the chain to the flush lever so that the chain has only about ½ in. of slack in it (Fig. 16).

If this does not correct the problem, expect that mineral deposits have made the flush valve seat rough, preventing a good seal. In that case, remove the flapper or ball and sand the valve surface until it feels smooth. Then replace the flapper.

If this still does not solve the problem, the flush valve is simply too pitted and rough to hold water. Until recently, this meant separating the tank from the bowl and replacing the entire flush valve assembly.

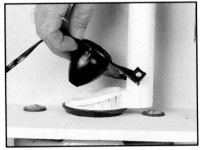

**15** If a bad seal causes tank water to leak into the bowl, replace flapper valve with new valve attached to flush-valve pegs.

**16** Finish installing new flapper valve by attaching the valve chain to the flush lever, leaving about ½ in. of slack.

**17** If flush valve seat is severely pitted, install flush valve kit with new seat. First, press epoxy onto worn flush valve seat.

**18** Press the new seat and flapper onto the epoxy putty, connect the chain and wait at least 15 minutes for epoxy to set.

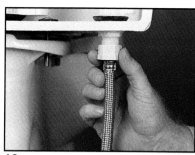

**19** To replace a fill valve (ballcock), first remove all water from tank. Then, disconnect the fill valve supply tube nut.

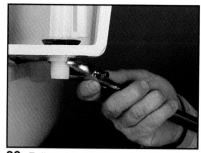

**20** Follow by undoing the fill valve's jamb nut with an adjustable wrench to free the fill valve from the bottom of the tank.

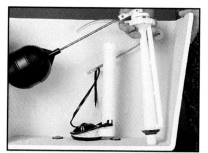

**21** Finally, remove the old fill valve by disconnecting the fill tube and lifting the old assembly up and out of the tank.

**22** Coat new fill valve's washer with pipe-joint compound to form a good seal with tank and insert through tank opening.

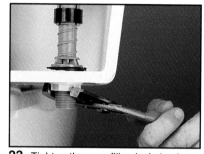

**23** Tighten the new fill valve's jamb nut to lock the valve in place. If the jamb nut is round, use pliers to tighten it.

**24** Feed the plastic fill-tube hose into the overflow tube and reconnect the tank water supply tube. Then, turn on the water.

As this is a real chore, you might consider a retrofit kit. Most cost about $8. One kit has a flapper-type seal attached to its own stainless-steel seat. You'll simply remove the old flapper and bond the new seat kit to the old flush valve with an extra-sticky epoxy putty provided in the kit (Figs. 17 and 18). After connecting the chain, wait about 15 to 30 minutes and then turn the water back on.

### Replacing a Fill Valve

A defective fill valve, or ballcock, is indicated when the toilet won't shut off completely. When this happens, a steady trickle of water hisses through the valve on a more or less continuous basis. While some fill valves are easily repaired, it's often difficult to find the parts. In many cases, it's just as easy to replace the entire valve.

To remove the old valve, you'll need to shut off the water and drain the tank completely, sponging the final few cups from the bottom of the tank. This done, loosen the supply tube nut from the shank of the valve (Fig. 19). Then, using an adjustable wrench or pliers, remove the jamb nut that secures the valve in the tank opening (Fig. 20). This will allow you to lift the old valve up and out of the tank (Fig. 21).

Before inserting the new valve into the opening, coat its rubber gasket with pipe-joint compound or, lacking that, liquid dish detergent (Fig. 22). Then insert the shank of the new valve into the tank opening and tighten the jamb nut until it feels snug (Fig. 23). Next, reconnect and tighten the supply tube nut.

Finally, attach the plastic fill-tube hose to the overflow tube of the flush valve (Fig. 24) and turn the water

**25** To clear a clogged shower head of mineral deposits, unthread the shower head from the arm with an adjustable wrench.

**26** Soak the shower head in hot vinegar for 15 minutes to soften the deposits. Then use a paper clip to clear the openings.

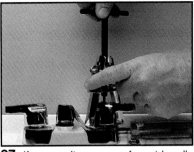

**27** If you can't remove a faucet handle by gentle prying with a screwdriver, use a handle puller to free the stuck handle.

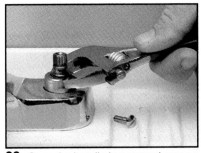

**28** Once the handle is removed, use an adjustable wrench to loosen the bonnet nut that secures the valve stem.

**29** To replace a worn compression washer, undo washer screw, slide off old washer and install a new one of the same type.

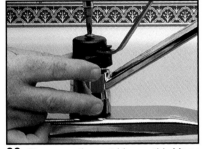

**30** To access the cartridge on this Moen faucet, take off the hood, remove the handle screw and tip handle back to free it.

**31** Once handle is off, use a pair of adjustable pliers to loosen the nut that conceals the valve cartridge.

**32** To free the valve cartridge from its housing on this single-faucet unit, pull the small, U-shaped brass key from its slot.

**33** Simply lift out the old cartridge and install a compatible replacement. Lock the new cartridge in place with the brass key.

back on. As the tank fills, adjust the float so that the valve shuts off with the water roughly 1 in. below the top of the overflow tube.

## Cleaning Fixtures

If your water is even slightly hard, you can expect some precipitation of minerals to form on your faucets and shower heads. If left unchecked, your shower heads can actually become completely blocked.

When components such as showerheads, faucet handles and aerators can be removed, your most effective approach will be to soak them for 15 minutes in a bowl of hot vinegar. Most of the accumulation will fall off in the solution, and the remainder can be scraped away with a knife or fingernail (Figs. 25 and 26).

## Basic Faucet Repair

Faucet repair is one area where prompt attention really pays off. While a dripping faucet will cost little to repair in the beginning, no amount of repair will help if you wait too long.

The problem is that once water leaks past a rubber O-ring or washer, it begins to cut a channel across the brass half of the seal. When this happens, you may need to replace the entire faucet. Moreover, a dripping faucet can cost you hundreds of gallons of water each year.

The type of repair needed will depend on which type and brand of faucet you have. There are two basic types, both with a myriad of design variations. Yours will be either a compression faucet, with a brass stem and rubber washer, or a cartridge-type faucet with either a single or double control.

**34** To remove the spout when replacing O-rings, lift up firmly and twist the spout to release it from the faucet.

**35** With new, appropriate O-rings on hand, use a sharp utility knife to cut the old O-rings from the faucet riser column.

**36** Grease the new O-rings and roll them over the column until they seat themselves. Then, reassemble the faucet.

**Compression Faucet Repair:** With the traditional compression faucet, start by shutting off the water at the nearest valve and removing the index cap from the handle, if it has one. Then, remove the handle screws and use a screwdriver to pry carefully under the handles to remove them.

If the handles won't budge, don't force them. Instead, use an inexpensive handle puller from any hardware store (about $5). Insert the stem of the puller into the screwhole of the handle and slip the side grips of the puller under the handle. Then, thread the stem down until the handle breaks free (Fig. 27).

With the handle removed, use an adjustable wrench to loosen the bonnet nut that holds the stem in place (Fig. 28). Thread the stem out of the faucet and loosen the screw that holds the washer to the stem (Fig. 29). Find an exact replacement washer and fasten it to the stem using a new washer screw, if necessary. Coat the new washer with heat-proof faucet grease to prolong its life, and then tighten the stem back in place. Finally, replace the handle and move on to the other stem in the faucet.

**Cartridge Faucet Repair:** Cartridge-type faucets are the easiest to repair because you replace the entire cartridge without bothering with the minor components. With a 2-handle cartridge faucet, access the cartridge just as you would a compression faucet stem—start at the index cap and work your way down.

**Single-Handle Faucet Repair:** With a single-handle faucet, such as the Moen Chateau kitchen model shown in the photos, start by removing the handle. On the Moen faucet, the handle screw is concealed under a plastic hood. With other designs, you'll find a recessed handle screw on the front underside of the faucet handle.

In the case of the Moen faucet, simply lift the plastic hood from the handle to reach the handle screw. Loosen the screw and tip the handle back and then off (Fig. 30). Beneath the handle, you'll find a bonnet nut that simply threads off. Remove this nut to reveal the top of the valve cartridge (Fig. 31).

Looking closely, you'll find that the cartridge is locked in place by a U-shaped brass key. To remove the valve cartridge, pull this key out and then lift the cartridge out of the faucet body (Figs. 32 and 33).

Moen offers two replacement cartridges, one brass and the other plastic. The brass unit is sturdier, but is not meant for every situation. If you have hard water, for example, a brass cartridge will become stiff in operation within a few years. A plastic cartridge, by contrast, will remain smooth in operation for much longer and will cost several dollars less (about $12 to $14) than the brass unit.

In any case, insert the new valve cartridge and secure it with the retaining key. Then replace the bonnet nut, handle and hood.

### Fixing Spout Leaks

When a kitchen faucet spout leaks around its collar every time the water is turned on, you know it's time for a new set of spout-collar O-rings. As the handle assembly must be removed to reach the seals, it's best to make this repair when you replace the cartridge.

With the handle assembly removed, grasp the spout and pull straight up until it comes free (Fig. 34). With an exact, model-specific O-ring replacement kit on hand, use a knife to cut the old O-rings from the faucet column (Fig. 35). Then, grease the new O-rings with heat-proof grease or the small packet of food-grade grease that often comes with the kit, and roll the new rings into their slots (Fig. 36). Finally, slide the spout collar back over the O-rings until it seats properly.

Other faucet brands will have slightly different design features, but most are accessed in ways similar to the Moen. While it's possible to install new O-rings on some cartridges, and save a few dollars, this doesn't always work as it should. Often a plastic cartridge becomes warped slightly and imperceptibly, so that the new O-rings work no better than the old.

In most cases, it's better to discard the old cartridge completely and opt for a new replacement. That done, you can expect years of service from your existing faucet.

# Basic appliance maintenance

Routine maintenance of household appliances will pay for itself in improved efficiency, longer life and improved appearance. The same sort of diligence most of us give our automobile maintenance schedules should be extended to our appliances. While it's true that a refrigerator costs far less than a new car, taken in total, appliances are no small investment. Just keeping them clean, inside and out, can make a world of difference.

## Servicing Refrigerators

Like air conditioners, refrigerators move a lot of air across their condenser coils. With this air comes dust, pet hair and lint that clings to the coils, reducing their ability to dissipate heat. When this happens, the compressor runs longer and cools less. This makes for an inefficient appliance and higher electric bills.

Cleaning these coils twice a year makes a big difference and will take only minutes to complete. As for gaining access, the condenser coils are behind the grille below the door.

The location of the evaporator plate (or evaporator coil) will vary. On older models, the evaporator coil is next to the compressor motor at the back of the appliance behind an access panel. Newer models usually

Text and photos for *Basic Appliance Maintenance* by Merle Henkenius.

**1** The grille is held to the refrigerator with clips. Snap out the grille to access the condenser coil.

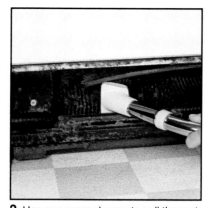

**2** Use a vacuum cleaner to pull the matted dust from the coil. If necessary, clean the tubes with degreaser.

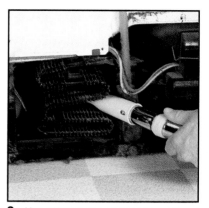

**3** Also vacuum the evaporator coil and compressor. Often these are at the back of the refrigerator.

**4** To inspect the burners and pilot light on a gas-fired range, lift its top and prop it up with a rod.

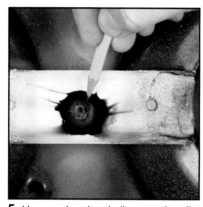

**5** Here, carbon has built up on the pilot flame shield to nearly ¼ in. deep. This restricts airflow to the flame.

**6** Clean soot and carbon from the pilot orifice using a safety pin. Work gently to avoid damaging the orifice.

have an exposed coil in the form of a large metal grid on the refrigerator's back.

Begin by lifting the grille from its place below the front door (Fig. 1). The coil probably will be loaded with clusters of greasy fuzz. Use a vacuum cleaner to pull the dust from the coil (Fig. 2). If the coil feels very greasy, use a spray bottle and some degreasing cleaner to rinse the fin tubes.

Next, pull out the refrigerator so you can work on the compressor compartment. Remove the access panel and vacuum the compressor and evaporator coil (Fig. 3). Finally, replace the grille and access panel and move the refrigerator back.

### Servicing Kitchen Ranges

Of the two types of kitchen ranges, gas-fired models require more maintenance than electric models. The reason is that gas is flamed from the burners, which can become clogged. Electric ranges come with direct electrical connections, which remain more or less intact.

Probably the most familiar sources of trouble are rangetop pilot flames. There are two problems. First, the pilot orifice may become clogged with carbon grit. Second, the flame shield under the cooktop can accu-

mulate carbon and soot, reducing the flame space between the orifice and the shield.

In either case, tip up the cooktop, and check for carbon buildup (Figs. 4 and 5). If you find buildup on the shield, remove the cooktop completely and scrape off the carbon with a knife. Then, for good measure, use a safety pin or thin wire to clean the pilot flame orifice (Fig. 6). Do this to both sides of the top before lighting the pilots. If the pilot flames seem too tall or too short, follow the pilot feed lines back to the mixing valve at the control panel and adjust the flames using the slotted adjustment screw.

While you've got the cooktop tilted up or removed, check the flame at each burner. If several openings in a burner appear to be clogged, clear them with the same pin or wire (Figs. 7 and 8). Then clean the area under the burners and replace the top. A similar approach can be used to correct a temperamental pilot near the oven burner.

As for electric ranges, the only maintenance you need to do amounts to keeping the various surfaces clean. This is often easier than it looks. Usually heating elements can be lifted out for easy access, as can the reflecting pans beneath the element (Fig. 9).

Another appliance associated with kitchen ranges is the vented range hood. The problem here is often a clogged filter. Remove the filter once a month and run hot water through it to rinse out the dust and grease that collect (Figs. 10 and 11).

## Servicing Dishwashers

Usually all you need to do to keep a dishwasher in good working order is to keep its door gasket and spray arms clean. You also should periodically clean any debris from under the heating element.

While the door gasket may appear clean where it is plainly visible, there's a good chance its bottom section is covered with slimy dirt, which can cause the door to leak. Hold a hand mirror to the bottom of the door to reveal any accumulation of dirt (Fig. 12).

Use a strong, nonabrasive household cleaner to remove the dirt from the gasket and door panel. You also can lift the water-level float from the base of the cabinet to check for dirt. If the float gets too dirty, it can stick in place, throwing the water level out of whack (Fig. 13).

While you're at it, check the openings in the spray arms for small shreds of plastic (Fig. 14). Remove these shreds with a pair of tweezers.

Finally, make sure some water remains in the base of the dishwasher. If you seldom use your dishwasher, add water periodically. If left to dry out, the pump seals may leak when the dishwasher is used.

## Servicing Washers and Dryers

The best things you can do for your clothes washer and dryer are to keep them level and clean. If they are out of level, their moving parts will wear unevenly and excessively. Service technicians can tell you that most of the laundry appliances they encounter are completely out of level. In some cases, "self-leveling" legs compound the problem because they don't always level the appliance. Instead, they're simply used to close the gap between the appliance and the floor.

To align an appliance properly, place a small level on the top frame of the unit to determine where the problem is (Fig. 15). Then, thread the legs up or down accordingly or, in the case of self-leveling legs, lift the low side of the appliance until that leg extends to the proper height.

To keep the finish on these appliances looking good, wash them regularly with a mild detergent (Fig. 16).

Some components, such as the fabric-softener reservoir on a washing machine, can be removed for better cleaning. The reservoir is often held in place by a friction ring. Just lift this and the reservoir will detach from the agitator (Figs. 17 and 18).

**7** Gas burners are not held in place with fasteners. Lift them out to inspect and clean them.

**8** Gently clean soot from the burner openings using a safety pin. Work around the burner's circumference.

**9** After removing the heating elements, lift out and clean the reflecting pan and the surface below the pan.

**10** Once a month, clean the underside of the range hood and remove the filter so it can be washed out.

**11** Rinse dust and grease out of the hood filter using hot water. Let the filter dry before reinstalling it.

**12** Use a hand mirror to check for a slimy accumulation along the bottom door gasket on a dishwasher.

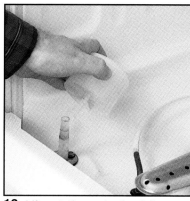

**13** Lift out the water-level float and clean the tube the float rides on. Dirt can cause the float to malfunction.

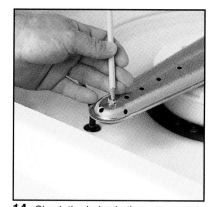

**14** Check the holes in the spray arm to be sure none are clogged. Here, a small piece of shredded plastic blocks a hole.

**15** Washers and dryers work best, and last longer, when level. Check the machine side to side and front to back.

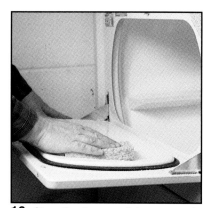

**16** Clean the drums and doors on washers and dryers to remove dyes that leach from new clothing.

**17** To release a soiled and sticky fabric-softener reservoir, lift up on the friction ring (in blue).

**18** The reservoir should lift free of the agitator shaft. Clean the reservoir in the sink using warm water.

Finally, you should fasten the washer discharge hose to the plumbing standpipe. A washer discharge pump is capable of moving 50 to 60 gallons of water per minute. That much pressure has a tendency to lift the discharge hose right out of its plumbing pipe. There are several devices made for this problem, including a friction-fit gasket (Fig. 19).

Use wire or duct tape to secure the hose. A loose discharge hose can do hundreds of dollars of damage.

Because dryers produce so much lint, you'll need to pay particular attention to the lint trap and the dryer vent tube. Remove and clean the lint trap with each load (Fig. 20). Failing to clean the lint trap regularly can cause the dryer to overheat and could start a fire. A clogged lint trap makes the dryer operate inefficiently.

Check the vent tube twice a year, especially if your dryer vents upward, as do most dryers located in basements. Pull out the dryer to get behind it. Then pull the vent from the dryer connection. This will allow you to shake any lint and debris accumulation from the tube (Fig. 21).

**19** Install a rubber friction fitting to fasten the washer discharge hose firmly inside the plumbing standpipe.

**20** Clean the lint from your dryer's lint trap after every load to prevent overheating and the danger of a lint fire.

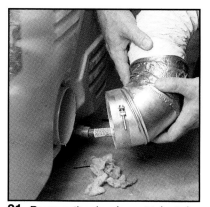

**21** Remove the dryer's vent tube twice a year and shake or vacuum out the accumulated lint and debris inside it.

# Ceramic tile maintenance

Ceramic tile is an attractive and durable material that is especially popular above bathtubs and inside showers. It's so popular, that alternative surface materials are often offered in styles that imitate the classic look of the real thing. Tile isn't maintenance-free, however. When problems arise, you'll have two simple choices. You can fix them right away, for a few dollars, or you can fix them later, for hundreds more. Once water penetrates the tile grout, wall damage can be extensive. Luckily, tile maintenance is easy and inexpensive, and requires only basic household tools.

## Tile Problems

Tile problems usually begin with damaged grout joints, and for one of two reasons. In today's housing market, installers need to move through a job quickly. The problem is that tile work resists speed with two obstacles. The first is that tile mastic cures too slowly; the second is that tile grout cures too quickly.

The mastic used to glue tile to walls will set in a day, but takes days longer to cure. If the spaces between tiles are grouted too soon, the gases that must escape as the mastic cures create pinholes in the grout that allow water to penetrate behind the tile.

As for curing the grout, the best approach is a wet cure, where the normal drying rate is prolonged. When cured properly, the grout becomes hard and water resistant. If allowed to dry too quickly, the grout will have a soft, chalky surface that absorbs water. As water is

Text and photos for *Ceramic Tile Maintenance* by Merle Henkenius.

absorbed, the grout swells, fractures and falls away. In either case, water reaches the drywall behind the tiles and destroys it.

## Assessing the Damage

How do you know when your ceramic tiles need help? To begin, look for discoloration in the grout. Dark spots in grout suggest that water is penetrating it, either because of pinhole openings or because the grout is loose.

As water penetrates these gaps, mold grows in them, holding more water and further weakening the grout in those areas. Where water mineral levels are high, the dark spots will be surrounded by lighter, yellow-orange discolorations. Of course, if small strips of grout have already fallen out, you'll have little time to waste. You also should examine the caulked seams in the corners and where tiles meet the tub. When you find spots of dark discoloration or cracks, a repair is in order.

## Preparing the Tile

The first step in bringing tiled walls up to standards is to remove any loose or degraded grout. Grout removal tools are available, but a simple carpet knife will do the job just fine. Force the blade into the problem area and dig out the grout a few inches on either side of the discoloration (Fig. 1). If grout has already fallen, extend the openings to make sure no loose grout remains.

If the caulk joints around the tub and in the corners are discolored or cracked, the best approach is to remove it all with a sharp knife or razor-type scraper. Simply cut along each edge of the caulk seam. This will loosen the caulk so that you can pull it away in strips (Fig. 2).

With the damaged caulk and grout removed, clean the entire surface thoroughly so that the new grout, caulk and sealer can adhere properly. Any of the tub-and-tile cleaners on the market will work. If you prefer a home remedy, try a formulation consisting of 1/2 cup of household ammonia, 1/2 cup of white vinegar and 1/4 cup of baking soda.

Scrub the tile with the cleaning mixture and rinse it lightly with water (Fig. 3). If a few grout stains persist, scrub those areas vigorously with a toothbrush, using either your tile cleanser or diluted household bleach (Fig. 4). Do not allow bleach to come into contact with any cleanser containing ammonia. When the entire surface is scrubbed clean, let it dry and wipe away any cleanser residue with a dry cloth (Fig. 5).

**1** Use a carpet knife or grout-removal tool to clear loose grout. Remove grout a few inches to either side of the affected area.

**2** Use a razor-type scraper or sharp knife to cut away damaged caulk from around the tub. Then, clean the joints thoroughly.

**3** Use a tub-and-tile cleaner or home-made solution to remove soap scum, mildew or hard-water stains from tile.

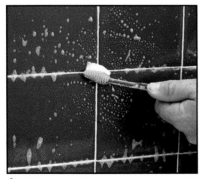

**4** Stubborn stains can be removed with a toothbrush. Use a tile cleaner or ordinary household bleach diluted with water.

**5** Rinse the cleaning solution with clean water and let the surface dry. Then, buff away the residue with a soft cloth.

**6** Mix powdered grout and a drying-retarder additive to the consistency of toothpaste. Use a clean container.

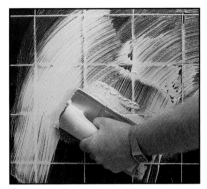

**7** Use a rubber float to apply grout. Force grout into the joints between the tiles and then squeegee away the excess.

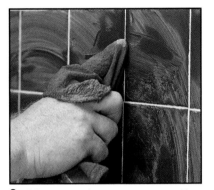

**8** Wipe away the excess grout with a damp rag. Then use the rag and your finger to smooth each joint individually.

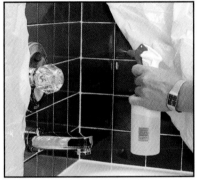

**9** To slow drying by wet curing, drape plastic sheeting over tiles and coat the tiles with a mist of water several times a day.

## Replacing Damaged Grout

Grout comes in a variety of forms, from small premixed tubes that handle patching jobs, to dry powder grout for bigger projects. While the small premixed packages have the appeal of simplicity, they are not always the best choice. Often they're difficult to match perfectly with an existing grout color, even when that color is white.

Dry grouts, on the other hand, are easy to mix in volume and can be used with an additive that retards drying. They also can be colored fairly precisely to match existing colors or to create new ones.

If you choose a dry mix, buy 1 to 3 pounds and make sure to get the drying-retarder additive as well. This is not the place to skimp on materials, and the additive will help assure a stronger grout. Begin by pouring about 2 cups of grout into a small bucket. Make sure the bucket is clean for best results. Follow by pouring a small amount of additive into the grout and mixing with a paint-stirring stick. You'll need to experiment, but the end product should have the consistency of toothpaste (Fig. 6).

Use a rubber float to spread the grout over the tiles (Fig. 7). Sweep the float in several directions to make sure the grout is forced deep into the joints. Finally, use the float as a squeegee to skim as much of the excess from the tile as possible.

Follow by wiping the remaining grout from the tile with a damp cloth, regularly rinsing the cloth with water until the surface is relatively clean. Finally, wrap the cloth around a finger and smooth the joints individually (Fig. 8). With this much done, let the grout set for 15 minutes, or until the residue on the tiles turns to a powdery white. Then buff the entire surface with a soft, dry cloth until it's completely clean.

With the use of the drying-retarder additive in the grout, the drying time will be substantially extended, so a wet cure is not absolutely necessary. Even so, the longer the drying time, the stronger the cure. If you choose to wet cure the grout, tape a sheet of plastic to the walls so it hangs over the tiles in a way that lets you reach inside easily. Then, use a spray bottle filled with water to mist the tiles several times a day for a day or two to slow down the drying process and achieve a stronger grout (Fig. 9).

## Caulk and Sealant

You'll have two types of caulk to choose from—either silicone caulk or latex tub-and-tile caulk. While the latex variety is much easier to use, it has far less elasticity than silicone. Because caulk needs to absorb the natural flexing of the floors and walls, silicone is the better choice.

Silicone caulk can be a mess when you don't know what you're doing, but is really very manageable when you do. Here are two basic guidelines: don't apply more than is absolutely needed to fill the joint, and don't apply more than you can smooth out before it gets tacky (usually no more than a 2- to 3-ft. bead).

Cut the smallest possible opening in the applicator tip and run the tip along the seam in an even, angled path while applying uniform pressure to the gun handle. Remember, apply no more caulk in the seam that is absolutely needed (Fig. 10).

To smooth the caulk, draw a finger lightly along the bead so that the caulk is arched against the opposing angles of the walls at roughly 45°. A light touch is important here—don't press so hard that some caulk is forced to the sides of your finger. Keep a bowl of warm, soapy water (water with a little dishwashing liquid) nearby. If the caulk begins to get tacky, dip your finger into the bowl regularly to keep things flowing smoothly (Fig. 11).

You'll need to apply a bead of caulk all around the tub at the joint where the tub meets the wall. In addition, caulk the two vertical corner seams and, if needed, the seam between the tub and the floor. For an important bit of added protection, you'll want to caulk the top half of the tub spout and the faucet trim plate.

The spout and trim will require a slightly different approach, as you'll want the bead to be all but invisible. Apply a thin bead in the joint between the tile and fixture pieces (Figs. 12 and 13). Then use a tissue to wipe away most of it (Fig. 14). The goal is for the remaining caulk to form a bead less than $1/16$ in. wide that just seals the gap between the trim and tile. Keep wiping until all that's left on the surrounding tile is a slight film. Buff away this film after the silicone caulk has fully dried.

When the caulk has cured (36 to 72 hours depending on the brand), seal the grout with clear silicone sealer (Fig. 15). This is an important step that takes only a few minutes. After all the seams have been sealed, wipe the entire surface with a soft cloth. For long-term protection, you may wish to apply another coat of sealer the next time you clean your tiles and periodically thereafter.

**10** Apply silicone caulk to the seam between tub and tile using even pressure and only enough caulk to fill the gap.

**11** Smooth the caulk so it blends with the surfaces. Periodically wet your finger with soapy water to keep caulk from dragging.

**12** Apply a thin bead of caulk between the tub spout and tiled wall. Then, wipe away excess with facial tissue.

**13** Sparingly apply a bead of silicone caulk around the faucet trim plate to keep water from traveling behind the wall.

**14** Use facial tissue to wipe all but a narrow bead of caulk from the trim-plate seam, so that caulk will be nearly invisible.

**15** After the silicone caulk has cured, seal each grout joint with clear silicone sealer and follow by buffing with a soft, dry cloth.

# H omeowner's tool kit

■ Moving into a new house may seem like a ticket to trouble-free living, but that's not always the case. A new home is like a new car, it sometimes take a little while to work out all the bugs. Even a high-end custom home will harbor a few blemishes and oversights that you need to straighten out. Combine these with the inevitable upgrades most of us make after moving in and you can see the usefulness of having some tools on hand.

### Claw Hammer

A good finishing hammer will last a lifetime and help you through a variety of improvement and repair projects. A hammer with a steel or fiberglass handle will be the most durable, especially when pulling nails. Get one with a curved claw and a 16-ounce head. This combination will work well on rough carpentry as well as on finish work. A quality hammer, in the $16-to-$20 range, can mean the difference between driving nails and bending them.

### Handsaw

Next on your list will be a good crosscut saw. Handsaws cost a good deal less ($10 to $16) than power saws and work just as well in limited-use situations. You'll also be able to reach into spaces too cramped for a

*Homeowner's Tool Kit* was written and illustrated by Merle Henkenius.

circular saw. A 10-point crosscut, having 10 teeth point per inch, will serve you well around the house and yard. This saw will cut clean enough for most finish work and quickly enough for most rough work. If you'll be doing mostly rough carpentry, a 6- or 8-point saw will speed your work substantially. Conversely, saws with more teeth per inch (12 and 14 are typical) cut slowly but leave a very fine edge.

### Hacksaw

There are many occasions when a hacksaw comes in handy, from cutting plumbing pipes to trimming downspouts and slicing through ceramic tile. The most important thing to look for is rigidity. A saw that flexes when used will bend or break the blade, or will simply refuse to cut straight. Most are adjustable and will accept 10- or 12-inch blades. Look for a brand that allows two different blade installations, either straight or at a 45° angle. A good hacksaw will cost between $12 and $16, and you should buy extra blades. These are often sold in packs of five for about $3.

### Tape Measure

The best advice one can give in selecting a tape measure is to avoid the short and narrow. For general household use, choose one that is at least ¾ in. wide and 16 ft. long. Beyond that, it's a matter of which style appeals to you most. Some tapes have the thumb-latch on the top, others on the front. Remember, a broken tape does not mean a ruined tape measure. Replacement tapes are available for most brands. The one shown here cost $11.

### Block Plane or Surform Tool

For trimming marginal amounts of stock from lumber and other materials, consider buying a plane or Surform tool. Because planes require exact adjustment and dull easily in untrained hands, a Surform tool is a good household alternative. This type of plane has a replaceable, slotted blade that gouges out narrow ribbons of wood, plastic, vinyl, and even aluminum without clogging. A Surform tool will not yield the clean, hard-edged surface of a block plane, but it's a snap to use  The one shown was about $12 for a 10-inch model.

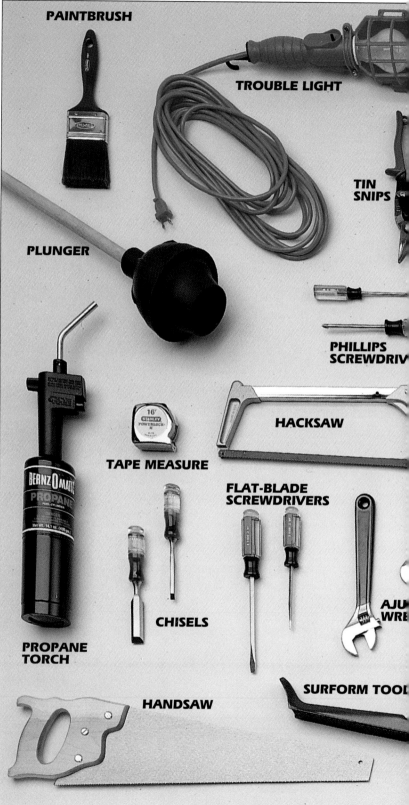

### 3/8-in. VSR Drill

Another tool that will quickly earn its keep is a ⅜-in. drill. While cordless drills are ideal for the quick fix, a cord-type drill is more versatile. It can be used for boring holes and running a wire brush or sanding wheel.

It's a powerful tool for driving all manner of screws. Because you won't be paying for a charger, you'll get more power per dollar invested. Look for one with a variable-speed reversible (VSR) motor capable of at

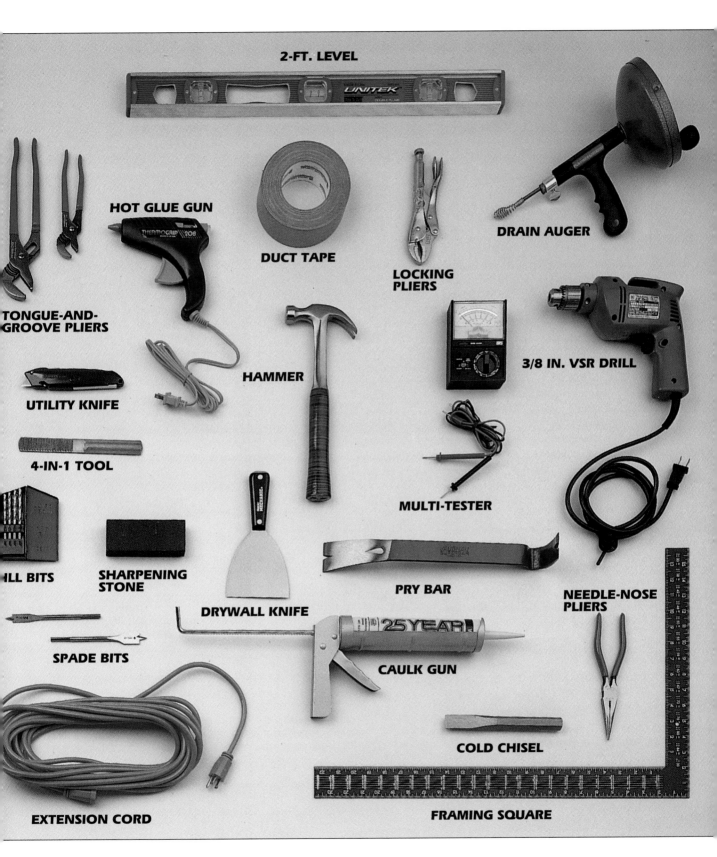

**2-FT. LEVEL**

**HOT GLUE GUN**

**DUCT TAPE**

**LOCKING PLIERS**

**DRAIN AUGER**

**TONGUE-AND-GROOVE PLIERS**

**HAMMER**

**3/8 IN. VSR DRILL**

**UTILITY KNIFE**

**4-IN-1 TOOL**

**MULTI-TESTER**

**LL BITS**

**SHARPENING STONE**

**DRYWALL KNIFE**

**PRY BAR**

**NEEDLE-NOSE PLIERS**

**SPADE BITS**

**CAULK GUN**

**COLD CHISEL**

**EXTENSION CORD**

**FRAMING SQUARE**

least 2000 rpm. The tool shown has 2.8 amps of power. It cost just under $70.

You'll also want a selection of drill bits and possibly a few specialty attachments. The one chosen here was a 13-piece high-speed steel bit set with sizes graduating from $1/16$ to $1/4$ in. Buying bits in a case makes selection easier and reveals at a glance which sizes you need to replace.

Besides the $16 bit set, choose a ½- and ¾-in. spade bit for larger holes in wood. Spade bits are reasonably priced, around $2.50 apiece, and are easily resharpened.

## Extension Cord and Trouble Light

To keep your project well powered and better lit, you'll need a grounded extension cord and a trouble light. An extension cord in the 30- to 50-foot range will serve most needs, but don't skimp on its wire size. A light-weight cord will allow too much voltage drop, which will in turn shorten the life of the tool or appliance it serves. Generally speaking, the longer the cord, the heavier it will need to be.

Shown here is a grounded 30-footer with 16-gauge wire and a carrying capacity of 13 amps, which was priced at just under $10. As for trouble lights, look for the same features. If the light you like does not have a receptacle, an ungrounded cord will do. The one shown cost just under $11, and it has a 25 ft. model with a plastic cage.

## Chisels and Sharpening Stone

Every household should have a chisel or two for rough-ing out wood that can't be reached with a larger, more precise tool. Wood chisels are handy for setting door hinges, and if they are sharp they can be extremely versatile, removing small amounts of wood in a variety of situations. Because many of us can blunt the edges of chisels just by picking them up, you'll also want a double-sided (fine/coarse) sharpening stone. When used with honing oil, a sharpening stone will return the sharp edge to all but the most abused chisels and knives.

You'll need to decide which sizes best suit your purposes, but two will often do. Shown are ¼- and ¾-in. chisels and a 2 × 5-in. combination sharpening stone. Expect to pay about $7 apiece for the chisels and $12 for the stone.

Finally, you may want a cold chisel in your toolbag for those materials not made of wood. A cold chisel can be used to chip concrete or split light-gauge metal. It's especially handy in cutting bricks, blocks and paving stones. The one shown, a hefty 1-in. model, was $6.

## Framing Square

A framing square in the hands of a pro can work wonders, but even the beginner will find this a useful tool, if only as a straightedge and angle finder. It can be used to check the squareness of a room before laying floor coverings or to ensure a square cut in plywood and dimensional lumber. You find them in steel and alumi-num for around $10.

## Caulk Gun

With everything from caulk to glue to grout to roofing tar packaged in tubes these days, a good caulk gun is a must. Expect to find two or three levels of quality in caulk guns. Cruise right past the 99-cent bargain on your way to those in the $4-to-$5 range. These mid-price guns will accommodate all 1/10-gallon tubes and are sturdy enough for years of casual use.

## Pry Bar

A pry bar is another useful tool, with more real-life uses than its manufacturer probably intended. A pry bar is designed to pry things apart, primarily pieces of wood that have been nailed together. It also provides an alternate means of removing nails, aside from your claw hammer. It has beveled nail claws at each end and has a curved shank ending in a sharp right-angle. When a block of wood is placed under one end, it makes a great lever and fulcrum. You can invest $8 or $9 in one of these.

## Knives

Everyone is familiar with the uses of a putty knife, but when headed out to buy one, consider upsizing to a 4-in. drywall knife for greater versatility. A flexible drywall knife can be used to apply spackling, scrape paint, strip furniture or press wallpaper into corners. Make sure that the model you choose has a chrome-plated blade to resist the corrosiveness of drywall compounds. Be-yond that, the choice is yours. Expect to pay about $8 for a good drywall knife.

You'll also want a sturdy utility knife for cutting open cartons, trimming wallpaper and floor coverings and a dozen other chores. Get one with a retractable blade for easier and safer storage. The better models have a cavity inside to store fresh blades. If your knife doesn't come with extra blades, pick up a pack. You'll find plenty of good utility knives in the $5-to-$7 range.

## Four-in-one Rasp/File

You also might consider a combination wood rasp and file in your toolkit. With a coarse and fine rasp and a coarse and fine file on each tool, you'll be able to shape wood and sharpen garden tools whenever the need arises, and for less than $9.

## Locking Pliers

Locking pliers first became popular in shipyards during WWII. Before long, they found their way into every mechanic's toolbox and have lately turned up in a good many kitchen drawers. This tool is popular because it can do so much. It's a makeshift wrench, a wire cutter, a pliers, and a sturdy clamp—which is about all you can ask of a tool costing $10 to $12.

## Tongue-and-groove and Needle-nose Pliers

Tongue-and-groove pliers make a good choice because the jaws are able to expand to meet the job require-ments. Their offset jaw configuration also provides a little more leverage than standard pliers. Get a 6½- and a 10-inch model. The smaller tool is good for many simple projects, while the larger version will easily handle the chrome or plastic trap nuts on plumbing fixtures. With new home construction going to almost all plastic pipes and fittings, this size makes a good substitute for a pipe wrench. Expect to pay $9 for the smaller tool and $11 for the larger one.

The 8-in. needle-nose has a long reach for getting into tight cramped spaces, which is where needle-nose models work best. This one also has a wire cutter built into the jaws. Expect a good tool to cost between $8 and $9.

## Drain Auger and Plunger
There's a perverse physical law that has drains clogging only when plumbers and drain services are hard to reach or frightfully expensive. Drain clogs like holidays best.

For those times and others, plan ahead and invest in an inexpensive drain auger. The one shown costs a mere $15 (a fraction of the typical daytime service call) and will work in most situations. Avoid the simple, bare-cable type augers, they won't give enough cranking power in problem situations.

A plunger is the other half of the drain clog solution. Most clogs can be broken free with a good plunger, almost to the complete exclusion of most drain chemicals. Look for one that has a large cup with a folding funnel. With the funnel folded in, this plunger will work well on sinks and tubs. Folded out, it's perfect for toilet clogs, and all for a mere $5.

## Hot-Glue Gun
A hot-glue gun used to be thought of as a hobby tool, but more and more of us are finding it useful around the house. It works very well in repairing small fittings on toys and other household items, especially plastics. Best of all, hot glue sets as soon as it cools, which speeds things up substantially. You'll find inexpensive versions that are fed simply by pushing the glue stick through the gun. Others feature a trigger-feed mechanism that offer better control when applying the glue. Expect to pay $17 to $19 for a trigger-fed model.

## Level
A good 2-ft. level is another tool you'll find yourself using repeatedly. It can level picture frames, start wallpaper, align appliances and provide a straightedge for a knife or pencil. You'll find them made of steel, aluminum, plastic and wood in a wide range of prices. The metal versions offer the most versatility for the money, which here was just under $14.

## Propane Torch
When making plumbing improvements, you will need a propane torch. You'll find two varieties in home centers. One will require that you light it with a striker or match. The other is self-starting. You can choose the substantially more expensive model simply because the self-starting feature is so handy. Just turn it on and pull the trigger for a clean blue flame. The price for the self-starter was just under $28.

## Tin Snips
Tin snips may seem a strange item for a household tool selection, but when you need them there's no substitute.

Try cutting in an extra heat register in an unfinished basement without them. If the need arises, choose one designed to cut along a straight line. These can be made to cut wide, sweeping curves as well. The one shown cost $17.

While you're at it, buy a roll of quality duct tape. You may never need it for ductwork, but you'll find a use for it just about everywhere else. Expect to pay $5 top $6 for a 2-in. roll 60 yd. long.

## Paintbrush
When it comes to paintbrushes, don't skimp. Cheap throw-aways have a way of finding their own revenge. A 2½-in. natural bristle or high-quality synthetic-fiber brush will do the best job and endure the most cleanings. Buy a natural bristle brush if you are working with oil based paint and stains, but buy only synthetic brushes for work with water based paints and stains. Brushes are available with tapered or straight bristles. The straight cuts work best on large areas, while the tapered versions work better as trim brushes. You may need both, but a straight-bristle brush is a good start. Expect to pay $8 for a 2½ incher.

## Adjustable Wrenches
Two adjustable wrenches are recommended for projects around the house and garage. A 6-in. wrench will work well in tightening furniture bolts, toilet bolts, appliance leveling legs and the like. A 10-in. spanner will handle many plumbing repairs and do double duty in automotive work. Adjustable wrenches are available at several price levels. Avoid the low-end import models, but the mid-price versions should service you quite well. Pay about $20 for the larger wrench and $14 for the smaller.

## Screwdrivers
Screwdrivers are typically the most abused tools in the toolbox. As such, steer clear of bargain screwdrivers. Look for handles that are large enough to be comfortable and shanks that are long enough to let you see your work. The better brands will have hardened steel tips and some may be magnetized. Two Phillips and two flat-blade screwdrivers are recommended in small and medium sizes. All four should cost about $10 to $12.

## Multi-Tester
A multi-tester is a good choice if you plan to handle your electrical problems. With it, you'll be able to test for voltage, continuity and ohm levels. It can be used in checking your home's electrical system—both wiring and devices—as well as the appliances within your home. Simple multi-testers start at around $25.

# Thickness planer users' guide

■ When you buy lumber, you take it for granted that you'll cut the pieces to length and rip them to width to suit your project. You don't expect the lumberyard to handle these chores—they are why you had a shop set up in the first place. Usually, however, you simply have to accept lumber in the few thicknesses offered and make your work conform to what's available.

Sooner or later, though, you'll want the same flexibility for handling custom thicknessing as you have with crosscutting and ripping. When that time comes, you'll want a thickness planer.

Not so long ago, thickness planers were rarely found in typical home workshops. The machines were large and expensive, designed essentially for commercial operations. Over the past several years, the picture has changed. Compact, affordable planers are now available to suit the needs of small shops and are increasingly popular with home woodworkers.

Text and photos for *Thickness Planer Users Guide* by Rosario Capotosto.

**1** Compact thickness planers are ideal for small shops and tight budgets. This model handles stock sizes up to 6x12 in.

**2** Shopsmith thickness planer features separate motors that drive the cutterhead and feed rollers so feed rate is variable.

**3** Sears planer also accepts molding knives. Open-side design permits molding the edges of a wide board.

Besides expanding the scope of your work, a planer allows you to work with rough-sawn lumber. You can access a wider range of woods, and take advantage of lower prices on species you'd normally buy as surfaced stock.

Thickness planers are designed to perform one simple operation—smooth a face of a board so it's parallel to the opposite face. Planing is accomplished by a rapidly rotating double- or triple-knife cutterhead that skims the surface of the work as it's held down against the planer table. Power-driven infeed and outfeed rollers grip and move the stock past the cutterhead. The depth of cut is controlled by one of two methods, depending on the design of the machine. With some planers, the table height is adjustable to bring the work closer or farther away from the cutterhead. In other designs, the table is stationary and the cutterhead assembly is lowered into the work.

Planer size is designated by the length of the knives—which determines the maximum width of stock that can be handled—and the maximum distance the table can be moved away from the blades. Small planers range in width capacity between 6 and 12 in., with maximum thickness ranging from 4 to 6 in. Minimum thicknessing capacities range from $\frac{1}{4}$ to $\frac{3}{32}$ in. (Fig. 1).

These small planers typically operate at a fixed feed rate. This means that the number of cuts per inch is not adjustable. One version, the Shopsmith Professional Planer, features variable speed capacity through separate motors for the cutterhead and feed rollers (Fig. 2). This allows you to increase the cuts per inch, producing a better surface on difficult woods.

Other planers accept molding knives in place of standard straight knives. The Craftsman planer/molder features an open-side design which doubles stock-width capacity and cuts moldings on edges, regardless of stock width (Fig. 3).

Besides dedicated thickness planers, some manufacturers offer their versions in combination with a down-scale jointer for conveniently truing stock before it's thicknessed.

## Basic Operation

The planer is a simple machine that requires no special skills to operate, but you do need to follow certain procedures for the best results. Typical planers have only one control—the elevation crank or wheel that sets the stock thickness. A scale and pointer indicate the current thickness setting (Fig. 4).

**4** Planer thickness setting is adjusted with a wheel that controls table height. Pointer indicates thickness on a scale.

**5** Long or heavy stock requires the extra support of adjustable roller stands at the infeed and outfeed sides of the planer.

**6** To flatten cupped work on a thickness planer, secure a shim on the concave side. Shim height lines up with stock edges.

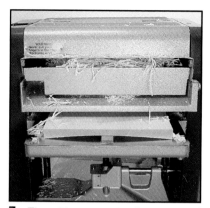

**7** The shim supports the center of cupped stock and eliminates any bending caused by feed-roller pressure.

**8** Heavy cupped lumber is often strong enough to resist feed-roller pressure. Always plane convex side first.

**9** To check for twist, lay a straight stick at each end of the work. If the sticks aren't parallel, the board is twisted.

**10** Adjustable jig holds twisted stock so it can be planed flat. Drywall screws placed in sidewalls hold work securely.

**11** Make successive passes to flatten twisted surface. Initial passes may have to be hand fed due to irregular worksurface.

Some small planers can remove as much as ⅛ in. in one pass. In general, a heavier cut will not produce as fine a surface as a lighter cut. When thicknessing work that requires much stock to be removed, make the final few passes with a light cut.

Planer tables are relatively short, so it's best to use a pair of roller stands to support long or heavy lumber on the infeed and outfeed sides (Fig. 5). You can buy adjustable stands or simply buy the rollers and make your own.

To operate a thickness planer, first set the planer table to slightly less than the maximum stock thickness. Then, turn on the power, stand to one side and feed the board under the infeed roller. Once the roller takes hold, move to the outfeed side to get the board as it exits. Whenever feasible, plane both sides of a board the same amount to equalize stresses in the stock that are relieved as material is removed.

### Stock Problems

Thickness planers are not designed to true or flatten irregular work—a job reserved for the jointer or a hand plane. Instead, they are designed to plane one face of a board so that it's parallel to the opposite face. Therefore, you'll find that warped boards will exit the planer at the thickness you desire, but not any flatter than when they entered the machine.

While the best procedure is to flatten one surface of the stock before thicknessing, there are a few techniques that enable you to do the job with your planer. These tips are especially helpful for truing stock that's too wide for your jointer. Whether your stock is badly warped or not, cut the lumber to rough size before planing. This reduces the effect of any warp, which allows you to realize the maximum thickness from each piece.

Because the feed rollers exert great pressure, stock that's cupped will be bent flat just as it's being planed. While this effect diminishes with heavier stock, you can eliminate the problem in thinner work by placing a shim between the bed and the concave side of the workpiece. Simply adjust the shim thickness so the edges of the work just contact the bed. Use hot-melt glue to hold the shim in place (Figs. 6, 7 and 8). Once one side is planed, remove the shim and plane the other side.

Before planing unjointed lumber, check for twist by laying a straight stick across each end (Fig. 9). If the sticks aren't parallel, the board's twisted. You can flatten twisted stock with a specialized jig to hold the work. The version shown is made of a double ¾-in. plywood bed and two sidewalls made from 5/4 stock. Make one sidewall adjustable to handle different stock widths by attaching it to the base with carriage bolts that fit through slotted holes.

To flatten twisted lumber with this jig, first adjust the sidewall to the stock width, and then position the stock so the highest corners are level. Secure the stock with drywall screws driven through the sidewalls (Fig. 10).

Make successive shallow passes until the surface is flattened (Fig. 11). Because of twist, the feed rollers may not remain in continuous contact with the work, and there may be periods when the assembly must be pushed and pulled through the planer by hand. Be sure to keep your hands a safe distance away from the machine and use roller stands to support the jig. After one side is planed, remove the work from the jig and plane the opposite side in the normal manner.

## Planer Problems

Once you've mastered a few basic techniques for flattening and truing stock, it's time to look at improving the quality of the planed surfaces your machine is producing. While this tool is a great time and labor saver, there are a few common problems that you can learn to control.

**Snipe:** If you've noticed a slight depression in the finished surface at the start, end or both ends of a cut, you're experiencing a problem common to most planers called *snipe* (Fig. 12). It's caused by a deflection of the board as it enters or leaves the area under the cutterhead.

Although you may be able to make certain adjustments in feed-roller pressure to help reduce the effect, it's often difficult to eliminate entirely. One solution is to feed a piece of scrap lumber through the planer first, followed by the workpiece butted against the end of the scrap. If you're planing several pieces, simply feed them one after the other, continually butting the ends (Fig. 13). Use a piece of scrap after the last piece to eliminate snipe at the end.

The other solution is simply to cut your stock long enough so you can saw off the ends after the wood is planed.

**Tearout:** If the grain is angled up toward the cutterhead, the knives will lift the wood fibers and tear out small chunks (Fig. 14). The fix is to make sure the predominant grain direction is angled down toward the direction of the feed. Wood with wild or reversing grain is best handled by making very shallow passes and by feeding the work diagonally for a smoother, shearing cut (Fig. 15).

**12** Snipe is a deeper cut at one or both ends of a board. It occurs as the board deflects under feed-roller pressure.

**13** Eliminate snipe by planing boards in continuous succession. Use scrap stock for the first and last pieces.

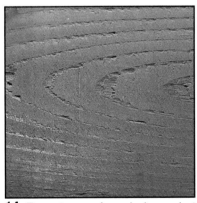

**14** Tearout comes from planing against the grain. Make sure that the grain slopes down toward the direction of feed.

**15** For wild or reversing grain, feed the work through diagonally for a smoother cut. Make shallow passes.

**16** Washboarding, or ripples across the board, is caused by coarse knife cuts. Check that knives are at the same height.

**17** Chips of wood that adhere to the feed rollers cause pockmarks in a planed surface. Clean rollers with alcohol.

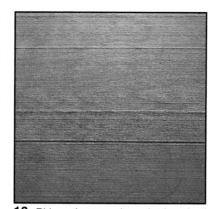

**18** Ridges that run along the length of the work are caused by nicks in knives. Resharpen knives to eliminate problem.

**19** Besides nails and other particles, glue lines can wear nicks in knives. Remove excess glue before planing.

**Washboarding:** This refers to uniform, parallel ripples that run from edge to edge across the board and are caused by individual knife cuts (Fig. 16). Washboarding may be caused by trying to remove too much wood in one pass, but also can result from an uneven knife setting. If one knife is set too high, it will do most of the work and the individual cuts will be spaced farther apart.

**Pockmarks:** Dents or impressions on the planed surface are caused by the imprint of wood chips stuck to the feed rollers (Fig. 17). Residue from resinous woods that collects on the rollers causes the chips to adhere. You can solve the problem by keeping the rollers clean with an alcohol-dampened cloth.

**Ridges:** If you begin to notice raised ridges that run the length of your work, your planer knives are nicked (Fig. 18). Such damage to the knives can be caused by gritty particles embedded in the wood or by nails hidden below the surface. It can also be caused by glue lines in laminated stock. Although it's difficult to avoid embedded particles, take special care to search for and remove nails in wood that you've salvaged for planing. To reduce the dulling effect of glue lines, remove all excess glue before running the work through the machine (Fig. 19). The best solution for nicked knives is

a resharpening. You can often reset the knives, however, so they're slightly offset and the nicks are no longer in line. This way, the good section of one knife follows the nick on the other knife.

**Special Tricks**

Of course, the bulk of your planing will involve bringing single boards to the uniform, parallel thicknesses necessary for most woodworking projects. You can, however, extend the usefulness of your machine with a few simple techniques.

**Planing Thin Stock:** While most planers are limited to a minimum thickness capacity of about $1/4$ in., you can produce thinner stock with either one of two methods. The work can be secured to a backer board, or you can use a shopmade auxiliary platform to raise the stock high enough to contact the cutters. Both methods simulate thicker stock.

To use a **backer board**, choose a board that's flat and has parallel faces. Then glue the stock to be planed to the backer board at the lead, infeed end only. Carpenter's glue is the best choice for gluing the end because it's strong and the glue layer is thin. You also can use hot-melt glue or a strong double-face tape to hold the work to the backer board (Fig. 20). The advantage of

**20** Plane thin stock by gluing it to a flat, parallel backer board. Apply the glue at the infeed end of the work only.

**21** Auxiliary platform effectively raises the table height for thin stock. Cleat on the infeed side holds platform in place.

these alternatives is that you're able to pry off and make use of the whole workpiece, although a thicker adhesive line causes the end to be planed slightly thinner. With carpenter's glue, you have to saw the workpiece off the backer board.

An **auxiliary platform** is simply a flat board placed on the bed with a cleat at the infeed end to keep it from moving through the planer (Fig. 21). The backer board is best for very thin work because the glued lead end resists the lifting action of the cutterhead. In either case, planing thin stock demands very shallow cuts, particularly when working with difficult-grain woods.

Keep in mind that there are limitations to how thin you can plane stock, and some woods can be taken thinner than others without breaking. Always proceed cautiously with shallow cuts, and stand to one side of the machine.

**Planing Bevels:** Another special technique allows you to plane bevels across the width of the work. Simply secure a shim to one side of the work so it's tilted at the required angle (Fig. 22). It's best to use a few dabs of hot glue to hold the shim in place. Take very light cuts—especially at the beginning of the operation. Until a substantial portion of the bevel is formed, the pressure of the rollers on a heavy cut will tend to flip up the work parallel to the bed.

**Planing Tapers:** To plane lengthwise tapers such as you might use for table legs, mount the work on a simple jig that holds it at an angle. To make an adjustable jig, cut two pieces of plywood slightly longer and wider than your work and attach them at one end with a hinge. Then, use a pine block to raise the opposite end of the jig to the desired angle and tack it in place. Cut several smaller blocks to support the angled platform at 4- to 6-in. spacings (Fig. 23). Secure the workpiece to the jig by tacking cleats to the inclined board, butting them against the work at each end. When feeding the jig through the planer, make shallow passes. It's also a good idea to use stock that's longer than required so you can cut off ends with snipe.

**Gang Planing:** Thickness planers also can be used to bring stock to a uniform width and to plan the edges parallel. Narrow stock—less than about 1 in. thick—or stock that's much wider than it is thick, however, will tend to lean over under the pressure of the feed rollers, resulting in an out-of-square edge.

You can, though, successfully plane stock on edge if you gang plane several pieces together (Fig. 24). This evens out feed-roller pressure across the planing area and reduces the tendency for the work to lean. Avoid taking heavy cuts as this can force the pieces to lean over, resulting in an out-of-square cross section.

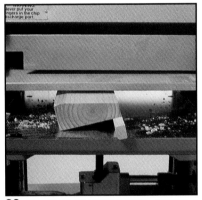

**22** To plane shallow bevels, secure a shim along the edge. Take shallow passes so feed rollers don't flip up stock.

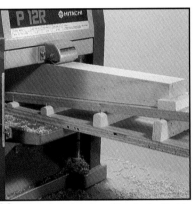

**23** Plane long tapers with a jig that holds stock at the correct angle. This jig is hinged at one end for a range of tapers.

**24** Trim several pieces to width by ganging them together and feeding them through the planer at the same time.

# Index

If you have not already ordered the new *Popular Mechanics Home How-To* book and would be interested in the many money-saving hints and tips it offers, please send a check for $29.95 to Hearst Direct Books, 645 Stewart Avenue, Garden City, NY 11530.
  We'll even pay for the postage!

# METRIC CONVERSION

Conversion factors can be carried so far they become impractical. In cases below where an entry is exact it is followed by an asterisk (*). Where considerable rounding off has taken place, the entry is followed by a + or a - sign.

## CUSTOMARY TO METRIC

### Linear Measure

| inches | millimeters |
|--------|-------------|
| 1/16 | 1.5875* |
| 1/8 | 3.2 |
| 3/16 | 4.8 |
| 1/4 | 6.35* |
| 5/16 | 7.9 |
| 3/8 | 9.5 |
| 7/16 | 11.1 |
| 1/2 | 12.7* |
| 9/16 | 14.3 |
| 5/8 | 15.9 |
| 11/16 | 17.5 |
| 3/4 | 19.05* |
| 13/16 | 20.6 |
| 7/8 | 22.2 |
| 15/16 | 23.8 |
| 1 | 25.4* |

| inches | centimeters |
|--------|-------------|
| 1 | 2.54* |
| 2 | 5.1 |
| 3 | 7.6 |
| 4 | 10.2 |
| 5 | 12.7* |
| 6 | 15.2 |
| 7 | 17.8 |
| 8 | 20.3 |
| 9 | 22.9 |
| 10 | 25.4* |
| 11 | 27.9 |
| 12 | 30.5 |

| feet | centimeters | meters |
|------|-------------|--------|
| 1 | 30.48* | .3048* |
| 2 | 61 | .61 |
| 3 | 91 | .91 |
| 4 | 122 | 1.22 |
| 5 | 152 | 1.52 |
| 6 | 183 | 1.83 |
| 7 | 213 | 2.13 |
| 8 | 244 | 2.44 |
| 9 | 274 | 2.74 |
| 10 | 305 | 3.05 |
| 50 | 1524* | 15.24* |
| 100 | 3048* | 30.48* |

1 yard =
.9144* meters
1 rod =
5.0292* meters
1 mile =
1.6 kilometers
1 nautical mile =
1.852* kilometers

### Fluid Measure

(Milliliters [ml] and cubic centimeters [cc or cu cm] are equivalent, but it is customary to use milliliters for liquids.)

1 cu in = 16.39 ml
1 fl oz = 29.6 ml
1 cup = 237 ml
1 pint = 473 ml
1 quart = 946 ml
       = .946 liters
1 gallon = 3785 ml
       = 3.785 liters
Formula (exact):
fluid ounces × 29.573 529 562 5*
     = milliliters

### Weights

| ounces | grams |
|--------|-------|
| 1 | 28.3 |
| 2 | 56.7 |
| 3 | 85 |
| 4 | 113 |
| 5 | 142 |
| 6 | 170 |
| 7 | 198 |
| 8 | 227 |
| 9 | 255 |
| 10 | 283 |
| 11 | 312 |
| 12 | 340 |
| 13 | 369 |
| 14 | 397 |
| 15 | 425 |
| 16 | 454 |

Formula (exact):
    ounces × 28.349 523 125* = grams

| pounds | kilograms |
|--------|-----------|
| 1 | .45 |
| 2 | .9 |
| 3 | 1.4 |
| 4 | 1.8 |
| 5 | 2.3 |
| 6 | 2.7 |
| 7 | 3.2 |
| 8 | 3.6 |
| 9 | 4.1 |
| 10 | 4.5 |

1 short ton (2000 lbs) =
907 kilograms (kg)
Formula (exact):
    pounds × .453 592 37* = kilograms

### Volume

1 cu in = 16.39 cubic centimeters (cc)
1 cu ft = 28 316.7 cc
1 bushel = 35 239.1 cc
1 peck = 8 809.8 cc

### Area

1 sq in = 6.45 sq cm
1 sq ft = 929 sq cm
      = .093 sq meters
1 sq yd = .84 sq meters
1 acre = 4 046.9 sq meters
      = .404 7 hectares
1 sq mile = 2 589 988 sq meters
      = 259 hectares
      = 2.589 9 sq kilometers

### Kitchen Measure

1 teaspoon = 4.93 milliliters (ml)
1 Tablespoon = 14.79 milliliters (ml)

### Miscellaneous

1 British thermal unit (Btu) (mean)
      = 1 055.9 joules
1 calorie (mean) = 4.19 joules
1 horsepower = 745.7 watts
      = .75 kilowatts
caliber (diameter of a firearm's bore in hundredths of an inch)
      = .254 millimeters (mm)
1 atmosphere pressure = 101 325* pascals (newtons per sq meter)
1 pound per square inch (psi) =
6 895 pascals
1 pound per square foot =
47.9 pascals
1 knot = 1.85 kilometers per hour
25 miles per hour = 40.2 kilometers per hour
50 miles per hour = 80.5 kilometers per hour
75 miles per hour = 120.7 kilometers per hour